French Lyrics in English Verse

French Lyrics

IN ENGLISH VERSE

WILLIAM FREDERIC GIESE
*Late Professor of Romance Languages
in the University of Wisconsin*

WITH A FOREWORD BY
FREDERICK MANCHESTER

Madison
THE UNIVERSITY OF WISCONSIN PRESS

PRINTED IN THE UNITED STATES OF AMERICA

FOREWORD

FEW men can have led lives more nearly after their own heart than William Frederic Giese. As a mere boy he felt to the full the enchantments of literature, and it was his great good fortune that the activities of his mature years, when he was student and teacher of Romance languages, never separated him from them. Reading was as natural to him as breathing—almost, one felt, as necessary; and it would scarcely be exaggeration to say that when he was not reading he was thinking, or talking, or lecturing, or writing, about what he had read. His books and essays on French literature, only a fraction of which have as yet been published, would fill many volumes. Altogether, his was such a career as Sainte-Beuve, perhaps his favorite critic, and a connoisseur of careers, would have contemplated with perfect satisfaction, suitable as it was to talent and temperament, and steadfastly pursued.

Yet "which of us has his desire"—*all* his desire? Not even, I think, my friend Giese, despite what I have said. To have had all his desire he would have had to give his life to the writing of poetry, above all of lyric poetry, and lyric poetry especially perhaps in its pastoral and idyllic moods. By inmost nature, by that part of him which was deepest and most personal, he was a poet.

Why then, with so pronounced a vocation, did he become primarily teacher and critic? The explanation lies no doubt partly in circumstances, but chiefly, I am sure, in his modest conviction that his poetical gifts, obvious though they must have been to himself, were insufficient to justify a

career. The renunciation, whether well or ill ad-
vised, has seemed to me a striking and too rare
example of the triumph of a disinterested critical
faculty over marked personal bent.

There were, to be sure, mitigations. His gifts of
poetical sensibility and poetical insight had their
large part in his abundant criticism, as similar
gifts had had their part in many a critic before
him. To be a poet in one's youth is no bad beginning for one who would occupy himself with the
imaginative writings of others, especially if his concern is predominantly, as was the case with Giese,
with their esthetic and psychological aspects. But
it was not only in this indirect way that Giese's
talent for poetry found outlet. Whom the muse has
once touched seldom forsake her utterly. How
much original verse he may have written through
the years, I do not know; many hundreds of lines,
ample evidence of his extraordinary facility and
grace, he read to me a decade ago. When, long
since, the University of Wisconsin celebrated its
jubilee, it was he who composed the official ode—a
few lines of which, lines that still echo in my
memory, I will not forbear quoting:

> *For is not life, that beats its little wings*
> *A little moment 'gainst the bars of time,*
> *A bird from dreamland that forlornly sings*
> *And singing new-creates that golden clime?*

Then there were his translations. Leconte de Lisle's
"Les Hurleurs," sonorously rendered, I recall
across many years. Of Molière he did, I believe,
three plays, one of which only, "The Misanthrope,"
has thus far seen the light. Last of all, and doubtless most important, was the collection of poetry

—he used to call it his "Golden Treasury of French Lyrics"—which these pages introduce.

The idea of this collection was for Giese a natural and an extremely happy one. In relation to it he had, to begin with, an intimate and prolonged acquaintance with the originals, and with the intellectual world to which they belong. As background, moreover, to his special knowledge of everything French, there was his large command of the European literary and artistic tradition generally, classical as well as modern. Finally, and incomparably most important, there was his poetical talent.

His circumstances at the time he set to work at his task, in the fall of 1939 or thereabout, were most propitious. A long professional career well behind him, he was living in easy retirement, in California, his daughter Rachel, always the brilliantly adequate and close companion of his intellectual life, by his side. Leisure he had in abundance, unqualified leisure, to read, to contemplate, to talk, to expand genially in the society of friends and neighbors—and now, glancing up and down the literature of his special concern, to choose what might seem its fairest flowers and plant them in an English garden.

One terrible cloud, it is true, soon or from the beginning, darkened his horizon. With the swift and triumphant advance of the Nazis, civilization, culture, art, humanity—everything he held dear, everything he had given his life to—were suddenly threatened with destruction; and it was with heavy heart, and without the slightest illusion, that he watched the drama unfold. Fortunate for him then was the literary task in hand. It was "of course a

great consolation"—the words are his daughter's—
"since it kept his thoughts in familiar and pleasant
channels, and yet kept him in touch with France,
with what he loved best of France, and what for a
time seemed alone likely to survive."

Happily, letters from Miss Giese afford us
glimpses of the translator at work. "Certainly,"
she writes, and I must give the entire passage,
"there is not much to say about the choice of the
poems. My father translated whatever he liked
particularly, at haphazard, as he came across it in
any volume that was handy—and sometimes without any text before him. The little madrigal from
Piron on the feathers from Cupid's wing was written from memory while he was rattling along Holly-
wood Boulevard in a streetcar. The lovely lines of
Marot on Venus and the roses were done—redone,
undone, as you choose—on a picnic, miles away
from the original text, and never, I fancy, compared with it. In a word, my father was writing for
pleasure, in a holiday mood, coming around full
circle to the early days when as a freshman at
Harvard he used to walk around with his pockets
full of sonnets. It is doubtless his lifelong interest
in the sonnet form that made him do so many from
Hérédia—whom in any case he admired more un-
reservedly than do many of his recent critics.
Baudelaire, you may notice, is very partially represented, and though Victor Hugo bulks larger, I
am sure, than any of his rivals, he has had to sub-
mit to considerable pruning. Of all the poets, I
believe my father cared most for André Chénier
and perhaps Louise Labé—or at any rate got more
satisfaction from his work on them."

Vivid and charming account of how enviable a

mood!.... But what was that, someone will surely
be exclaiming—a madrigal from memory! Lines
done "miles away from the original text and never,
I fancy, compared with it"! What conception of
translation could render such unconcern about
textual faithfulness even an exceptional possibility?

The answer we may hear directly from Giese's
own lips. "I have translated," he wrote to a cor-
respondent early in 1941, "virtually all that seemed
to me worth while of French lyric poetry, which
was a considerable undertaking, and one I enjoyed
more than all my efforts in criticism, poetry being
a field in which I feel very much at home—so much
so that I take liberties with my text so startling that
they would no doubt make every individual hair
stand on end on the head of ――――, who solemnly
maintains that the one and indispensable virtue of
verse translation is absolute faithfulness to the
original—which would deprive the translator of
every vestige of that liberty which the original
poet enjoyed of turning his thought at his own
bon plaisir according as rhyme and rhetoric and the
capricious muse may suggest—as if one could be
graceful in fetters! Unhappily nine readers out of
ten hold to this traditional notion in spite of the
fact that almost no literal verse translations are
readable."

There it is, expressed with characteristic ease
and verve—the theory of the least pedantic of
scholars; of an excellent, ingenious, and subtle
critic; of one who loved letters passionately and
deeply and for their own sake: a theory which
firmly asserts, as I conceive it, that the responsi-
bility of the translator is not to reproduce his
original word for word, image for image, thought

for thought, to the last potentialities of the language in which he works, but instead, operating with such freedom as in the individual instance may seem necessary or desirable, and within such limits employing to the full his own talent, to create if possible, or rather to recreate, a living work of art.

The pleasant quarrel between those who hold one view of verse translation, and those who hold another, is not a new one; and it will probably never end. I pursue it here only to remark that Professor Giese might smilingly invoke, so far at least as the question of literalness alone is concerned, the shining example of Edward Fitzgerald. The "Rubáiyát of Omar Khayyám of Naishápúr" (what vague splendor of suggestion in the full title!) is perhaps the most widely celebrated poetical translation in the English language, and the most admired; yet of a total of one hundred and ten quatrains it is said that for only some forty can an original be identified.

For the rest, the reader of "French Lyrics in English Verse" should not, from what has been said, draw too hasty a conclusion regarding the degree of its actual departure from the original poems. "In general," writes Miss Giese, "I should say that my father's translations were more faithful than his own theories required. He didn't feel that he was under bond to reproduce weak lines and redundant stanzas, but when his originals were true to themselves he stuck to them pretty closely. Of course there were occasions when a minor poem merely served as springboard for a flight of his own, but they were rare . . . The virelay of 'The Nightingale's Daughter,' one or two of Marot's posies, an epigram of Piron, and the sonnet on 'The Sleeping Beauty' are perhaps the most free and easy pieces in the collection . . ."

My high estimate of the poetic merit of Professor Giese's translations is no doubt apparent in all that I have said; but it is a pleasure to express it formally here, and to predict for the collection, on the part of lovers of English poetry generally, a cordial and enduring welcome. At the close of a Foreword to his version of "The Misanthrope"— a brief apologia composed in whimsically archaic style—Giese wrote: "For full surely if thou canst with a ready delight peruse this most agreeable divertisement in the original numbers, thou wilt not mistakenly turn away from the incomparable Molière to spend thy time with his most zealous yet all-too insufficient interpreter." It is easy to imagine that if he were offering the present anthology to the public, he would accompany it with the same modest hint—though in considering his remark one cannot but reflect that probably in all times excellent translations have brought even to those best acquainted with the originals a special and real pleasure. For an excellent translation doubles its original, adds a second delight to the first; and though the new delight may be less rare than the old, it is fresh and different, and so by the charm of its novelty tends to cancel its imperfections. But, be that as it may, the devotee of English poetry who comes to "French Lyrics in English Verse" will find in it an art that is pleasantly familiar: familiar stanza forms, familiar rhythms, familiar diction. The diction, to speak of that more particularly, he will at once recognize as the rich, musical vocabulary of our central lyric

heritage. Above all, perhaps, he will be struck by
an engaging spontaneity, suggesting easy mastery
of wide resources. What is possibly less noticeable,
amid the sustained adequacy of word and melody,
is the variety of poetical effects represented, and
especially the rise here and there to an excellence
not often attained in translation—or, for that
matter, in original verse. For variety, compare, for
example, this graceful stanza from an *aubade:*

> *My love and I we roamed the wood*
> *Where shone so white the moon*
> *That every leaflet silver-hued*
> *Danced to the wild birds' tune.*

with the crisp realism of Villon's "Fair Armoress":

> *Thus doth all human beauty end:*
> *The long arms shrink, the hands grow coarse,*
> *The shapely shoulders bow and bend,*
> *The bosom dries up at the source,*
> *The body wears away, the head*
> *Wags on its base, and shanks and shins*
> *Seem cased in spotty sausage skins.*

or with the massive sweep of Leconte de Lisle's
"Condor":

> *Night rolls up from the East, where one by one*
> *The mountain chains unfold. Toward their broad*
>   *base*
> *The trackless pampas stretch a sea of grass.*
> *The darkness mounts from every deep morass*
> *And slowly steals round bays and curving shores*
> *Till like a billowy ocean-swell it pours*
> *Its heaving tides in whirling vortices*
> *Past the pale skyline and the Western seas.*

or with—though I must resist quotation—the impassioned love sonnets of Louise Labé; and for that
ascent to the higher levels of poetry, listen, for
example, to the exquisitely picturesque close of
Victor Hugo's "Boaz":

> *In Ur and Jerimadeth all is still,*
> *Bright stars enamel the abysmal sky,*
> *And the new moon that lights each jutting hill*
> *Shines in the west, while Ruth asks wonderingly,*
>
> *Seeing that fine and splendent crescent hung*
> *High on the far horizon's pearly bars,*
> *What god, what heavenly harvester, has flung*
> *His golden sickle in the field of stars.*

or to the opening quatrain of Hérédia's "Antony
and Cleopatra"—in its last line an accent hardly
to be distinguished, if at all, from that of England's
organ voice:

> *On their high terrace throned triumphantly,*
> *They watched the sun-god over Egypt ride*
> *And lordly Nilus through the delta glide*
> *Past Sais and Bubastis to the sea.*

or, finally, to the sestet of the same beautiful sonnet, with its brilliant rendering of one of the most
audacious and at the same time most successful of
images:

> *Her pallid face, ringed round with odorous hair*
> *That shed its perfume on his quickened sense,*
> *Proffered red lips and azure eyelids fair;*
> *But in her eyes imperial Antony*
> *Saw, leaning toward her kiss, on an immense*
> *High-tossing tide a hundred galleys flee.*

It is proper to add that Professor Giese did not live to prepare his manuscript for the printer, and that in consequence it never received his final attention. This is of course to be regretted—though in the circumstances as little as possible, since what remained to be done fell to the hand of his daughter. Because of military service abroad, however, Miss Giese was unable to see the book through the press; and in this connection, and on her behalf, certain important acknowledgments should be gratefully made. The notes on authors were compiled by Dr. Selim Ezban, the index of French titles by Professor Casimir D. Zdanowicz. To Professor Zdanowicz, moreover, and to Miss Livia Appel, Managing Editor of the University of Wisconsin Press, special thanks are due for the warm interest they have taken in the publication, and the great care they have bestowed upon it, from the time it was first projected.

FREDERICK MANCHESTER

CONTENTS

JOACHIM DU BELLAY (1522–1560)

ANTOINE DE BAÏF (1532–1589)

RÉMI BELLEAU (1528–1577)

PONTUS DE TYARD (1521–1605)

CHARLES BAUDELAIRE (1821–1867)

LECONTE DE LISLE (1818–1894)

French Lyrics in English Verse

ANONYMOUS

FROM THE PROVENÇAL

Twelfth Century

Aubade

WHERE THE WHITE hawthorn bush embowers,
Two lovers lay among the flowers,
Nor heard the night watch call the hours.
        Ah God! that dawn should come so soon!

O night! O night! more slowly flee,
O love! O love! bide here with me,
And may the watch drowse sleepily.
        Ah God! that dawn should come so soon!

Hush, lover mine, your softest word
Might rouse anear some jealous bird
To mock the sweetness he had heard.
        Ah God! that dawn should come so soon!

Sweet love, lie close and kiss and cling,
Though birds to greet the daybreak sing
And faint afar the church-bells ring.
        Ah God! that dawn should come so soon!

OLD FRENCH
Twelfth Century

Aubade

MY LOVE AND I we roamed the wood
Where shone so white the moon

That every leaflet silver-hued
Danced to the wild bird's tune.
But all too soon the daybreak came,
And came the waking lark,
To put our amorous sport to shame
And drive away the dark.
Her matin song it pierced our heart
And paled the white-orbed moon.
O why, shrill bird, bid lovers part?
It is too soon, too soon!
False-piping bird, fly, fly away!
This light is not the light of day,
Not yet the stars do swoon.
O love, so dear! O love, so fair!
A little longer bide:
Not yet I scent the morning air—
The jealous lark has lied!

Reverdie

When in May the year is young,
When the meadows turn to green
And, in briars with rose o'erhung,
Nightingale sings all unseen,
   Hush, hush!
In the grass so green and lush
Sleep we by the hawthorn bush.

I did hear his fluting song,
Hidden in the clustered bloom,
Slumbering a half-hour long,
Drunk with music and perfume.
   Hush, hush!
In the grass so green and lush
Sleep we by the hawthorn bush.

When I roused me from my sleep
Through the branches I did peep,
And I thanked the merry bird
For the sweet tunes I had heard.
        Hush, hush!
In the grass so green and lush
Sleep we by the hawthorn bush.

On my lute I played a strain
Dear to every shepherd swain,
And the birdling sang with me,
Fluttering down from his green tree.
        Hush, hush!
In the grass so green and lush
Sleep we by the hawthorn bush.

But, flown near, he scanned my face:
"Ah," he cried, "what sore disgrace
That a peasant carl hour-long
Should lie and listen to my song!"
        Hush, hush!
In the grass so green and lush
Sleep we by the hawthorn bush.

The Nightingale's Daughter

A LINEN sark enfolded her,
A soft pelisse of ermine fur,
    Silk gown to shield from showers;
Her knees were ringed with lilies bright,
And her small feet, so dainty white,
    Ran slippered in May flowers.

Her girdle was a leafy wreath
All dew-sprent from the verdant heath,
    And gold the clasps thereof;

Her wallet was a pretty thing
With flowery bands that smelt of spring
    To mind her of her love.

She rode a mule whose tinkling shoon
Rang silvery 'neath the silver moon;
    Her saddle was of gold;
Three boughs weighed down with many a rose
Leaned round her like a garden-close
    To shadily enfold.

Her father is the nightingale
Whose song thrills all the bosky dale
    Around his tree-top home;
Her mother is the white sea-maid
Who sings her nightly serenade
    From cliffs adrip with foam.

GUILLAUME DE MACHAULT

c. 1292–1377

Under the Cherry-Tree

WHERE THE grass grows deep and high
There I sat and there did sigh,
Pouring in my lady's ear
Words that she alone should hear,
Letting on my shoulder press
That sweet load of loveliness.
All my heart was filled with joy
As she lay there, birdling coy,
Nestling soft on my warm breast—
Did she sleep, or only rest?
   Then Dan Cupid from some green
Thicket where he lurked unseen
Of a sudden startled me,
Lighting by my cherry-tree.
From the branch a leaf he strips,
Lays it on my lady's lips,
And then bids me, amorous thief,
Steal the kiss hid 'neath the leaf.
Soon my hesitating head,
O'er that green leaf anchorèd,
Downward sank, half loth, half glad,
To snatch what courtesy forbade,
For my heart, by fancy led,
Longed to do as Cupid said.
   As I near and nearer leaned
Cupid, laughing, intervened
And the leaf so slily snatched
That my lips 'gainst hers were matched.

It was but the lightest touch,
Yet I paled and trembled much;
It was but the lightest kiss,
And I took no more than this,
Half repenting while I took it
Lest my sweeting might not brook it.
Suddenly in shy surprise,
Opening her winking eyes,
She rebuked what I had done,
But rebuked in gentlest tone.
"Friend, sweet friend, be not so bold:
Kiss again, and I will scold!"
So she chid, and chiding smiled,
And, smiling, we were reconciled—
So I guessed, ere we should part
Each would steal the other's heart,
Since she let me steal a kiss
With no more reproach than this.

Rondeau

WHITE AS THE lily, vermeil as the rose,
Splendid as rubies of the Orient,
Such sovran loveliness your cheeks disclose,
White as the lily, vermeil as the rose
That buds and blushes in the garden-close,
So ravishing that all my hope is bent
To serve that heavenly beauty's blazonment,
White as the lily, vermeil as the rose,
Splendid as rubies of the Orient.

JEAN FROISSART
1337–c.1410

They Tell Me I've a Bonny Face

THEY TELL me I've a bonny face
Where rose and lily bide,
And wear it with as fine a grace
As any maid beside.

This morn ere break of day I rose
To greet the coming dawn
And stole into the garden-close
Across the dewy lawn.

I thought to be the first to roam
Under the greenwood tree,
But my true love betimes had come
To pluck a wreath for me.

I gave to him a trembling stem
Of blossoms plucked yestreen,
And one by one he counted them
And kissed me still between.

They tell me I've a bonny face
Where rose and lily bide,
And wear it with as fine a grace
As any maid beside.

EUSTACHE DESCHAMPS

c. 1340–1405

Virelay of the Dainty Maid

Am I not a dainty maid?
Lissom body full of grace,
White my brow and fair my face,
Lips with coral overlaid,
Cheeks of rose and sparkling eye.
                    Reply, reply,
Am I not a dainty maid?

I've a deal of fine array,
I've a cape with tippet gray,
I've a vest with crimson braid,
I've a solid silver pin
With two clasps that golden bin.
                    Am I, am I,
Am I not a dainty maid?

Loyal lover must he be
Who shall wooing come to me;
Only such his heart shall trade
For a damsel such as I.
                    Reply, reply,
Am I not a dainty maid?

Ne'er will I, if heaven aid,
To my love be renegade,
If in turn my lover sigh
Only when I am not nigh.
                    Am I, am I,
Am I not a dainty maid?

Where this side of Paradise
Is a mistress such as I,
One so winsome, one so wise,
One so fond, and leal, and staid?
                    Reply, reply,
Am I not a dainty maid?

ANONYMOUS
Fifteenth Century

Birdsong

I HEARD the lark at break of day,
I heard the nightingale,
Sing from the same green tree this lay:
"Behold my lover's sail;
His galliot floats upon the Seine,
All shaped of yellow pine;
Of satin are the white sails twain,
The rigging silken twine;
The rudder is of shining gold,
The mast of ivory;
The skipper and his sailors bold
Hail from a far countree;
The tallest is the prince of France,
He wears the lily-flower:
In times agone we two did dance
By moonlight in my bower."

The White-Cross Knight

"I BEG YOU, gallant knights of France,
Who fare o'er land and sea
To fight for Christ with sword and lance,
Oh, greet my love for me!"

"My lady fair, you do but sport:
How should we know your knight?"
"You'll know him by his valiant port
And armor dazzling bright.

"He wears a white cross on his breast,
His casque has golden bars,
And on his shield he bears impressed
Three shining silver stars."

"Sad lady, stanch your flowing tears:
Upon a Breton heath,
By Breton hands and Breton spears,
Your lover met his death.

"Your White-Cross knight so young and brave
Sleeps under greening grass;
We heard beside his new-made grave
Four Cordeliers say mass."

ALAIN CHARTIER
c. 1385–1440

Spring Song

FLY AWAY, pale melancholy!
Let me wear a cheerful face;
Welcome, love and lovers' folly!
Spring is coming on apace.
     Thus I sang, and in the fields
Sought the pleasure nature yields.
All alone I trod the wood
Where the new grass pierced the ground,
And I pretty comfort found
In that perfumed solitude,
Comfort for a heart bereaved
And by faithless love deceived.
     All around the birds were winging
And their sweetest songs were singing.
Every heart was filled with joy.
Loud they caroled, heavenward flying,
Bird with bird unwearied vying;
Naught did grieve them, naught annoy,
For the sky was clad in blue,
Golden sunbeams shooting through,
And a thousand violets
From their grassy coverlets
Lifted up their little faces,
In a thousand pleasant places,
Sprinkled all with beads of dew.
Birds sang loud from hill and hollow,
These did lead and those did follow,
Opening wide each tiny throat

To let the airy music float,
Singing now the same refrain,
Now each bird a diverse strain,
Soft crescendos pyramiding
Wildly sweet, at nature's bidding.
    I, hid in the echoing grove,
More and more did nature love
That such music could instill
In each birdling's horny bill.
Doubly sweet the love-notes sound
From the songbird's swelling breast
As he circles round and round
His mute consort in the nest.
    Trees were budding, bushes flowering,
Hares and rabbits quit their lair,
Spring its hoarded sweets was showering
On the clover-scented air.
Love, tranced by that odorous breath,
Took no thought of grief or death,
Seated by a plashing fountain
Whence the shallow brooklet's bed,
Slowly winding down the mountain,
Was by limpid waters fed.
Little birds with chirping cries
Levied war on crickets, gnats,
And the bright-winged butterflies
In their leafy habitats.
Falcons fierce and taloned hawks
Sailed on high, and honey bees
Built their hives in hollow trees
That lined the lonely forest walks
Or graced the meads where nature's hand
Decked with bloom the smiling land,
White and yellow, red and blue,

While the trees appeared to strow
Not white flowers but flakes of snow,
Dotting all the champaign green
Till it seemed a painted scene.

CHARLES D'ORLÉANS
1394–1465

The Summer's Heralds

THE SUMMER's heralds bring anear
The season of soft-falling showers
And carpet every meadow sere
With weft of verdure and fresh flowers.
O'er grassy lawn and shining mere
Flutter the rosy-footed Hours:
The Summer's heralds bring anear
The season of soft-falling showers.
Sad hearts enchained by sullen fear
No longer now a-tremble cower
While north winds blow and tempests lower;
No longer, Winter, tarry here,
The Summer's heralds draw anear.

Time Has Now His Mantle Shed

TIME HAS now his mantle shed
Of wind, and cold, and rain,
And his robe is all o'erspread
With shining gold again.
Beasts all round and birds o'erhead
Sing the glad refrain,
Time has now his mantle shed
Of wind, and cold, and rain.
Fountain, stream, and river-bed,
Freed from winter's stain,
Hail the season garlanded
With dew-dripping bloom again:
Time has now his mantle shed.

So Sweet Is She to Look Upon

So SWEET is she to look upon,
So gracious, kind, and debonair,
All those on whom her eyes have shone
Call her the fairest of the fair.
What churl could bid such charms begone,
What lover that blithe face forswear?
So sweet is she to look upon,
So gracious, kind, and debonair!
Nor here, nor yet beyond the sea,
Is there a maid that e'er will seem
So gracious, kind, and fair to me;
Her beauty is a heavenly dream,
So sweet to look upon is she!

Farewell to Love

Away, AWAY! Depart, depart!
Woe, care, and melancholy!
Think not to nestle in my heart,
Think not to rule me wholly.
I swear to play a braver part
And yield no more to love's sweet folly:
Away, away! Depart, depart!
Woe, care, and melancholy!
Come not again to plague my heart,
O cursèd company!
Flit far away, all three!
God shield me from love's smart!
Away, away! Depart, depart!

Pedlar's Song

LITTLE pedlar, little basket!
If I have no merchandise
Fit to please a lover's eyes,
From my pack you must not ask it,
Such rich wares would overtask it.
Penny-foolish, penny-wise,
Are the customers who prize
Little pedlar, little basket!
Hide your frown, good folk, and mask it,
Idle chatter I despise;
I must empty out my casket,
Lucky is the man who buys:
Little pedlar, little basket!

FRANÇOIS VILLON
1431—after 1463

A Ballade of Dead Ladies

TELL ME WHERE, in what dim Thule,
Roman Flora dwells, the fair,
Where Archippe, Thais where;
Echo, too, sweet nymph who duly
Mimes all sounds that mountain steep
Sends o'er river-bank and mere—
Where doth all this beauty sleep?
But where are the snows of yesteryear?

Where doth Heloise repose,
For love of whom Pierre Abelard
To Saint Denis bore wounds and woes
And lived in cloister, evil-starred?
Where is the queen who did ordain
That Buridan, once held so dear,
Be sewed in sack and tossed in Seine?
But where are the snows of yesteryear?

Where bides Blanche, the lily-white queen,
She who sang a Siren strain,
And Bertha, mother of Charlemain;
Where are Beatrice, Alice seen,
Haremburg, who ruled in Maine,
Or the virgin of Lorraine,
In Rouen by English burned—
To what far heaven hath she returned?
But where are the snows of yesteryear?

ENVOI

Ask not, Princes; 'tis in vain,

Whether they be far or near—
Still recall this sad refrain:
But where are the snows of yesteryear?

Ballade
For His Mother to Our Lady

QUEEN OF THE skies and regent of the earth
And sovran empress of the realms of hell,
Receive me, Mary, though of little worth,
Yet heavenward bent, a child of Christian birth;
Through your grace only can I enter in—
For your great goodness, as I know full well,
Is greater than the burden of my sin.
O queen of heaven, your servitor am I,
And in this faith I mean to live and die.

Tell your blest Son I am His own, and thus,
Even as Egyptian Mary was forgiven
Or that most learnèd clerk, Theophilus,
Who once did seal a compact with the devil—
May God forbid I fall into like evil!—
So may I also be absolved and shriven;
For I hold true, howe'er unworthily,
Since I am weak, and sinful too alas,
The holy things that I have heard at Mass,
And in this faith I mean to live and die.

I am a woman poor and very old,
Who cannot read and nothing know at all,
But in the cloister, when my beads I've told,
I see God's paradise upon the wall,
All gay with harps and lutes, and, underneath,
A flaming hell where damned souls boil and seethe.
Hell frightens me, and heaven fills with joy:

O heavenly goddess, let the joy be mine,
For you to every sinner are benign
Whose faith is free of weakness and alloy—
And in this faith I mean to live and die.

ENVOI

Virgin and blest princess without stain,
Thy Son was He who shall forever reign,
Jesus, who, wrought on by our feebleness,
Left His bright heaven to succor our distress
And offered on the cross His lovely youth.
Our Lord is He: this do I hold for sooth—
And in this faith I mean to live and die.

The Fair Armoress

I HEARD a withered courtesan,
No longer now proud-helmeted,
But worn and wan, her beauty dead,
And sad her shrill complaining ran:
    Out on thee, Time, to spoil me so!
Thy curst hand has my visage shent
So fiercely I could be content
To stab me with a mortal blow.
Where is my vaunted beauty gone
That once made slaves of clerics shorn,
Merchants, aye princes, every one?
For never man of woman born
From my red lips did coldly turn,
Though kisses, certes, cost him dear,
Full many a coin, full many a tear—
Kisses a beggar now would scorn!
    Full many too did I refuse,
Though ne'er from chastity, beshrew me!
But for a worthless lad who used

My weakness only to undo me.
How did I coax and cosset him!
Ah! by my soul, I loved him true!
Though robbed and periled, life and limb,
And bruised and beaten black and blue.
Though he betrayed and played me false
And trampled me beneath his feet
And filled my house with hellish brawls,
I found his blows and kisses sweet,
Remembering only how we loved
And how we kissed when first I came. . . .
But ah, that day how far removed!
What gain for me but sin and shame!

      He has been dead these thirty year,
And here I crouch, grown bald and blear,
Thinking, alas! of those blest times,
And what I was, and what I am,
No longer sung in lilting rhymes,
But a poor bawd the passers damn.
When I behold so altered quite
My naked body, once so white,
Now shrunken, squalid, sickly-sad,
Almost the sight doth drive me mad.

      Where is that smooth white forehead now,
Those flashing eyes, that taking glance,
Those golden braids around my brow,
That made all hearts, and purses, dance,
That chiselled nose, nor large nor small,
Those dainty ears, a pearl in each,
That saucy chin, most sweet of all,
And red cheeks, downy as a peach,
Those sloping shoulders, slender-shaped,
Arms white as snow, and tapering hands,
Pink budding breasts, and loins well draped
In flesh more soft than velvet bands?

My brow is wrinkled now, my hair
A wisp of gray, my red eyes shock,
My eyebrows peel, my smiling air
Is turned a grin at which men mock;
My nose is crook'd, unbeautiful,
My ears sag down, my spittle drips,
My face dead-pale and peaked and dulled,
My chin o'erplumbed by wizened lips.
Thus doth all human beauty end:
The long arms shrink, the hands grow coarse,
The shapely shoulders bow and bend,
The bosom dries up at the source,
The body wears away, the head
Wags on its base, and shanks and shins
Seem cased in spotty sausage skins.
    So sit we here, forlorn old crones,
Mourning the years when we were young,
Low-huddled on our marrow-bones
Like a dry bunch of faggots flung
Upon a fire of blazing fir
That burns so bright but burns so brief—
Poor things that once such darlings were:
Thus many and many come to grief.

A Ballade of the Gibbet

O HUMAN brothers who live after us,
View not with hardened hearts our cruel fate;
If ye have pity on our wretched state
God's grace for you will flow more piteous.
Some five or six we hang on high unshriven,
Whose flesh, of old to wanton riot given,
Long since has rotted from our skeletons—
Here hang we, five or six unhappy ones,

Whose shrunken bones in ashy dust-flakes fall:
O pray that God have mercy on us all!

When thus we cry to you, O brothers, heed
Our plea and curse us not, though we be shent,
As well ye see, for our just punishment:
Some men are strong, but some are weak indeed;
O intercede for us with gentle heart
Unto the Virgin Mary's blessed Son
That His compassion save us, every one,
From hellish fire and its eternal smart.
We are dead men—no more our sins recall—
But pray that God have mercy on us all.

The rain has soaked and washed our flesh to shreds,
The sun has baked and burned our tender clay,
Magpies and crows have pierced like arrowheads
Our hollow eyes and torn our beards away.
Never a minute do our bodies rest,
Tossed hither, thither, by the changing wind,
And pierced like thimbles by this flying pest
That leaves them swinging mutilate and skinned.
O never be, like us, the devil's thrall,
But pray that God have mercy on us all.

ENVOI

Prince Jesus, You who hold the world in sway,
Preserve us from the mastery of hell,
Cleanse us from sin, and make our spirits well;
And ye, our brothers, mock not at our fall,
But pray that God have mercy on us all.

CLÉMENT MAROT
c. 1496–1544

Cupid's Blunder

LOVE CHANCED TO meet with her who loves me not:
I too was there, but Cupid stood between us.
"Good-day," he cried, "good-day, my mother
    Venus!"
Then smiled amazed, while sudden doubt begot
A shamefaced blush that mantled cheek and brow
That he had blundered thus, he knew not how.
"Nay, Cupid, nay," I cried, "be not aggrieved:
Some clearer-eyed than you have been deceived."

With a Gift of Roses

WHY IS THE ROSE, fair Venus' sacred flower
That thrills the trancèd senses with delight,
Now clothed in glowing red, now in pure white,
While in your face both bloom with equal power?
Love only, love eternal, was the cause:
One day the goddess her Adonis sought,
Running through wildering meadows without
    pause,
Among rude briars and bushes, love-distraught,
Unshod, bare-armed, her magic zone unbound;
And many a thorny hedge that girt her round
Was dyed with blood celestial, till each rose
That whitely bloomed was, by those droplets shed,
Emblazoned with a deep vermilion red.
O lady mine, these blossoms that I bring

Are some as white and some as red as those;
Lay on your breast this whitest bloom of spring,
And 'gainst your cheek this vermeil-tinted rose.

Since That You Love Me Not

SINCE THAT YOU love me not, let me depart
And like a hermit in the desert dwell;
God grant some lover with as pure a heart
Sue for your love as honestly and well.

Farewell, my sweet, farewell those heavenly charms,
Those rosy cheeks, those eyes, that dainty air,
That beauty that disdained my circling arms;
One less in love perchance may better fare.

The Fair Musician

WHEN I BEHOLD the rose-enameled cheek
Of her I love, her grace, her royal port,
And hear her voice, her hands, her spinet speak
Soft sounds that up and down the keyboard sport,
Ravishing eyes and ears with such sheer joy
As though I heard a heavenly chorister,
Then do I taste a bliss without alloy,
Knowing I am a little loved by her.

Yes and No

A SWEET *No, no,* said with as sweet a smile,
Has such fine grace I fain would have you learn it,
While a smooth *Yes,* though spoken without guile,
Hints of excess, whatever way you turn it.

Not that I long the less for your sweet kiss,
So sweet that lost I ever should regret it,
Still fain were I, the while I snatch my bliss,
To hear you say: *No, no, you shall not get it!*

In Days of Yore

In days of yore love ruled in such sweet wise
It had small need of art or ornament,
But a bright nosegay made the heart content;
If love saw love shine out of answering eyes,
Not the wide world could swerve it from its bent;
And if perchance it won a dear consent,
Would you fain know how long its blandishment
Wore through the years? It did but wax the more
    In days of yore.

Now love no longer rules in this fond wise,
Now tears are feigned, now fickle hearts repent:
Why should I then pursue a barren prize?
Nay, I'll not love till love's sweet babblement
Shall be once more as true and kindly meant
And bear the world of tenderness it bore
    In days of yore.

Love's Votary

My life has had its blossom-time,
No magic will its bloom restore;
Sweet-scented spring, gay summer's prime
Have come and gone, to come no more.
O Love, that brought such bliss and pain,
Love, dearest of all gods to me,
O Love, could I be born again,
How doubly would I worship thee!

HUGUES SALEL

1504–1553

On Passing through a Wood

YE NIGHTINGALES that sit and sing
A-twitter on these greening boughs,
No longer make the woodland ring
With songs of love and lovers' vows.
Since vanished joys but sharpen pain,
Sing me no lilting strains today,
But o'er and o'er chant this refrain:
My love, my love, has gone away.

JACQUES PELETIER
1517–1582

The Lark

WHEN THE dawn with rosy hue
Paints the curtain of the skies,
From her nest, all drenched with dew,
Swift of wing the lark doth rise
Toward the fields of cloudless blue.

While the light grows ever clearer,
Clearer swells her liquid voice,
Skyward soaring, near and nearer,
With her music to rejoice
Phoebus, who makes pause to hear her.

Borne on Zephyr's buoyant wing,
Through the air she steers and veers,
And so prettily doth sing
That she makes the welkin ring,
Rivaling the chiming spheres.

Whether Juno purge the skies,
Whether Jove descend in rain,
Still her pinions heavenward strain,
Still resound her melodies,
Till white winter comes again.

Ne'er her tiny beak she closes
E'en to hatch her chirping brood,
But her tuneful airs composes
As if songs alone were good
For her little larklets' food.

When the sun rides high o'erhead,
She outsoars the watchful eye,
Then, with wings tight-gatherèd,
Dropping from the azure sky,
Hides her in some tree-top nigh.

PIERRE DE RONSARD

1524–1585

On the Forest of Gastine

No MORE, O FOREST, shall your rustling drown
The bird-notes in your boughs, nor the lone deer
Roam in your shady aisles; your verdant crown
No more shall veil Apollo's golden sphere;
No more against a gnarlèd oak inclined,
Tuning his reedy pipe, the amorous hind,
His mastiff at his feet, his crook flung down,
Shall sue his shepherdess to be more kind.
All sound shall cease and Echo's voiceless hush
Rule o'er the fields; gone every tree and bush
Whose shifting shadow played with every wind,
Gone music's charm, Pan and the wood-nymphs
    gone,
And gone the doe that wandered with her fawn.
Farewell, ye flowery banks where Zephyr sported,
Where first my fingers teased the new-strung lyre,
Where Phoebus, by the Muses nine escorted,
Thrilled my fresh senses with his heavenly fire.
Here first I worshipped fair Calliope,
While all her sister nymphs from Castaly
Crowned me with wreathèd roses soft as silk
And bland Euterpe fed me heavenly milk.
Farewell, ye antique woods, ye marble gods
Whose heads were ever garlanded with flowers.
No shrine smokes here, no shady tree-top nods
Above the bare earth in the noontide hours.
May every god the apostate disavow
Who levelled low the Muses' sacred bowers!

Farewell, ye groves of Dodonaean oaks,
Jove's trees, whose foliage wreathed the victor's
  brow
And nursed the ungrateful tribe whose fatal strokes
Cut down the trunk and burned the sacred bough!
O changeful universe, that mocks our trust!
How stern, ye gods, the iron rule of fate
That shatters all things mortal into dust,
And only from that dust doth recreate!
Thus Tempe's vale shall heave up mountain-high,
Steep Athos' top wear down to grassy plain,
Neptune's salt-wash with harvests fructify,
And new worlds bloom and fade, and change forever
  reign.

To the Fountain of Bellerie

Silver fount, in sunlight glowing,
How thy crystal waters gleam,
Through the greening meadows flowing
In a slow meandering stream.

When the harvesters of summer
Bowing ranks of wheat assail,
Like the music of a drummer
Sounds the beating of the flail.

May thy sacred springs, upwelling,
Echo like a holy hymn
To the ox and oxherd dwelling
Near thy moss-girt rocky rim.

May the white moon, wanly shining,
See at midnight in the vale
Nymphs, their snowy arms entwining,
Foot it round thy flowery pale.

To the Snowdrop and the Rose

WHAT other flower encloses
The odorous charm of roses,
Or of that lesser flower
That in the vernal hour
Lifts up a shining face
From its snow-circled vase?
No daffodil, fresh-budded,
No gillyflower, no pink,
No daisy golden-studded,
No pansy streaked with ink,
Nor bells that dot the lawn
Like gems flung by the dawn—
Not one among all those
Vies with the purple rose,
Or charms the matin hour
Like springtime's snowy flower.
How then can I reward ye,
What happy boon accord ye?
May every breeze that blows
On thee, O purple rose,
Bring dew to fill thy chalice
Till moisture bend it down,
And ne'er may summer's malice
Thy ripening buds embrown.
O snowy flower of March,
Ne'er may the dry winds parch
Thy leaves, or thy loved head
On broken stem hang dead;
But may thy perfumed breath
That ever wandereth
Through woods where wild birds sing,
On green boughs sojourning,

Blow over holt and heath
To tell us Sol is turning
A kinder face toward us
While gentle Zephyrus
Leads in the jocund spring.

To the Hawthorn

HAWTHORN, whose white bloom between
        Branches green,
By this streamlet serpentine,
Yields its wealth of snowy charms
        To the arms
Of this circling purple vine!

Rival hosts of ants lie spread,
        Glowing red,
On thy boughs; and in his home
In the hollow of yon tree
        The blithe bee
Shapes his golden honeycomb.

Nightingale, the amorous bird,
        Here is heard
Uttering his melodious cry
To his tawny-feathered love
        High above,
Where the branches pierce the sky.

In the tree-top hangs his nest,
        Deep-recessed,
Where he rears his callow brood;
Threads of silk through tangled moss
        Softly cross
Wisps of straw all golden-hued.

Put forth, hawthorn, all thy flowers;
   Ne'er may showers,
Never axe, nor icy blast,
Never blighting thunderstorm,
   Thee deform
Or thy green boughs earthward cast!

Spring Song

Welcome, ye heralds of the spring,
Swift swallows, singing on the wing,
Hoops, cuckoos, nightingales,
And every other quavering bird
Whose trills and staves all day are heard
In heathery hills and greening dales.

Welcome, thou queen of garden flowers,
Sweet rose all wet with dewy showers,
And daisies white and clover red
And hyacinth that first did bloom
Where young Narcissus met his doom
Or where, of old, mad Ajax bled.

Welcome, ye gaily colored band
Of butterflies that scour the land
And dance on flowers, nectar-fed;
Welcome, gay swarm of new-born bees
That drain down to the last sweet lees
The winy blossoms white and red.

Welcome, ye martins homeward coming,
Your happy songs, your blithesome humming—
Fresh life that flows through everything,
Glad din that chimes from shore to shore,
Proclaiming that the winter frore
Has fled before all-conquering spring.

The Lark

WHAT SWEET envy do I prove
When I hear you greet the dawn,
Telling earth and heaven your love
From your nest in this green lawn,
Spreading wide your quivering wings
Where the silver streams flow past,
Bathing in the crystal springs
Where bright Phoebus' face is glassed,
Shaking from your downy limbs
Dewdrops on the sailing cloud
While you trill your joyful hymns
Now low-toned, now pealing loud,
Till fond lovers all do rue,
Hearing such sweet caroling,
That they are not birds like you
So they might as sweetly sing—
Then from heaven's utmost top
Of a sudden down you drop,
Like the spindle that a maid
From her opening hand lets sink
When sweet sleep, too long delayed,
Makes her weary eyelids wink.

To the Fountain of Cassandra

HAIL, CLEAR fountain skyward springing,
Crystal current softly singing,
Mirror of the blue above!
In thy limpid wave my love,
Where the foamy tide o'erbrims,
Came to bathe her snowy limbs.

How her beauty charmed the sun!
How her tresses golden-spun
Floated on the amorous air!
Ceres' self did never wear
Half so long or half so fair;
No, nor Cupid, nor Apollo,
Whom the choiring Muses follow,
Guided over hill and hollow
By the streaming golden hair
Curling round his shoulders bare.
It was here the nymph I love
Leaned thy silver tide above,
Mirroring her magic eyes
Like twin stars in smiling skies,
Eyes the Paphian goddess might
Deem more excellently bright
Than the triple Graces' own,
Or the jewels of her zone,
Eyes like violets newly blown,
For the which she fain would change
Her love-lighted orbs that range
Through Elysium, flinging darts
At mortal and immortal hearts.
    Many a time, O happy stream,
Did thy argent waters gleam
Round my lady's tapering fingers
Where the rose tint fades or lingers
As it waxes, as it wanes,
With the pulsing of her veins.
Prisoned in her ivory skin,
It irradiates from within
All that row of five small pearls,
Circling in translucent whorls
And escaping from eclipse
In five little rosebud tips.

Many a time, O beauteous fount,
Did thy cooling waters mount
Round those alabastrine feet
That with Thetis' own compete,
And those lithe limbs that disclose
Here a lily, there a rose.
Many a time, loved fountain, thou
Didst asperge her ivory brow;
Many a time thou hast caressed
The carnations of her breast
And those lips of crimson dye
Where the wells of nectar lie.
When the dog-star Sirius
Hangs his lantern over us,
Oft upon thy shaded bank,
Where the earliest Mayflowers prank,
Thou hast seen her drooping head
Pillowed on a grassy bed,
While fond Zephyr slily played,
Wantoning, yet half afraid,
Prisoned in her odorous bosom
Like a bee within a blossom,
Watching with delighted eyes
Its soft fall and its soft rise.
Lying by the fountain's side,
She might seem Pygmalion's bride
Out of veinèd marble wrought,
If her golden hair, upcaught
On the fanning breeze, had not
Proved her mortally begot.
  Craning out their lissom necks
In graceful arches circumflex,
Tender birdlings perch and sing
On each branch, soft jargoning,
And between the foliage peeping

Watch her as she lies there sleeping,
And in ravishment forget
They should not be flying yet.
In their nests no longer sitting,
From their leafy mansions flitting,
They shake a thousand blossoms down
Till they form a petalled crown
Round my lady's head, or rest
Beauteous on her marble breast.

    But farewell, loved fount, farewell,
In thy verdant citadel!
While millenniums come and go,
Still thy singing rills shall flow,
Never silent, never dry,
Changeless evermore; while I,
I, alas! must pass away
When I've lived my little day;
Like a faded rose I must
Be dissolved again in dust,
And no more of me remain
Than a casket may contain,
Or a little earthen vase
Under turf where cattle graze.
Yet before my eyes shall close
On the beauty of the rose,
O thrice-lovely fontanet!
My last prayer do not forget:
When thou hear'st I am no more,
Whisper to thy echoing shore
That Ronsard in happier days
On his golden lyre did praise
The sweet murmur of thy waves,
In which fair Cassandra laves
Her white limbs by silver springs
Where the tender swallow sings.

On the Choice of His Sepulchre

YE CAVES, and limpid fountains
That spurt from cloud-capped mountains
And down their grassy side
        Soft-flowing glide,

Ye solemn woods, ye waves,
Whose crystal water laves
These meadows, oh rejoice,
        Hearing my voice!

Heave not from the dark womb
Of earth, to grace my tomb,
Some shaft of granite rock,
        Some marble block;

But let this fruitful ground
In ivy-bloom abound,
And let its garlands wave
        Above my grave.

Here let the twisted vine
And fronded ivy shine,
Decking with tender grace
        My resting-place.

And let the shepherds here
Hold festival each year
Or on the greensward sleep
        Among their sheep.

Let them invoke my shade
With the sweet verse I made,
And cull the stainless bloom
        That hides my tomb,

Crying: "Ye Muses nine,
Come dance around his shrine;
You to his pastoral song
    Did ever throng.

"May blossoms wall him round
And murmurous music sound
From fountains stealing soft
    Through wood and croft."

So let the shepherds sing
While I lie slumbering
In the white asphodel
    Where spirits dwell,

Where never falleth snow
Nor boisterous north winds blow,
Where never tempests lower
    Nor thundershower,

Where always fields are green,
Where evermore is seen,
Mid blossoms burgeoning,
    Eternal spring.

To Cassandra

THE EVER-roaming moon
Doth monthly wax and wane;
But neither late nor soon
Shall we roam here again,
Once couched in the cold earth
Waiting another birth.

Dear love, whilst yet we live,
A warm kiss warmly give,

And then a thousand more:
Love brooks no scanted measure
But scatters his sweet treasure
Out of an endless store.

To The Same

SEE, LADY, how the selfsame rose
Which in the morning did disclose
Its purple petals to the sun,
Amid the twilight's darkening shades
With drooping damask petals fades—
Sweet damask hue, so like your own!

Alas! see how each flitting hour,
My Lady, this pale purple flower
Doth of its fragile beauties reave.
Ah, Nature, why so pitiless!
And why should roses flourish less
Than dures a day from morn to eve!

Nay, heed, oh heed me, Lady mine,
While yet the roses bud and twine
Athwart the marble of your brow,
And cull youth's blossoms, lovely Maid,
Lest all untouched they faint and fade
As this sweet flower is fading now!

To an Angevine Girl

O LOVELY blossom of Anjou,
Your smooth brow speaks a virgin soul,
All simpleness and self-control;

Yet are you neither good nor true,
And your sweet-seeming manners hide
A vein of perfidy inside.

Give back to me, O cruel maid,
The heart that I too lightly gave,
That heart whose service you parade,
Whose master you proclaim your slave:
Nay, you shall not my love retain
Who find your pleasure in my pain.

I will bestow it otherwhere:
I know a maid less fair than you,
But she is fond and she is true,
And she shall comfort me, I swear,
And haply teach me to forget
My Angevine with eyes of jet.

But no—I cannot bring my heart
To quit its prison and its chains;
Sweet Angevine, we must not part;
Too much I love my hopeless pains
To seek a cure for my despair
With one more fond but not so fair.

Mortal Life

Let me on the tender grass
Lie beneath a laurel tree,
And let some sweet-spoken lass,
Some white-limbed Terpsichore
Bent loose-girdled over me,
Fill with wine my lifted glass!

Mortal life is but a day,
Hour by hour it ebbs away
As the waves die on the shore,

And when the last call has sounded,
When our little span is rounded,
We are dust forevermore.

Do not waste your rich perfume
In libations on my tomb,
Dead men need no incense showers;
But while here I lie supine
Fill my cup with ruby wine,
Crown my head with rosy flowers.

Pluck the rose and shun the thorn;
Never spare the wine and corn;
I'll be heir unto myself:
Foolish they who toil and moil
And their precious moments spoil
That their sons may get their pelf.

Death's Captive

YOUTH, so sweet, has passed away;
One by one my powers decay;
Black my teeth, my hair is white,
And my strength has vanished quite;
In my veins the languid flood
Is of water, not of blood.

Heavy hangs my weary head,
From my cheek the rose has fled;
Care and sorrow haunt the street
Where I walk with laggard feet,
Turning oft with anxious breath,
Fearing I am dogged by Death.

For I know he soon will come,
Soon will lead his captive home,
Numbed and chilled by venomed spells,
To the cave where Pluto dwells,
In whose mirk no lantern burns
And from which no man returns.

Anacreontic

Cupid, dainty little god,
Sported on the velvet sod,
Where the buzzing yellow bees
Hid their hives among the trees.

Where the flowers clustered deep
Lay a tiny bee asleep
In a budding lily-pod.
Out it flew and stung the god!

Staring at his wound, big-eyed,
"I'm undone," the urchin cried;
Then straight to his mother ran,
Bidding her his finger scan.

"Mamma, see my swollen hand!"
Cried Dan Cupid, quite unmanned,
Big tears rolling down his cheeks,
"See what harm this fury wreaks!"

Venus turned and smilingly
Kissed the infant deity,
Blowing on his bitter wound
Till her sweet breath made it sound.

"Speak," she cried, "O wanton boy!
Who hath worked thee this annoy?

Was't my rosy-fingered Graces
Marred your flesh with these red traces?"

"Nay, 'twas something serpentine
Creeping on a leafy vine,
Poised on filmy, fluttering wings—
Sudden it alights and stings!"

"Now I know," fair Venus spoke;
"The Hymettan village folk,
When these buzzing things they see,
Cry: *Beware! A honey-bee!*

"Now if insects small as this
Can so wound us with a kiss,
How much worse you hurt men's hearts
When you shoot your cruel darts!"

Greeting His Mate

GREETING HIS MATE, the questing matin bird
Amid the trembling boughs is dimly seen;
The amorous vines the pliant elms engird,
And all the earth laughs in its robe of green.
Then scorn not nature: be not foe to love!
See how the songbirds preen their glossy wings,
Moved by desire; hark how the turtle-dove
Coos in its nest, how sweet the fond lark sings.
Beside her spinning-wheel the shepherdess
Sings passioned ditties, while her rustic swain
In some dark copse stands listening motionless,
And all things throb with love's delicious pain—
Save only you, who, more than Dian cold,
Your loveliness from love's approach withhold.

Skies, Stars, and Winds

Skies, stars, and winds, green meads, and moun-
    tains bare,
Summits twin-domed, and peaceful landlocked
    coves,
Curved shores, and silver fountains hung in air,
Bird-haunted greensward, and reverberant groves,
Moss-covered caves that scorn the peeping sun,
Sweet-scented flowers, fresh buds, and burnished
    grass,
Hillsides vine-clad, and you, my Helicon,
My Loire, and you, my plaintive Muse, alas!
Alas! in sudden scorn of her sweet spell,
I left my love, and spoke no fond farewell
To her whose image colors land and sea.
O hear me then, air, sky, wind, meads, and moun-
    tains,
Caves, forest glades, and silver-flowing fountains,
Trees, buds, and blossoms, say farewell for me!

Here Is the Wood

Here is the wood where roaming all alone,
Among ten thousand blossoms burgeoning,
Down winding ways with mossy rocks bestrown,
My angel love trilled greetings to the spring.
Here is the champaign dressed in gold and green
That made her white hands smell of meadowsweet
Whenas she stooped to pillage it between
The shining grass-blades curling round her feet.

Here did I see her sing, and there shed tears,
Here smile on me, and there with tender glance
Wake wistful visions of the eager years,
Here did she sit, and yonder did she dance:
Thus on the loom of dream-spun hopes and fears
Love weaves its cloudy fabric of romance.

Up, Lady Mine

UP, LADY MINE, and ope those drowsy eyes!
The merry lark already greets the morn,
And the amorous nightingale from yonder thorn
Wakens the echoes with her pretty cries.
Come, darling, come and tread the dew-pearled
    grass;
Your fair hand watered every rosy bud
And daisies pied that the green turf bestud;
See how they lift their heads to watch you pass!
Last night you vowed to put the sun to shame,
And me your lover, waking ere the dawn;
But morning slumbers that feed beauty's flame
Seal your bright eyes and keep their curtains
    drawn.
Nay, I will kiss that white breast and those eyes
To teach you, lazy maid, betimes to rise.

Receive This Nosegay

RECEIVE THIS nosegay of fresh flowers pulled
In golden meadows, blossoms all full-blown:

Had they not ere the vesper-bell been culled
The dawn had seen their petals wind-bestrown.
O sad example of the too brief date
Of beauty's bloom! Like them, sweet lady mine,
Only a little while your charms will shine
Before they share the fading blossoms' fate.
Time flits away, time flits away, my love;
Alas! not time, 'tis we that flit away
To sleep alone in some dark cypress grove.
Then of this love so tender-true today,
We being dead, no mortal tongue will speak:
Ah! love me while still blooms that rosy cheek.

In Vain the Meadow's Fairest Blooms I Cull

IN VAIN THE meadow's fairest blooms I cull,
In vain my skill their thousand tints disposes:
What blossom matched with you is beautiful?
O flower of flowers! O rose among the roses!
You and the roses differ but in this:
Harsh winter lays their beauty in the tomb,
While your blithe spring knows no fell Nemesis
And through all seasons keeps its perfect bloom.
O garden spoils, so lovely yet so frail!
Shun that fair bosom where the Graces dwell,
Nor brave compare with those red rosebuds' spell.
The luster of your damask leaves would pale
Even as in me youth's ardors faint and fail
For this dear love I feel, yet may not tell.

To Helen

In after days, when time shall quite consume
Your beauty's bud, in the dim candlelight
Spinning your wool, you'll cry, "O wondrous night,
When Ronsard sang me in my springtime bloom!"
At your proud word each weaver by her loom,
Though toil and slumber seal her weary sight,
Will wake to life, and marvel and delight
That thus your glory doth outlast the tomb.
I shall be then a disembodied ghost,
Treading the myrtle-sprinkled fields of death;
You, bent with age, will mourn the love you lost
Through your disdain that deemed it idle breath:
Nay, heed my prayer, avert a tardy sorrow,
And cull today the rose that fades tomorrow.

Take This Red Rose

Take this red rose, yourself the queen of roses
Whose fairest blooms are copied after you,
My very flower of flowers, whose cup encloses
Scents sweet as roses and of livelier hue.
Take this red rose, and with it take my heart
To nestle near your own. It has no wings—
In vain, O cruel one, you cry, Depart!
It still sits by your side and still it sings.
We differ but in this, my rose and I:
One single day beholds it bloom and die,
A thousand days have seen my passion grow
And thousands wait in vain for its decay.
O too fond heart to be deluded so!
Would, like the rose, love lasted but a day!

In Sweet May Month

IN SWEET MAY MONTH the red rose on its branch,
At the fresh season of its heyday prime,
Made every rival flower with envy blanch
As the dawn kissed its petals time on time.
In its frail chalice grace and love reposed,
It made the garden balmy with its scent,
Till cruel heat and beating raindrops bent
Its beauty earthward and its buds upclosed.
Even so, my loved one, in your vernal bloom,
While all the earth smiled on your loveliness,
Death laid you low! As offerings to your tomb
I bear this jar of milk, these flowers that press
So softly on your limbs—these roses red.
You loved them living, let them grace you dead.

Beside This Singing Fount

BESIDE THIS singing fount I plant a tree
And carve on its smooth bark your name and mine
That after-times may read them and divine
Our ancient love and its brave witchery.
Ye fauns, whose cries the woodland echoes rouse
When by the river-edge you lead the dance,
Nurture this tree with tender sustenance
Lest summer parch or winter sere its boughs.
And thou, sweet shepherd with the oaten reed,
When to this spot thou bringst thy flock to drink,
Pour milk and wine upon the mossy brink,
And every year renew the ancient screed
By time effaced, and carve these words above:
Sacred to Helen and to Ronsard's love.

Nor Dawn of Day

NOR DAWN OF DAY glassed in the opening rose,
Nor lilies floating on a silver fount,
Nor song of lute, nor larks that skyward mount,
Nor starry gems that clasps of gold enclose,
Nor the white bosom of the wingèd wind,
Nor dryads dancing where cool waters glide,
Nor shallops wafted on the whispering tide,
Nor Spring returned from shores of odorous Ind,
Nor high-piled arms where glittering lances cross,
Nor curtained caves o'ertapestried with moss,
Nor tangled tree-tops waving in the blue—
Not all of these can such sweet pleasure yield
As roaming lovelorn in a poppied field
Or silent meadow where I dream of you.

JOACHIM DU BELLAY
1522–1560

The Winnower's Song

Ye zephyrs fleet of wing
That musically sing
Down hill and dale,
Or 'mong the flow'rets drift
And tenderly uplift
Their odorous veil,

These purple violets yet
With globèd dewdrops wet,
I offer you;
Lily and rose I bring,
Sweet buds just opening,
And pale pinks too.

Breathe soft, ye fanning airs,
Down these green thoroughfares;
Cool this parched soil,
While in the noonday heat
I winnow my ripe wheat
With weary toil.

Rome

O WANDERER that seekest Rome in Rome,
Though naught of Rome in Rome doth now appear,
These crumbling fanes, these ancient piles that rear
So high their heads, were once the Roman's home.
See Rome in ruin, that once like a king
Beheld all lands 'neath its dominion cast,
And, spoiling all, despoiled itself at last,
A prey to Time, who conquers everything.
Rome is of Rome the last sad monument,
And Rome alone wrought Rome's abolishment;
Now Tiber only in his seaward flight
Flows past old Rome. Thus age succeeds our prime:
All that stood firm is levelled by Time's spite,
But that which flows withstands the flight of Time.

The Same

HE THAT WOULD learn the stretch of nature's
  power
Or spell of art, let him survey thee, Rome!
Let him conceive thy glory in its flower
And read thy greatness in its ruined home.
Rome is no more. If its gigantic walls
Retain some trace of beauty once so brave,
'Tis like the ghost the necromant recalls
At midnight from the darkness of the grave.
The frame of Rome is unto ashes turned,
Its soul has vanished from this marble tomb
Wherein its mighty body lies inurned:
But its immortal poesy shall bloom
Unscathed, athwart Time's cloudy dust upwhirled,
A radiant image wandering through the world.

Confession

WHERE IS IT NOW, that scorn of changeful fate
And that proud heart that bore all strokes un-
  shocked,
That love of fame that early strove and late
And that far flight that baser natures mocked?
Where is the ecstasy, the golden dream
The Muses woke when, in the pale twilight,
On the green bank of some meandering stream
I led their dances through the moonlit night?
Now Fortune rules me, and my wavering heart
That once was steadfast mistress of my powers,
Is doomed to play the servile courtier's part,
Consuming in regrets its ill-spent hours,
While the bright Muses, seeing me so changed,
Whom once they loved, have fled away estranged.

Happy the Man

HAPPY THE MAN who travels distant seas,
Like shrewd Ulysses or the Argonauts,
Then homeward fares, admonished by sage
  thoughts
To pass his waning age in careless ease!
Alas! when shall I see among the trees
The blue smoke curling from my cottage roof,
And those green hedgerows where I sat aloof
From the proud world and its vain pageantries?
More dear to me is my forefathers' home
Than all the splendors of Imperial Rome,
More dear than marble walls its mossy tiles,
My Gallic Loire than Latian Tiber's streams,
More than the Palatine these wooded aisles;
And sweetest of all climes my Anjou seems.

My Ancient Nurse

FRANCE, MOTHER of the arts, of arms, of laws,
Long didst thou feed me at thy fecund breast;
But now, poor lamb, by fear and thirst oppressed,
I call my ancient nurse and know no pause.
If thou hast loved me as thy foster-child,
Turn not away, nor leave me sick and faint!
O France, O France! lend ear to my complaint,
Which mocking Echo mimics in the wild.
Among the cruel wolves I roam the plain
And watch the wintry tempests blanch the hills.
Sweet mother! lock me in thy fold again!
Thy other lambs in the green pastures feast,
Safe from the wolf, and wind, and nightly chills:
Yet of thy flock I am not last nor least.

Already Night on Heaven's Azure Steep

ALREADY NIGHT on heaven's azure steep
Was gathering her flock of wandering stars;
Already through the Western Ocean's bars
Day drove his coursers from the caverned deep;
But when the Indian skies grew rosy-red,
And the new morn shook from her golden curls
A glittering shower of Oriental pearls
On thousand shining isles and mountains shed,
Then, like a star that shoots up in the west,
Sudden I saw a fair nymph, golden-tressed,
White-raimented, blaze in the Occident,
And rising Day, shamed by this rival dawn,
Flung shafts of light from skiey fountains drawn
On Anjou and the Indian Orient.

Soft Sleep, Best Gift of Heaven

SOFT SLEEP, BEST gift of heaven, on my tired eyes
Flowed honey-sweet, and on its fluent streams
Moved Love with all his retinue of dreams
That from the fountains of enchantment rise.
Methought I kissed my lady's mouth and twined
My eager arms around her marble breast,
Like wanton vines that round the elm-trees wind
Where lordly Loire rolls through the fertile West.
And now the mounting flame of sweet desire
That burned between the roses of her lips
Lured my sick spirit, like a star on fire,
Toward that dark Lethe where the senses swoon,
Till envious dawn, returning, ah! too soon,
Dispelled my dream in day's apocalypse.

To His Lady

FOR ALL THE GRIEFS, my dear, I have sustained,
For all the love that year on year I lavished,
For all those tears and sighs that passion ravished
From my sad soul, with yet no guerdon gained,
I asked one kiss, such as could never move
Envy or blame, or make the mockers sport,
Favor oft granted to an honest love
Even by the chastest lady of the court.
But you, alas! whether indifference sway
Your heart, or pity, lest a grace like this
Should make my swooning soul die on a kiss,
Deny me still. Oh drive this fear away!
I would adventure all for such fond bliss,
And, dying so, deem death a holiday.

To the Same

WHILE YET MY hearing, which is withered now,
Could grasp your speech and revel in its grace,
You hid from me the glory of that face
And the calm beauty of that sovran brow.
Too late do you your coldness disavow,
Too late you sorrow at my piteous case,
Too late, like the fond ivy, you embrace
A sere tree barren to its utmost bough.
O haunting passion, O relentless pain,
To gaze on that loved face, yet gaze in vain
At beauty that can but increase my woe,
To touch that yearned-for hand, so white, so dear,
See those so lovely eyes, yet never know
That gentle voice I fain would die to hear.

The Ideal

IF OUR BRIEF SPAN yield like a flitting day
To endless night, if each revolving year
Hasten a death foredoomed, and if so near
To man's maturity lies man's decay,
Why, captive soul, would you prolong your stay
In the dark cycles of this terrene sphere,
Having immortal wings with which to steer
Your flight to heaven's eternal holiday?
There is the good which every heart desires,
There the repose to which all life aspires,
And there is love, and peace that knows not fear;
There, O my soul, in heaven's utmost height,
Thou may'st discover that diviner light
Of perfect beauty thou didst worship here.

Elegy on His Cat

I HAVE NOT lost my rings, my purse,
My gold, my gems—my loss is worse,
One that the stoutest heart must move.
My pet, my joy, my little love,
My tiny kitten, my Belaud,
I lost, alas, three days ago.
O little friend, adieu, adieu!
Would that I too were dead like you!
Dame Nature never shaped a cat
So sleek as you, so soft to pat,
So sweetly bred, so midget-sized,
So fit to be immortalized.
        His like in France you will not meet,
But only in a Roman street.
Gray was his coat, yet not all gray,
But streaked with many a silver ray,
All satin-smooth; and down his spine
In little billows argentine
It rose and fell, then vanished quite
Beneath a belly ermine-white.
Tiny his head and small his joints,
And short his ears, with pinkish points;
Under his nostrils coraline
A little muzzle leonine,
And all around it, bristling bright,
Twice seven whiskers, silver white.
Cruel death has struck at him
And has chilled each furry limb.
Death, alas, had never seen
Belaud frolic on the green,
Seen him leap, and run, and scratch,
Or with lightning motion catch

Some poor mouse which scurried past,
Catch him, loose him, hold him fast.
Oh, how soft would Belaud climb
On my couch at napping-time,
Or with sudden impulse shrewd
Ravish from my lips the food,
Or with frenzied jerk and bound
Like a wheel spin round and round,
Following the speeding trail
Of his own revolving tail,
Or, displaying all the fur
Of his ermine stomacher,
On his velvet haunches perch
Like some Doctor of the Church.

    Sweet Belaud, you cunning actor,
You were sure no malefactor!
E'en your sins did halfway please.
It was you who stole my cheese,
You, alas, who killed my linnet,
Wrecked the cage with birdie in it,
Feeling sure you did no wrong
Since it irked you with its song.
I forgive you, little pet,
I, too, am not perfect yet.

ANTOINE DE BAÏF
1532–1589

To the Swallow

BABBLING swallow, why so shrill?
Wherefore with your piercing screams
Drive away my glad daydreams?
Babbling swallow, hush, be still!

Babbling swallow, cease that trill!
If you do not let me rest
I will trap you in your nest.
Babbling swallow, hush, be still!

Babbling swallow, your smooth bill
And your glossy wings I'll clip
And your bonny plumage strip.
Babbling swallow, hush, be still!

Babbling swallow, many an ill
Threatens you and your sweet brood
If your piping be renewed.
Babbling swallow, hush, be still!

RÉMI BELLEAU
1528–1577

April

APRIL, pride of all the year,
    And of sere
Woods and meadows sweetest hope,
With ambrosial savors pent
    Redolent
In lush buds that wait to ope;

April, queen of hillsides green,
    Opaline,
Where the wild flowers grow untrammeled
Like the stars in multitude
    Rainbow-hued,
With ten thousand tints enameled;

April, wooed by Zephyrs soft
    That aloft,
Flitting through the perfumed aura
Of the wildwood, sigh and soar
    Evermore
Round the garden goddess Flora;

April, that hast ta'en for nest
    Nature's breast,
Fountainhead wherein has birth
All this harvest of rich flowers
    Which she showers
Breeze-borne o'er the balmy earth;

April, on the verdant heath
        Cull a wreath
And let blossom bound with blossom
Slowly wind with soft caresses
        Down thy tresses
Till they kiss thy snowy bosom.

April, thy enchanting smile
        Might beguile
Cypris' self to steal thy breath
And her cheeks divine illume
        With thy bloom
Bastioned there from blight and death.

Thou from far Hesperides,
        Where tall trees
Hang their golden fruit on high,
Bring'st the swallows home again
        O'er the main
To proclaim that spring is nigh.

Hawthorn, thyme, and eglantine,
        Columbine,
Lilies, pinks, and roses red,
Every blossom, every vine,
        Bud and twine
In thy glowing garden-bed.

Now the timid nightingale,
        In the vale,
On her bough the whole night long
Frames a thousand babbling trills
        Till the hills
Ring with echoes of her song.

For the springtime's glad return
          There doth burn
In our veins a long-pent fire
'Scaping from the sullen shade
          Winter made,
Foe of Love and young Desire.

Now on every plant are seen
          Libertine
Swarms of bees with nectar filled
Stol'n from every odorous petal
          Where they settle
Till their honey is distilled.

Vainly May doth vaunt her beauty
          And the fruity
Odors of her laden trees
And the incense that she brings
          On her wings
To embalm the lingering breeze.

April, month of golden days,
          Thee I praise,
From the goddess named who sprang
Skyward from Aegean seas
          While Naiades
And Tritons mounting peans sang.

PONTUS DE TYARD
1521–1605

Sleep

SLEEP, FOUNTAINHEAD of dreams and bland re-
   pose,
Now that the night, enwrapt in sable clouds,
This air serene in humid shadow shrouds,
Come, blessèd Sleep, and these tired lids upclose.
Thy absence drear prolongs the languid hours
And makes love's torment seem unparagoned.
Come, balmy Sleep, with wafture of thy wand
Point me toward dreamland's visionary bowers.
Already stilly Silence leads his bands
Of phantom dancers in their nightly round,
Yet thou disdain'st to medicine my wound.
O come, sweet Sleep, to lay thy gentle hands
On this tired head, and when day dawns I'll twine
A wreath of scarlet poppies round thy shrine.

JEAN PASSERAT
1534–1602

Villanelle

I HAVE lost my turtle-dove,
'Tis her mate, not she, I hear:
Let me go to find my love.

Thou art sick with grief and love,
So to both do I lend ear:
I have lost my turtle-dove.

Thy lost mate thy grief doth move,
Mine to me was no less dear:
Let me go to find my love.

Thy sad plaining fills the grove,
Mine re-echoes far and near:
I have lost my turtle-dove.

Naught to us can beauteous prove,
Naught our heavy hearts can cheer:
Let me go to find my love.

Death, let us thy pity move,
We would bide no longer here:
I have lost my turtle-dove,
Let me go to find my love.

May Song

LET US FLEE from bed and sleep
    On this happy day,
Over vale and hillside steep
    Dawn lights up the way.
Now while all the heavens are gay,

In this merry month of May,
      Buss me, buss me, dear:
Let us taste love's sweetest treasure,
In this world they have no pleasure
      Who to take it fear.

Come, my sweet, let us go maying
      In yon shady grove:
Hear the twittering birds essaying
      Their sweet songs of love,
Hear, oh hear, o'er all the rest
Nightingale, who sings the best,
      Sings, yet never tires.
Think no more of grief and pain,
Youth will ne'er return again
      When it once expires.

Time, the foe of lovers' blisses,
      Time that knows no ruth,
Steals away love's joys and kisses,
      Steals away our youth.
Ah! when wrinkled eld draws nigh,
You will say with many a sigh,
      How I do repent me
That I let my beauty fade:
See what havoc age has made,
      See how time has shent me!

Leave vain tears and sad repining
      Till old age arrives.
See the globèd dewdrops shining
      On the golden hives:
Now while all the heavens are gay,
In this merry month of May,
      Buss me, buss me, dear:
Let us taste love's sweetest treasure,
In this world they have no pleasure
      Who to take it fear.

OLIVIER DE MAGNY
1529–1561

To Pales

IN THIS meadow blossomy,
Sacred, Pales, unto thee,
In this meadow where I sported
With my love a little time,
Whom I pleasured, whom I courted
With my lute and with my rhyme
While the birds peeped o'er the edge
Of the snowy hawthorn hedge,
And with hundred melodies
Lauded love and love's sweet ease—
Unto thee, my goddess, I
Raise this altar here on high,
Girt around with daisied turf
Rolling up its flowery surf,
Little altar built of clay
O'er which ivy tendrils stray,
Sprinkled all with rose and lily
Gathered in the regions hilly:
You may pin them on your gown,
Or weave them, Pales, in your crown.

LOUISE LABÉ
1526–1566

I

Soon as these weary eyelids 'gin to close,
My tristful thoughts incontinently spurn
The feathered nest where soft my limbs repose,
And fly to thee to seek more sweet sojourn.
Ah! then meseems within this tender heart
I lock the golden flower of my desires,
That blissful love to which my soul aspires
With deep-drawn sighs that rend my breast apart.
O happy slumber! O auspicious night!
O sweet repose! Kiss shut these tear-stained eyes
And evermore renew that blessèd sight:
For if my lonely heart unloved must live,
To salve my wounds let night benignly give
In dream-wrought semblance what the day denies.

II

When I behold your head with laurel crowned
And hear the gentle plaining of your lute,
That might persuade with magic of its sound
The trees and rocks to stand no longer mute,
When I behold such sovran worth adorn you
As in no rival finds a counterpart,
My love that would to answering love suborn you
Voices its passioned pleading in my heart:
These golden virtues that all men approve,
Making you of all men most beloved,
Might they not also teach you how to love?
Might not that liberal heart at last be moved
Through very pity to bestow this grace,
To give me in your thoughts a little place?

III

O MELTING GLANCE, O eyes so full of charms,
Like little gardens rich in amorous flowers
Where ambushed Cupid hid his perilous arms
And where I roamed in incense-breathing bowers!
O cruel love! How often have I bled
To see those gardens now with weeds o'ergrown!
How many bitter tears in slumber shed
Since one dear heart was shut unto my own!
Alas! my wanton eyes, renounce your quest,
Nor longer in those gardens cull delight,
While you, my heart, the more my sight is blest,
Languish the more and dwell in sadder plight:
Ah, doubly cruel is the part I play,
Whose eyes say *Yes* the while my heart cries
      Nay!

IV

IF I COULD LAY my head on his loved breast,
In which sweet comfort I were fain to die,
If in that happy haven all the rest
Of my brief span could glide unenvied by,
If, thus enfolding me, my love should cry,
"Sleep, my beloved, in this downy nest,
Where never storm nor grief shall break thy
      rest,
Thy faithful lover being ever nigh,"
If prisoned in my arms I held him fast
As climbing ivy holds the bending tree,
If he with thousand kisses showered me
Till all my soul hung on his fevered lips,
To pay a joy I knew too sweet to last
I were content to swoon in death's eclipse.

V

WHILE YET THE tear-drop's gather in mine eyes
When I recall the bliss I had with you,
While yet I can, despite my sobs and sighs,
Find voice to sing a love so tender-true,
While yet my hand can touch the trembling
    strings
Of my loved lute to hymn your thousand graces,
While yet my soul, save you, disdains all things
And, barring yours, turns from all human faces,
So long I will not yearn for easeful death:
But when the years shall dim these tearful eyes,
When my hands drop the lute, and my slow
    breath
Faints from my song, when my worn cheek denies
To flaunt love's banner, then let endless night
Forever hide me from the day's glad light.

VI

WHEN, ROBED IN GOLD, the all-renewing sun
Is crowned and sceptered by attendant spring,
Bare fields and frozen streams, new-wakening,
Herald his reign. The singing waters run
Down murmuring slopes where many a peerless
    flower
Lifts its red clusters in the golden corn,
While mating larks salute the rising morn
Safe-citadeled from hurt in their green bower.
The Oreads with thousand sports beguile
The moonlit night and dance the grasses down.
Ah, Zephyrus, would you bring back a smile
To these pale lips and my long sorrows crown
With sudden joy? Bring back my kingly sun
And 'mong the fair I'll seem the fairest one.

VII

Do NOT, YE FAIR, my passion disapprove,
Though hotter than a thousand torches' glow
Burns its fierce flame and sears my heart-strings so
That day and night I weep for very love.
Do not, alas, my folly's height reprove:
If I have erred, do not my fortunes show
I was predestined to this utmost woe?
Then let my sorrows your compassion move,
For though no god Olympian charm your heart,
No, nor no fair Adonis' counterpart,
Yet Love may bend you to his sovran will
Till more than me you passionately sigh,
Though lured by less of beauty than was I.
Alas! alas! may you not fare as ill.

VIII

ALAS! WHY HAVE I lived to see the day
When two loved eyes consume my longing
  heart?
Why must my rosy morning turn to gray?
Why must the sunshine in my soul depart?
Had I foreseen love's course in its completeness,
Its aftermath of tears and self-reproach,
Divined how soon its flower must lose all sweetness,
How soon the night must on its day encroach,
Had I perceived what way my passion led,
How fell its power, how deep its poignant pain,
How surely had I paused, how swiftly fled!
But nay, not so! Could that day come again
When first I saw my love, how quickly I
Like a light bird would to his bosom fly.

VAUQUELIN DE LA FRESNAYE
1536–1606

Idyl

ON A BED of lily flowers
Phyllis through the matin hours
Slumbered in the balmy air;
Little Cupids round the maid
Danced and frolicked unafraid,
Seeing her so heavenly fair.

Could I spy unmoved those charms,
Rose-tipped breasts and snowy arms?
Nay—my heart admonished me—
All too heavy is the cost
Of sweet hours forever lost:
Youth can ne'er recovered be.

Wiser grown, I stooped above her,
Softly, slily, wanton lover,
Stole from her red lips a kiss.
O delights of Paradise,
O seraphic ecstasies,
Can your joys be sweet as this?

O Gentle Breeze

O GENTLE BREEZE, whose incense-burdened
  breath
Fills the night air with balm of thousand flowers!
O smiling mead, where half in love with death
Two parting lovers counted the sad hours!

O shadowy forest and swift-flowing stream,
That saw at last their sorrows turn to bliss
And their long severance ended in a kiss
When love renewed their interrupted dream!
Now age has weaned them from love's wayward
    folly,
And wisdom sanctifies their ancient fire,
Blunting the too sharp edge of young desire:
Yet still they feel a gentle melancholy
When some sweet chance brings back as in a
    dream
This breeze, this wood, this mead, this flowing
    stream.

GUILLAUME DU BARTAS

1544–1590

The Pyrenees

T IS NO MERE mount, this guardian of the plain,
This rock Titanic whose proud top impends
Above the pass, and evermore defends
Spain's frontier from the French and France
from Spain.
Pause, traveller, nor transgress this mountain-
chain,
Along whose flanks a rock-ribbed wall extends
And toward whose base the leaping stream de-
scends,
Bringing new beauty to this wide domain.
Holding one arm to Spain and one to France,
It props the load of Atlas on its head;
Its feet toward two confronted seas advance;
Vast forests on its mighty shoulders spread;
Its body is of rock, and down its side,
Like bands of sweat, the foaming rivers glide.

PHILIPPE DESPORTES
1546–1606

Invocation

O Sleep! I bring thee this long-cellared wine,
And milk, and poppies dark, with crownèd heads,
To lure thee where the old crone Sibyline
Sits with her maids, pulling her last long threads
Of fresh-spun wool. Over the chill hearth bent,
With twisted thumb upraised and moistened lips
She plies her task. Softly her eyes eclipse,
Arrest her distaff, end her brabblement,
And let me all night, without harassment,
Still kiss and kiss that dimpled little maid,
Fond Ysabeau, who waits and waits, afraid.

The Fountain

How cool this fountain, whose smooth-flowing
    tide,
All silvered o'er, invites to thoughts of love!
Soft herbage rims its brink on every side,
And alders spill their shadows from above.
Low-twittering birds among the boughs alight,
And amorous Zephyr finds a still retreat
While flaming Sol shines from his mid-noon
    height
And earth lies arid in the parching heat.
Love's pilgrim, by long ways dispirited,
Burned by the sunshine and by drought op-
    pressed,

Pause in this spot where happy chance has led:
Here weariness is turned to blessèd rest,
Here sunbeams play, with shadows interspersed,
And this clear current will allay your thirst.

GILLES DURANT
1550–1615

The Lover's Lament

IN VAIN 'mong wooded nooks,
Green dells and plashy brooks,
        And rocky belvedere,
I've sought my love all day!
Ah! who has stol'n away
        The nymph I held so dear?
Ye pretty shepherdesses,
With flower-entangled tresses,
        Whose silver voices clear
Trill love's sweet roundelay,
Tell me who's stol'n away
        The nymph I held so dear.
Farewell, ye somber woods!
Sing a sad dirge, ye floods,
        Beside my leafy bier!
Why should I longer stay
If death has stol'n away
        The nymph I held so dear?
She's gone—I know not where,
My love that was so fair!
        Has some god wandering here,
Thinking her gone astray
From heaven, snatched her away,
        The nymph I held so dear?

JEAN BERTAUT
1552–1611

To His Lady

TIS TIME, MY FAIR, 'tis time the woes to end
Those dear eyes cause, sweet fount of my de-
  sires;
Let them on me with greater kindness bend,
Or else consume me quite in their fierce fires.
Holding the issue of my life or death,
Judge what return my faith has merited:
Is it pure faith, or is it idle breath?
Do I deserve your love, or hate instead?
If that your heart be not of adamant,
Scorn not my love for that it still endures,
Nor spurn a lover whom your charms enchant.
Beauty breeds love, and beauty such as yours
Must bear the blame, that breeds it everywhere:
If love be sin, 'tis scandal to be fair.

FRANÇOIS DE MALHERBE
1555–1628

To Louis XIII

I YIELD UNTO the conquering hand of age;
Only my mind, unbated in its course,
Can show even yet upon my latest page
      Its primal force.
The Muses came to crown my infant brow
With gracious wreaths of never-fading bays;
I had their favors young, I have them now
      In my last days.
So shall you learn how great a gift is mine,
How great my skill; and from my Muse's wings
Shall flash such rays as never yet did shine
      On crownèd kings.
Whether your martial feats my song inspire
Or in my verse your royal goodness shine,
What bard is there so vain to think his lyre
      Can equal mine?
Amphion, who a city raised from naught,
And won the plaudits of the universe,
Though great his fame, no greater marvel wrought
  wrought
      Than my proud verse.
My lines shall fill the world with thy renown;
The very peoples of the Nile shall bring,
When this they read, their fairest flowers to
  crown
      Louis our king.

OGIER DE GOMBAUD
1570–1666

To a Lady Who Gave Him Roses

IN DIVERSE ways the heart discloses
 The secret love with which we burn;
O lovely maid, you send me roses,
 And I send verses in return.
Roses are sweet, yet in their stead,
 Prithee, more lasting pledges give:
Already your fair flowers are dead,
 My verses will forever live.

MATHURIN RÉGNIER
1573–1613

Epitaph

LIVING without a thought,
Taking what Nature brought,
Drawing untroubled breath,
I wonder curiously
Why Death should think of me,
Who never thought of Death.

JEAN DE LINGENDES
1580–1616

The Sad Shepherdess

PHYLLIS by a shady elm,
Seated on the stony ground,
While her lambkins sport around—
Phyllis whom love's woes o'erwhelm,
Loitering in this lonely spot,
By her fickle swain forgot
And no more with roses crowned,
With wet eyne and trembling hand
Scrawls this posy on the sand:
"I love one who loves me not!"
Ah! tormented shepherdess!
There is cure for love's distress:
Straight a gentle zephyr rose,
Blowing through that woody close
Till it cooled her amorous smart,
And with fanning breath erased
Both the posy she had traced
And the passion in her heart.

FRANÇOIS DE MAYNARD
1582–1646

A Declaration

Dear object of first love and latest praise,
Whose worth my tongue is hourly caroling,
Sweet Chloris, change the tenor of my days
And turn my winter to a balmier spring.

My love is not a flower of yesteryear;
Four decades have been as a passing day,
Making that lovely head, those locks, more dear:
I loved them brown, I love them dearer gray.

It was those eyes that charmed my youthful heart,
They were the first, the last, that I adored.
Silent I watched you play your wifely part:
I kept my secret, and love spoke no word.

I breathed my passion to the voiceless hills
And to the rock-ribbed vales and antique woods,
From whose green depths a silent peace distils
That, though it cure not, soothes our saddest
    moods.

Consumed with love and fruitless melancholy,
I roamed distraught through orange-scented lands,
Conjuring far-off seas to share my folly
And make your name resound on alien strands.

Yet still your beauty shines as in its prime,
The fleeting years are impotent to harm
Its calm perfection, and relentless time
Forgets his errand and renews your charm.

Care cannot lessen it, nor grief consume;
Your glorious day knows no dim evening,
Still on your cheeks the rose and lily bloom,
And winter is for you a second spring.

But not for me—my head, all bowed and white,
Leans toward the tomb and the funereal urn,
And my spent fire would be extinguished quite
Did not love's deathless flame more brightly burn.

THÉOPHILE DE VIAU
1590–1626

To Corinna

IN THIS unpeopled shady valley
The stag that bays the murmuring stream
Bounds lightly from some verdant alley
To spy the water's silvery gleam.

A naiad dwelling by the spring
Throws open wide each evening
Her door of shining crystal made
And sings a joyful serenade.

Here silence deep and shadows dim
Amid the clustered elm-trees hover,
While amorous Zephyrs rock each limb
And every leaf with kisses cover.

Come, my Corinna, come and lie
At ease upon this mossy bed,
Or if you fear some envious eye,
We'll choose this hollow grot instead.

Here love has built a fragrant bower,
Here Venus' self has set her shrine,
And in this haunt of vine and flower
No feet shall tread but yours and mine.

How I love your lawless tresses,
That wander daintily remiss,
Touching your cheek with warm caresses
Till I grow jealous of their kiss.

O lovely lips of rose and amber,
Lips to melt the heart of Jove,

Here where the honeysuckles clamber,
How can ye speak of aught but love?

O dainty fingers, snowy white!
If by the streamlet's mossy brink
Some god should stray, in his delight
He'd kiss them and forget to drink.

Nay, hide those lily hands away,
Nor in the brook your beauty glass;
In my fond eyes your charms survey,
And let the god unheeded pass.

Here where pale myrtles dot the ground,
And peeping violets feed the sight,
And waters make a pleasant sound,
We'll sit and kiss from morn till night.

Shrill the chaffinch and the linnet
In the rosebush tune their lay,
With a trembling passion in it
Born of springtide and the May.

Come, then, come, my trembling dryad!
By this music-making stream,
With the lark we'll form a triad,
And we'll sing of love's sweet dream.

I will bathe my eager fingers
In the billows of your hair,
Like a devotee who lingers,
Saying o'er and o'er his prayer.

Fear no harm from Cupid's wiles,
Listen to the love I plead,
And your answer in your smiles
And your blushing cheek I'll read.

My Corinna, let me kiss you,
There's no witness near but Love;

Sol's bright arrows here will miss you:
This is Cupid's sacred grove.

Gossip Zephyrs overhead
Watch us in our leafy bed
While we whisper, hand in hand,
Things no Zephyrs understand.

CLAUDE DE MALLEVILLE
1597–1646

Morning Beauty

CALM SILENCE ruled on land and on the deep,
Soft airs played round Olympus, rosy red,
And amorous Zephyr, wakened from his sleep,
Kissed every rose and raised its drooping head.
Aurora came her matin rites to render,
And sprinkled rubies on the sun-god's track,
Who through the heavens rode in all his splendor
While paling stars before their lord drew back.
But lo! my Phyllis walked with smiling face
Forth from her palace toward the orient light,
And the new day turned pale, the sun less bright:
O golden Phoebus, deem it no disgrace
If, matched with hers, your state more dimly
    shone
Than did the fires of night beside your own.

VINCENT VOITURE
1598–1648

Evening Beauty

WITH ROSES crowned, the nymph that I adore
Walked in the evening glow across the lawn,
Her cheeks and eyes so bright that all men swore
'Twas not my love but reappearing dawn.
The earth to greet her sprouted thousand flow-
  ers,
The birds on every bough held jubilee,
And paling stars forgot to count the hours,
Deeming new day was rising from the sea.
The sun forspent, that hovered on the deep,
Infused new splendors in his golden beams
And bade his fiery chariot eastward sweep,
Unbarred by Neptune and the ocean streams,
Till, love-bedazed yet fearing her disdain,
He seaward plunged and dared not come again.

TRISTAN L'HERMITE
1601–1655

The Lovers' Walk

NEAR THIS LOW grot with vines o'ergrown
And pendant flowers, the loitering stream
Coats with white spray each mossy stone
Where broken lights through shadows gleam.

In this wild spot the ruddy Faun,
Pausing his fortunes to bewail,
Mirrors himself at earliest dawn
To see if love has made him pale.

The floating faces of the flowers,
The pictured reeds that softly weep,
Appear in these crystalline bowers
Like dreams of waters fall'n asleep.

No leaf in this still air is stirred,
No hunter treads this lonely land,
Or if some echoing horn is heard,
'Tis but of Dian and her band.

The melancholy nightingale,
On whom King Tereus worked such woe,
From branch to branch prolongs her wail,
Singing a mournful tremolo.

Still rings her song, the selfsame one
She sang of old by Thracian streams;
Still through the darkling boughs the sun
Plays hide-and-seek with fitful beams.

On yonder ash two turtle-doves,
Filled with the languor of the spring,
Tired of their pretty bickering loves,
Sleep side by side and wing to wing.

Here let us sit, my lovely one,
Watching the silver waters mount
Until the setting of the sun
Shall veil the crystal-flowing fount.

List! how the lovelorn Zephyrs sigh
As, spellbound, in your cheeks they view
Red roses of a richer dye
Than e'er in mortal gardens grew.

In this clear fount, so silver bright,
The mirror of the shepherd lasses,
See how your image with delight
Smiles back at the fair face it glasses.

Yet tremblingly I see it drift,
Convoyed by my too fond desires,
Lest some stray god his torch uplift
To lure it shoreward with his fires.

Fill with this lymph more sweet than wine
Your snowy palms and hold them up,
And let me sip a draught divine
From those white hands that form my cup.

But see! upon my humid mouth
How many telltale drops remain:
O love, breathe like the balmy South
And kiss them dry—again, again!

ANONYMOUS

From The Misanthrope *of Molière*

If the King Should Say to Me

If the king should say to me,
"Come, my lad, I'll give to thee
    My great city Paris,"
And instead would take away
Her whom I shall love alway,
    That so sweet and fair is—
I would say, "King Henry, nay!
    Keep your city Paris,
But take not my love away,
Her whom I shall love alway,
    That so sweet and fair is!"

JEAN DE LA FONTAINE
1621–1695

The Cicada and the Ant

THE SHRILL cicada piped her song
    All summer long,
But found herself without a crumb
When the wintry days had come.
There was not a grub to fill her,
Not a worm or caterpillar,
So she hopped off to her neighbor,
The wise ant, that friend of labor,
Begging for a little grain
Her frail body to sustain
Till the spring should come again.
"If you'll help me in my plight,
I'll repay you, honor bright,
When the crop comes in next fall,
Interest and principal."
Now the ant is not a lender:
"Pray," she cried, "what were you doing
While my stores I was renewing
In the time of summer splendor?"
"Night and day with cheery spirit
Still I sang—don't look askance!"
"Ah! you sang? I'm glad to hear it:
Now then, bundle off and dance!"

The Oak and the Reed

THE OAK ONE day said to the reed,
"At nature's ways you well may be chagrined:

A kinglet is for you a load indeed,
And the least breath of wind
That paints a ripple on the tranquil river
Makes your whole body quiver,
While my proud top, like giant Caucasus,
Confronts the sun and braves the impetus
Of frost and storm.
Zephyrs for me, for you are deadly blasts.
You should have grown here in the warm
Protective shadow that my foliage casts—
But no, you lift your puny head
By the moist borders of the river-bed,
A prey to every random gust.
Fate is indeed to you unjust!"
"Your pity proves," replied the reed,
"That you're my friend in word and deed;
But be not troubled for my sake,
'Tis you, not I, should quail and quake:
When blustering north winds blow
I bend but do not break.
Till now, full well I know,
The tempests never made you bend,
But let us bide the end."
Even as the little reedling spoke,
Over the high horizon's edge there broke
A storm wind such as never yet
The frozen Arctic did beget:
The tree held firm, the lithe reed bent,
The wind waxed trebly violent
And, roaring like an avalanche,
Levelled to earth both trunk and branch
Of the great tree that pierced heaven with its head
And, with its roots, the empire of the dead.

The Two Pigeons

THERE WERE two pigeons, tender friends—
The one was happy in his home,
But the false charm that distance lends
Made his companion long to roam.
        "How!" cried the first, "what scheme is this?
You weary of fraternal bliss?
Is absence not the bane of love?
No? Not for stony hearts! At least,
If friendship fail, let prudence move.
Think of the highways unpoliced,
The tempests, lightnings, icy weather—
Nay, let's awhile abide together
Till Spring has clad the earth in green
And forests spread their leafy screen.
A dreadful omen I have heard:
Just now beneath yon hollow oak
Echoed a raven's bodeful croak,
Presaging death to some ill-fated bird.
All my dreams now will be of tragic things,
And pigeons beating with their broken wings
At nets and gins. Alas, I'll cry,
How is my brother bird bestead?
Has he found supper and a bed?
Has he a roof above his head?"
        By these words just a little daunted,
The imprudent traveller made pause:
But wild desires obey no laws,
And foreign parts are so much vaunted,
He needs must go. He cried: "Come, dry that tear:
Three fleeting days are not a year.
In three short days I shall be back,
And I'll delight you telling all

The gay adventures that befall
Those who desert the beaten track.
Ah! what a tale I'll tell to you!
I'll say: In this spot have I been—
This have I done—this have I seen:
You'll almost think you've seen it too!"
      With many a fond farewell and many a tear
The traveller starts. Anon a thundercloud
Filled all the heavens. A single tree stood near,
A scanty shelter. Louder and more loud
The tempest swelled, then of a sudden ceased.
The sun shone out—the bird was off again,
His plumage dripping with the icy rain.
Soon hunger came—his weariness increased.
Near by he spied a field of golden grain,
A pigeon perching there. Toward it he flew,
And straight was caught—the wheat stalks hid
    from view
A traitorous snare. Awhile it held him fast,
But it was old and worn. Our bird at last,
Using his wings, his beak, his sharp claws, broke
    away,
Yet many a feather perished in the strife,
And with these spoils he almost lost his life.
A hovering vulture, armed with steely claws,
Saw the poor biped impotently trail
The broken cord and ever lamely pause,
Like a scared convict stealing out of jail.
That hour had been his last, but, by good luck,
An eagle now swooped earthward. Horror-struck,
The pigeon through the embattled foes slipped out
And, looking round about,
Espied a wretched hut. Alighting here,

He thought to bid farewell to fear;
But a young scamp (children are pitiless)
Discharged his sling at him with such address
The bird was well-nigh killed,
And, with new terror filled,
Cursing his nomad mood,
With drooping wings and dragging feet
Retraced his journey as he could.
Half dead, half lame,
He homeward came,
And found homecoming strangely sweet.
The pair were joined once more, and you may
   guess
After such woes how deep their happiness.
     O lovers, happy lovers, would you roam?
Then seek some flowery bank in sight of home.
Be each to each a world, forever true,
Forever diverse and forever new;
Be all in all and count the rest as naught.
I too once loved. The Louvre and all its treasures,
Or Paradise and its celestial pleasures,
Could not on my rapt spirit so have wrought
That I would leave for them the sacred spot
Pressed by the feet and lighted by the eyes
Of the fair shepherdess
Whom Cupid's self did press
My happy heart to idolize.
Alas! When will those blessèd days return?
Shall eyes like those no longer wake desire
Nor kindle a fond fire?
Oh, that this heart once more might dare to burn!
Must I forego these tender spells at last?
Is love's sweet season past?

The Plague-Stricken Beasts

A CURSE THAT dogs the sinner's path,
A curse that Heaven in its wrath
Conceived to punish mortal crime,
The plague—to call it by its name—
Was raging once upon a time
Among the beasts both wild and tame.
'Twas pitiful to see them sicken:
Not all died off, but all were stricken.
Their velvet feet no longer scurried
Through brake and marsh in search of food;
No more the busy songbirds hurried
Toward nests where chirped their tender brood;
The wolf and fox no longer spied
Their guileless prey; the turtle-doves
From one another sought to hide,
Forgetting all their pretty loves—
All hopes repel, all comforts cloy,
When love has fled and with it joy.
The lion called his council and thus spoke:
        "My loved and loyal friends,
For some misdeed the Lord this evil sends.
Let the most guilty of our folk,
To serve the common good,
Upon the altar shed his tainted blood,
For history teaches that in such a crisis
The cure is found in bloody sacrifices.
Then let us each with searching eyes
His conscience sternly scrutinize.
I own up to a gluttonous appetite,
And sheep and lambs are my delight,
Though these poor innocents do me no wrong.
Sometimes I even eat, with ram and ewe,
        The shepherd too.

I'll die, if that seem well; yet let's prolong
The session till each member has acquitted
His conscience of the sins he has committed,
And then, as is but just, the guiltiest
Shall die to save the rest."
     "Sire," cried the fox, "you are too good a king!
Your scruples show a conscience too refined.
What! to kill beasts of this stupid kind,
Is that a sin? No, no! 'Tis no such thing:
You do them honor by devouring them.
As for the shepherd, who would not condemn
This cruel wretch who overruns our states,
Our woods, our fields, our hills, and arrogates
Dominion over every quadruped
The teeming earth has bred."
Thus spoke the fox—the flatterers applauded.
Not one dared to suggest
That tiger, bear, or wolf make a clean breast
Of how he murdered and marauded.
The snarling mastiff was all self-restraint,
And every long-toothed creature was a saint.
Then spoke the ass in turn: "I recollect
How one day in the monastery grounds,
A place where always luscious grass abounds,
Hunger, the tender grass, and, I suspect,
Some devil, urging me unseen,
I gnawed some straggling shoots of herbage green;
I was at fault no doubt, to tell the truth."
Straight every beast assailed him without ruth.
A wolf that dabbled in the law harangued
The crowd and proved the donkey should be
   hanged,
Or, in default of hangman and of halter,
Be bled upon the altar.
This scurvy, mangy author of their woes—
His pecadillo merited the noose.

What, eat another's grass! Such horrid crime
Was past excuse.
There was no use
In wasting further breath:
All voted death!

Those who have power, and those who lack,
The court by turns makes white or black.

The Cobbler and the Financier

A COBBLER sang from morn till night;
To hear him was a sheer delight;
His songs to him were more than wages,
And he was happier than the Seven Sages.
Not so his neighbor; though in wealth he rolled,
Little he sang and slept still less;
His thoughts were all of gain and gold,
And if at dawn sleep came to bless
His weary lids, the cobbler's matin song
            Woke him ere long.
Loud he inveighed against the heavenly powers
That licensed sale of food and drink
While all Golconda could not buy a wink
Of healthful sleep to speed the leaden hours.
He summoned to his halls the cobbler gay:
"Grégoire," he asked, "what do you earn per
    annum?"
"Per annum, sir? That's not my way
Of reckoning. I do not count by years;
I am content if I can only span 'em
By stitching day to day without arrears."
"Well, then, what are your earnings day by day?"
"Why, sometimes more and sometimes less, Your
    Honor.
With steady work, each day would give

          Enough to live;
But when there is no work there is no pay.
There are so many idle days, you see.
The Church does this; there's sure some plague
    upon her;
There is no week but we have two or three
To ruin us, for every week the priest
Loads one or two new saints on us at least."
The nabob, smiling at his simple air
And artless speech, cried out: "Indeed,
My good man, you shall be a millionaire!
Here, take these hundred crowns; hoard them with
    care
Against the time of need."
The honest cobbler thought he now possessed
More money than the whole world could produce
In hundred years for mankind's use.
He hies him home and locks up in a chest
His money—and his joy!
For money doth all peace destroy:
Farewell, sweet poverty; farewell, content!
His song fell mute, his voice was spent.
No longer now he knew the charm
Of easeful sleep, but vain alarm
And dark suspicion broke his rest.
All day he watched; at night, if some sly cat
Stole through his hovel pit-a-pat,
That cat was sure a thief! At last
The poor man, when a weary week had passed,
His folly now deploring,
Took down his strong-box from the shelf,
Ran to his wealthy friend—and found him snoring.
"Give back," he cried, "my songs and sleep,
       And keep
Your hundred crowns yourself!"

NICOLAS BOILEAU
1636–1711

Silvia

T WAS HERE by this green garden bed
My Silvia first appeared to me.
O dear delight forever fled!
How true I loved! How fair was she!
Poor wounded heart! That time has sped.
Have you forgot that love lies dead?

Here roaming in the dewy fields,
I decked her with embroidery
Of every flower the season yields.
How true I loved! How fair was she!
Be still, sad heart! Have you forgot
That she was false and loved you not?

ABBÉ DE CHAULIEU
1639–1720

The Woods of Fontenay

O SHADY grotto, crystal spring,
Here let me lie on petalled flowers
That dot the moss, and lose the hours,
Lulled by the brooklet's murmuring.

What pleasure still to watch the flocks,
When noon lies faint on flower and grass,
Under the shady elm-trees pass
To the cool stream and dripping rocks,

Or hear, when slow-paced evening
Steals sable-veiled through field and city,
The milkmaid trill her blithesome ditty
While sheep-bells ring and shepherds sing.

O Muse, that in this still retreat
Charmed my first years; O arbors green,
Where vine and blossom first were seen
That soon shall deck my winding-sheet!

Reclining in this leafy shade,
Still let me sing, still let me smile,
Until in my green peristyle
Grim death shall find me unafraid.

O Fontenay, delightful spot!
Here was I born and here would die
And by my blest forefathers lie,
At peace like them, like them forgot.

Here let my dead bones lie at ease—
White blossoms round, green leaves above—
Soft slumbering in this lovely grove,
Still shaded by my cypress trees.

CHARLES DU FRESNY

c. 1654–1724

Love's Progress

PHYLLIS in the meadow straying
(O the pretty avarice!)
Tricked Sylvander into paying
Thirty sheep to win a kiss.
On the morrow, changeful maid,
Fain the shepherd's love to keep,
She in amorous passion paid
Thirty kisses for one sheep.
Two days passed, and yet more tender,
'Neath a wreathèd clematis,
Phyllis waited to surrender
Thirty sheep to win a kiss.
Next day Phyllis, ever blander,
Offered flock and dog to buy
That sweet kiss which false Sylvander
Gave Lisetta on the sly.

ALEXIS PIRON
1689–1773

Love's Miseries

How SAD a thing a man in love,
His heart transfixed by beauty's eye!
He imitates the mourning-dove
And has no language but a sigh.

If he take heart and tell his passion,
His lady frowns in cold disdain—
But to persist is lovers' fashion
In spite of aches and plagues and pain.

Yet if the lady love, new worries
All unforeseen invest her charms:
Her tears, her fears, her foolish flurries,
Her spouse, her parents up in arms.

And what is worse, she has her honor,
That pale antipodes of pleasure;
Ere you at last prevail upon her
What qualms, what quarrels, hedge that treasure!

A rival comes: in vain you scowl;
Your peace is gone, your sleep takes flight;
Jealous, you fret, and spy, and prowl,
And find no rest by day or night.

Then after all this mighty pother
She clings to you when you'd be going.
Alas! She was not worth the bother:
The meadow was not worth the mowing!

With Cupid's Aid

You found my missive very tender,
But pleasure mingled with surprise
That I whose talent is so slender
So sweetly should extemporize.

Your beauty, dear, was half my wit;
Alone, 'twould serve a better poet.
But whence the other half of it?
I'll tell you if you fain would know it:

I wished to write; I had no pen—
When lo! a little wingèd thing
Flew past me, then returned again
And dropped a feather from his wing.

The Portrait

The god of love one day in airy flight,
Spying the shepherdess that I adore,
With folded wings stood transfixed in delight:
So fair a face he never saw before.

"I will eternize her," he promised, vaunting
His brush, his palette, his celestial art,
But could not yet begin—one thing was want-
    ing,
A canvas—and for that he took my heart.

Epitaph

MY EARTHLY journey now is done;
A breakneck course I've had;
Through light and darkness I have run,
And I was wise and I was mad.
Now yawns the abyss, the horrid spot,
Where madmen and where sages slip.
My destination? I know not!
Good-bye, Piron! A lucky trip!

VOLTAIRE
1694–1778

A Sorry Jest

I LOVE, UPON my own green garden walls,
To watch the fruits of Persia and of Ind
Slow ripening, sheltered from the boisterous
    wind,
Till from the stems the luscious booty falls.

A garnished pheasant has a savory smell,
And a plump partridge, if it's roasted well,
Tickles my palate and regales my sight—
But age has robbed me of my appetite.

On flowery slopes where the Pierides
Disport beneath far-shining laurel trees
By Heliconian streams, I fain would touch
With flying feet 'mong dancing Dryades
The smooth mead—where I stumble with a
    crutch.

I love the vermeil cheeks, the lustrous eyes,
The charm, the grace life's budding years im-
    part,
Youth's songs and ecstasies and melting sighs—
Let age go hang that only has a heart!

Some day you'll be as lean and bald as I,
Frisk prelates, abbés, churchmen purple-stoled,
Princes and kings who now are all the cry;
Like me you will be sadly wise and old.

Ours are but pleasures of a day,
Pale hollow joys that fade away;

Life holds no lasting zest:
You made, great Jove, in shaping our dull clay,
     A sorry jest.

To Madame du Châtelet

IF YOU WOULD have me love you still,
Bring back to me the age of love,
And while I totter down the hill
Let evening a new daybreak prove.

From bowers where Bacchus plucks the grape
And Cupid bends his twanging bow,
Old Father Time, that grisly shape,
With threatening gesture bids me go.

Then let me bow to Time's fell rage
And from his spite some profit wring:
Who spurns the wisdom of old age
Bears all the burdens age doth bring.

Let's leave to youth love's sprightly charms,
Love's bliss, love's dainty melancholy,
Let our first years know love's alarms,
But let our last be free from folly!

Alas! must you forever flee,
Illusions sweet and dear delights,
That once made life so fair to me,
That charmed my days and thrilled my nights?

We die not once, but twice, alas!
Ceasing to love and to be loved—
What pang can such a grief surpass,
And when has death so painful proved?

Thus did I mourn to see depart
The all-too-pleasing dreams of youth,

And craved with fondly feeble heart
The bubbles sold in Folly's booth.

But clad in a serener splendor
Fond Friendship came from heaven above,
And proved perhaps more truly tender
Though not so bitter-sweet as Love.

I gave my heart into her keeping—
Her charm was new, her worth was known:
I followed her, but followed weeping,
Because I followed her alone.

To Madame Lullin

DOES IT amaze you or amuse
That after eighty winters past
Even now my doting, dribbling Muse
Can turn a rhyme—perhaps my last?

Yet oft in frozen fields mayhap
A random blade of grass will sprout
And greenly shine in nature's lap
Though with the day its life goes out.

And oftentimes a tardy bird
Still sings on some autumnal bough,
Although no melting notes are heard,
No songs of love re-echo now.

Thus do I strum with awkward fingers
My all-too-unresponsive lyre,
While plaintively my weak voice lingers
On notes that falteringly expire.

"When I shall breathe my last farewell,"
Tibullus cried, "O mistress mine,

On thee let my last glances dwell,
My dying hand still rest in thine."

Alas! When Death our heart disarms,
When the faint soul grows numb and chill,
Do we have eyes for Delia's charms,
Or hands that can caress her still?

In that grim hour no hope can move,
No passion thrill us as of yore:
What lover ever won from Love
A rendezvous beside Death's door?

Fond Delia too your fate must share
And vanish into endless night,
Forgetting that she once was fair
And only lived for love's delight.

We're born, we live, sweet shepherdess,
And then depart, we know not why:
We come here out of nothingness,
And where we go, God knows, not I.

To Phyllis

SWEET PHYLLIS, where have fled the days
You rode with me in hackney cab,
No footman, naught to draw men's gaze,
Save your sweet face and gift of gab?
Contented with a ten-sou supper,
Which your sweet lips to nectar turned,
You threw yourself with all your charms
Into your happy lover's arms—
And sometimes into those of others:
In those gay days all men were brothers
And love a blessing never spurned.
Heaven gave you in that joyous time

No rank, no wealth, no worldly treasure,
But gave the charms I used to rhyme,
Your youth, your warmth, your love of pleasure,
Your fickle heart, your artful lies,
Your snowy breast, your roving eyes.
　　　But ah! Madame, how changed your lot
Since you became a lady fine—
So fine that you have quite forgot
Those far-off days when you were mine.
This gorgeously appareled porter,
This Cerberus who guards your door,
Scowls as if he would draw and quarter
The dainty god whom Venus bore.
Aye, Cupid, though a god, would fear
Among these splendors to appear—
But in old days he used to come
And in your chamber found a home,
For if it chanced your door was locked,
The window served, and none were shocked.
　　　No, Countess, no, the times have changed,
And love and lovers are estranged.
These splendid carpets that I see,
Woven at La Savonnerie,
These Persian stuffs and silver plate,
With gems that gleam and fascinate,
These cabinets whose curious art
Outdoes their Chinese counterpart,
These painted vases Japanese
And countless marvels like to these,
These diamonds Orient queens have worn,
These pendants that your ears adorn,
These pearls on golden ribband strung—
All this, Madame, I swear, all this
I value less than one sweet kiss
Of your red lips when you were young.

CARDINAL DE BERNIS
1715–1794

Love's Constancy

Iris, Themira, Danäe,
I've sued and wooed all three by turns;
Yet my fond heart, fair Merope,
For thee alone, my darling, burns.

Young Iris' voice so charms the ear
And thrills the soul so tenderly
That, hearing her, I thought to hear,
To see, to kiss, to fondle thee.

Enraptured by her winsome smile,
I made the gay Themira mine,
Inly persuaded all the while
That sweet smile was not hers but thine.

When Danäe floated, all undressed,
Where billowy breaks the silver sea,
I kissed the rosebuds on her breast,
Believing she was Merope.

Thus in my sport Love's doting blindness
Sought everywhere thy sovran charms,
Thy eyes, thy voice, thy amorous kindness;
I pressed thee only in my arms.

Iris, Themira, Danäe,
I've sued and wooed all three by turns;
Yet my fond heart, fair Merope,
For thee alone, my darling, burns.

BEAUMARCHAIS

1732–1799

Chérubin's Song

I SAT BESIDE a purling stream
(My heart is heavy, my peace is fled);
My lovely lady was all my dream,
For her my tears I shed.

I carved her name on every tree
(My heart is heavy, my peace is fled);
The king rode past, but saw not me,
On a milk-white steed he sped.

"Sweet page," cried out the winsome queen
(My heart is heavy, my peace is fled),
"By bitter sorrow well I ween
These flowing tears are fed."

"Alas, alas! my gracious queen"
(My heart is heavy, my peace is fled),
"My grief will flourish ever green:
I mourn my lady dead."

"Sweet page," cried out the rosy queen
(My heart is heavy, my peace is fled),
"From a lady dead your heart to wean,
Come, love your queen instead."

NICOLAS LÉONARD
1744–1793

To Doris

LET JOY ITS blushing roses twine
Around our brows while love is new;
Tomorrow's sun again will shine
Bright as today's on me and you.

But when the beckoning hand of fate
Points toward the meads of asphodel,
For amorous sports it is too late,
And love must breathe a last farewell.

Then give me, while its season lasts,
A thousand kisses ere the dawn,
And thousand more when sunset casts
Our lengthening shadows down the lawn.

And if some long-faced Pharisee
Should stumble upon our retreat,
Kiss on to spite his jealousy
And make our love seem doubly sweet.

ÉVARISTE DE PARNY
1753–1814

Elegy

THE GRACE OF childhood still was hers,
    Hers its blithe innocence
And rosy charm in which scarce stirs
    The bloom of dawning sense.
Soon, without hint of guileful art,
Love would have blossomed in her heart.
But fairest things have swiftest wing
    And briefest vigil keep;
Just entered in her budding spring,
    She softly fell asleep,
Rapt in a sweet beatitude
As fades a smile on a fair face,
As dies away without a trace
A birdsong in the wood.

CLARIS DE FLORIAN
1755–1794

The Journey of Life

To START ERE daybreak, groping in the night,
Not knowing and not caring where we go,
To fall, and rise, and stumble on, and so
Make half the journey with no end in sight;
Then at full noon to see the gathering clouds
And whirling sands enwrap us in their shrouds;
To run with hurried steps through storm and
    wind,
Braving the angry elements in quest
Of some chimeric goal where we may rest;
And then, rain-drenched, into some refuge
    creep
At nightfall, stretch, and fall asleep—
Thus are we born, and thus we live and die:
        The Lord knows why.

ANDRÉ CHÉNIER
1762–1794

The Young Tarentine

WEEP, GENTLE halcyons, by the moaning deep,
Loved birds of Tethys, sacred halcyons, weep!
  The young Tarentine, Myrto, is no more!
Myrto who sailed for Camarina's shore,
Where Hymen for her coming, all day long,
Sat waiting, myrtle-crowned, with flute and song
To lift her past the threshold as a bride.
Her wedding-robe lay shining, Tyrian-dyed,
In cedarn chest, and golden bands lay there,
And odorous nard to sprinkle on her hair.
  Charmed by the stars, all heedless of the gale
That rose afar and puffed the bellying sail,
She seaward leans—no sailor at her side—
She shrieks, she falls, she sinks below the tide.
The young Tarentine in the sea is lost,
Her lovely body by the salt waves tossed.
  White Tethys, grieving, in a hollow rock
From dragon jaws and the mad ocean's shock
Hides her away, and ever-weeping bids
The band attendant of her Nereids
Lift her, thus sepulchred, from out the deep
To where a promontory rises steep,
Sacred to Zephyr. Here the golden-tressed
Tarentine virgin lies in lonely rest.
Here all the sister nymphs flock from their foun-
    tains,
Fair Dryades and Oreads from the mountains.
In slow procession round her tomb they move,
Mourning her early death and hapless love,

Beating their breasts and crying loud, "Alas!
Alas, that thy brief day so soon should pass!
Thou hast not rested in thy lover's arms,
No hymeneal robe has graced thy charms,
Thy slender wrists no golden circlets wear,
No bridal wreath perfumes thy floating hair."

Neaera

As on a silver stream a stately swan
Melodious sings, till ebbing life is gone,
His last lament, so, faint and nigh to death,
The pale Neaera sang with failing breath:
    "Ye naiads wandering by Sebethus' wave,
Lay your shorn locks on my untimely grave!
Clinias, farewell! Why is our love forgot?
Why must this grief be your Neaera's lot,
Neaera whom you lured from Hellas' shore,
Whom once you loved—whom now you love
    no more?
O earth! O sea! O mountain-girdled spot,
Flowers, vocal woods, dim vales, and rock-
    rimmed grot!
Recall to him again and yet again
How once I did not feed on his disdain,
How once his heart by these poor charms was
    moved,
And how he loved me even as I loved.
Tell how for him with guilty feet I fled
My mother's home, by his loved image led.
Tell how Neaera, whom he called his own,
Roamed for his sake in banishment, alone,
A hapless wanderer, driven from place to
    place,
Hiding from human kind her shameful face.

"Where, Clinias, are you now? Does the
  twin star
Of Helen's brothers, shining from afar,
From Neptune's wrath your tossing bark to
  save,
Light at your prow the blue Ionian wave?
Or do you still on Paestum's templed strand
See twice a year from Flora's brimming hand
The reddening roses on your garden wall
In festooned wreaths and hanging garlands fall,
Such roses as you fondly used to twine
Around my brow while yet your heart was
  mine?
  "If at the twilight hour a mood more kind
Bring back the lost Neaera to your mind,
Oh then, my Clinias, whisper soft my name,
And I'll float near you: like a tenuous flame
My wandering soul will quiver in the vines,
Or haunt the breeze that sways the sighing
  pines,
Or hover in the clouds, or from the sea
Rise like a shining wraith that longingly
Thrids the thin ether, praying you to hear
The plaintive voice that woos your startled ear."

Lovers' Meeting

Chloe

YE ECHOING groves and softly nodding reeds,
And rivers singing through the sunlit meads,
Does Mnasylus the herdsman loiter near?
Ye know, alas! how oft to my charmed ear
From these dense hazels and these alder-trees
His tuneful song swells on the sighing breeze!

Mnasylus

O goddess of the stream, white water-sprite,
Pacing these odorous dells with footsteps light,
Is Chloe here? These wooded mountain flanks
She daily haunts, and these soft-sloping banks.
And I—how oft down these green paths I pass,
Kissing her footprints in the dewy grass!

Chloe

Ah! could he know how dear this woodland dim
To her who seeks it but to dream of him!
Could I but dare some day with furtive smile
To lure his steps down this same forest aisle!

Mnasylus

Oh that some god, more skilled in amorous art,
Might speak for me and all my love impart!
Or that I dared, myself, in tender tone
Persuade her to be loved and be my own!

Chloe

My heart, 'tis he! Ye gods! I cannot speak.
I'll turn aside to hide my blushing cheek.

Mnasylus

The leafage quivers. Lo! a rustling dress!
'Tis she! Be still, my heart! Hide thy distress!

Chloe

What, Mnasylus! Alone I wandered here,
In this cool grove. I knew not you were near.

Mnasylus

Alone I sought the linden's noonday shade,
Nor dreamed to meet you in this distant glade.

Hylas

THE ARGO, shaped of stout Penneian pine,
Toward Colchos steered across the Aegean brine
And the broad Euxine, home of Boreal gales,
Then swanlike, furling all her snowy sails,
Lay havened in a windless landlocked bay
Where peaceful Zephyrs hold eternal sway
And never tempest mars the perfect day.
    The sailors spread a banquet on the strand,
And the blond Hylas, youngest of the band,
To fetch them drink ran with his earthen urn
Through reed-fringed paths and meads all rain
    bow-hued
With thousand flowers and banked with sedgy
    fern
Where a clear fountain sang in shady wood.
Three naiads, sirens of the silver fount,
Spy him afar and toward the blue air mount.
Lured by the singing stream, he forward wends
And, urn in hand, o'er the blue water bends.
His blithe face dances by the fountain's brim,
His lips, his eyes. The naiads softly swim
Through the tall rushes, where they float unseen,
The nodding reeds and lily-cups between.
The stream more limpid runs; the breeze, more
    soft,
Wafts spicy odors over field and croft;
Fresh flowrets bloom with colors more intense,
And sighing music lulls the languorous sense.
The boy, enchanted by these miracles,
Forgets his errand and a garland culls.
But still the fountain woos him back again;
He views it stealing through the grassy plain

With many a sinuous curve or sudden turn,
And in its crystal dips his heavy urn—
When lo! the naiads from the dripping sedge
Dart forth and draw him past the rock-bound
    ledge.
They woo him on their mossy bed to rest,
Or in their arms, or on their snowy breast,
While with slim fairy finger-tips they seek
To press the roses on his vermeil cheek,
And brush away the first quick tears that rise
Half-glad, half-grieving, in his startled eyes.
    "When first I saw," he cries, "with such
        strange grace
Float on the tide each snowy limb and face,
I deemed they were but images of me,
One in the air, but in the water three."
    Meanwhile Alcides, longing for his friend,
Roams the dark wood and seeks him without end
In vain through rocky vales and hills he climbs
And calls his Hylas' name a thousand times.
Young Hylas dimly hears that mighty cry,
Whose echoes in the bubbling waters die,
And from the fount, to ease the hero's pain,
He vainly calls, again and yet again.

Lyde

"THE TORRID sunshine on my hot cheek burns,
And my white feet are reddened by the thorns.
Lured by the tinkling bells of wandering flocks,
All day I've strayed among the mossy rocks
And met a hundred shepherds—but not you,
Who shun me. Down what wooded avenue,
O fairest man of men, do your sheep roam?

In what lost valley do you make your home?
O charming youth! See what warm tears bedew
These paling cheeks, grown wan for love of you,
Of your smooth brow, your grace, your modest
    mien,
And your dear face, the loveliest ever seen.
Nay, fear not me, but trust your tender soul
To these soft hands and to love's sweet control.
Come, let me thrill your heart with joys unknown
Until it sigh and languish like my own,
Until no blushes dye your cheek but those
My kiss begets as spring begets the rose.
Abide to greet the dawn with me, and rest
In sun-kissed slumber on my pulsing breast,
And I'll hang o'er you, ever breathing low,
So you may drowse hour-long, while to and fro
I wave my linen scarf thus tenderly
To chase the gnat and scare the jealous bee."
    She sways toward him, halts, then with a
        sigh
She draws him to a grass-grown bank near by
And trembling casts her down. Slowly he yields,
And sinks beside her in the flowery fields,
Half-pleased, half-proud, and yet reluctant, too.
The nymph with soft touch labors to undo
The tangles of his golden hair, and then she sighs:
    "Come, let us nestle closer, happy pair,
You fair and young, and I, too, young and fair.
Lift up your eyes! How blest that mother is
Who on your dewy mouth imprints her kiss!
Or are you goddess-born? What! does your
    breast
Heave tremulous when touched? My own, if
    pressed

By your warm hand, with rounder curves will
    swell.
Or have you haply in some leafy dell
Wooed some young nymph that cared not to be
    shy,
Not half so fair—not half so fond—as I?
You smile! You blush! In those black eyes what
    light!
Those lips how vermeil, and those cheeks how
    bright!
Are you not Hyacinth, whom Phoebus loved?
Or Ganymede, whose charms great Jove ap-
    proved?
Or that Adonis, whom on Smyrna's shore
The hapless Myrrha unto Theias bore?
O youth! whate'er you be, those eyes divine
Have spells to win all hearts as they win mine.
For me in vain a thousand lovers sigh:
I love but you—then love me or I die."

The Young Sufferer

"DELIAN APOLLO, source of those strange powers
Of life and healing lodged in plants and flowers,
Dread Python-slayer, radiant deity,
Pity my only son and pity me,
Who else am doomed to shed unceasing tears
And live unfriended all my last long years.
O youthful god, have mercy on his youth;
Let not these withered hands with touch un-
    couth
Close his bright eyes. Bring him sweet rest,
And calm the fever in that childlike breast.
Could I once more but see him guide his flock

On fountained Maenalus by bush and rock,
These aged hands would bear, O lord divine,
My onyx cup to deck thy laureled shrine,
And, each revolving year, a snow-white bull
Should fall before it, young and beautiful.
  "My son, my child, are you still pitiless?
Have you no words to comfort my distress?
Are you still bent to die? And will you leave
Your white-haired mother here alone to grieve?
Must I outlive my son, so long my pride,
And set his ashes by his father's side?
These pious cares my age had hoped from you,
These deathbed kisses and this fond adieu.
Speak, speak, my child; whence this consuming
 grief?
Sorrow that's mute is stranger to relief.
Nay, lift those heavy lids!"
      "Mother, farewell!
I suffer from a hurt I may not tell.
Your son is doomed. I die. A fatal wound
Drains my sick heart. No herb was ever found,
No medicinal plant, that holds the power
To stretch this weary life a little hour.
I cannot speak my woe. It is too late.
All things oppress and crush me with their
 weight.
I faint beneath my heavy coverlet.
Oh! I could welcome death! And yet, and yet
 ..."
  "Come, my loved child, this healing potion
  drink;
It can bring back the soul even from the brink
Of black Cocytus' stream. The leech's craft
Has mingled mallow, dictame, poppy, in the
 draught.

A witch Thessalian of a hundred years
Compounded it, moved by my prayers and tears.
Three times the circling sun has made his round
Only to see those eyes fixed on the ground,
Sleepless; thrice has it sunk in black eclipse
Since Ceres' gifts have passed those icy lips.
Yield, darling son, to your old mother's prayer,
You, her sole comfort and her dearest care.
'Twas she who steered your first unsteady walk,
With tearful smile drank in your lisping talk,
Poised you upon her knees, twined with fond
     arms
Your trembling limbs and soothed your sweet
     alarms,
Taught you to love her, and to say you loved,
And by your sole emotion still was moved,
Still with her song could many a time beguile
From tear-stained lips a momentary smile."
        "Ye hills that line the Erymanthian stream,
Whose waters through the tremulous foliage
     gleam,
Ye vales and woods and music-making breeze
That thrills the heart of nymphs and dryades,
Lifting the light folds of their tunics white
In purple meads aglow with pale moonlight!
No ravening wolves lurk here, no venomed snake
Winds silently athwart the tangled brake.
O flowery fields, blithe songs, Elysian dreams
Of linkèd steps beside the purling streams!
What region smiles so bright in nature's bounds,
So full of lovely sights and liquid sounds?
Gods! shall I see no more such golden hair,
White lifted feet, and faces heavenly fair?
O carry me to Erymanthus' banks
To watch again the dancers' swaying ranks

And that proud virgin, loveliest of the band!
Let me behold once more that wonderland,
That vine-clad cot, sweet haven of repose,
That shaded bench, where, seated by her sire,
She charmed to sleep regrets and vain desire!
There, one day, gazing through the thick-set
    hedge,
I saw her, lying on the marble ledge
Of a white sepulchre, forlornly weep
Her late-lost mother, lapped in wakeless sleep.
How soft those tender eyes, how fair that face!
Ah! could I dying hope that dearest grace,
To hear your voice, O loveliest of all maids,
Mourn my descent among the loveless shades!"
    "What! does the dark fatality of love
In your sick soul this frenzied passion move?
O wretched son! O sore-tried mortal men!
Love is your curse, as it has ever been!
But tell me, child, what nymph has wrought this
    spell?
Does she in Erymanthus' valleys dwell?
And tell me, why must son of mine despair?
If she be lovely, are not you, too, fair?
Yea, none was fairer till that luckless hour
When passion paled your cheek and nipped its
    flower.
Speak, is it Egle, naiad of the sea?
Is't some reluctant sylvan deity?
Or she whose charms all mortal charms eclipse,
Whose praise runs like a flame on all men's lips,
In woods or temples, meadow-land or mart,
The queenly Daphne—?"
               "Hold! speak not her name,
Lest it consume me in a sudden flame.

Oh, never speak my Daphne's name aloud!
Her wild heart is intractable and proud
As Juno's own; not Dian is more cold;
She walks 'mong thousand lovers, virgin-souled
And passion-proof. I had but wooed in vain,
And love reproved had brought me double pain.
Nay, let my secret perish with me here!
O death, not sweet but dread! O mother dear,
Behold what torments rack my feeble heart!
Pity your dying son, aye, play his part.
Go—seek her out—and let your careworn face
Her mother's love recall, her hopes retrace.
Bring her this osier crate of earliest fruit,
Our ivory Cupid, my smooth-polished flute,
Your onyx cup, rarest of Corinth's spoils,
And my young kids, the prize of all my toils;
Bring her my heart, my life—tell her your son
Expires for love of her, by her undone;
Fall at her father's feet, implore his aid;
Adjure the skies and seas, entreat, persuade!
If she refuse and come not back with you,
Your dying son must breathe his last adieu."
    "I still shall have a son! A golden hope
Dawns in my heart."
                        Her trembling fingers grope
Among his tangled locks, and falling tears
Wet the warm kisses fain to calm his fears.
She hastes away on restless, tottering feet,
No longer brisk with youth, no longer fleet.
Yet she returns—she sinks upon his bed—
An old man follows, by his daughter led.
He smiling stands; she, blushing like a rose,
Looks shyly toward the couch. The trembling
    boy

Half hides his face, aglow with sudden joy.
    "My friend," she murmurs, "three long days
      have passed
Since last our shepherds saw you, and since last
They heard your festive songs and mellow flute,
That was so sweet to hear, but now lies mute.
Why do you dote on death, why are you sad?
They bid me come to heal you, make you glad.
Oh, live, and let a son cheer my lone sire,
A daughter sit beside your mother's fire."

Homer

"Hail, lovely Scyros, hospitable shore!
I trod thy blessèd soil in days of yore:
I know this friendly land, I knew your sires
When they were young as you are, when the fires
Of Phoebus, the glad spring, the rosy dawn
Gladdened these eyes, ere night's dark veil was
    drawn—
Foremost of warriors then in martial dance,
In racing, wrestling, hurling of the lance.
The fertile banks of old Egyptus' stream
And Crete's fair land where hundred cities gleam,
Corinth I saw and Argos,
And many an isle in the Aegean Sea,
But wandering ways and age and pain at length
Have drained this body of its ancient strength,
And I am but a voice. So with spent wings,
Perched on a shrub, the tired cicada sings.
    "Begin we with the gods! Hail, sovran Jove,
All-seeing sun, stars that in order move,
Avenging powers of the infernal world,
And foaming streams from topless mountains
    hurled

To swell the seas and fertilize the earth,
And ye nine Muses of Olympian birth,
Who light in mortal minds the heavenly fire.
Of wisdom and the music of the lyre!"
    So sang the rhapsode, and the ancient trees
Rustled concordant with his harmonies.
The shepherds left unwatched their wandering
    sheep,
The woodmen gathered from the mountain steep,
Pan and the nymphs from darkling thickets
    peered,
And many a faun and satyr, shaggy-eared,
Listened enchanted. The great stream of song
Through earth and heaven majestic wound along:
It sang the birth of worlds, sang hill and grove,
And rivers flowing from the breast of Jove,
Old cities, templed shrines, and civic arts,
And love that rages in immortal hearts.
It sang the gods arrayed in hostile bands
And the world reddened by Titanic hands,
Achaian kings whose spears and clashing shields
Darkened the heavens with dust of battlefields,
Whose rushing cars lit up the Ilian plain
Like fires that leap along a mountain-chain,
Whose long-maned coursers, eager for the fray,
With human calls to battle led the way.
Next peaceful scenes and cities decked the song,
Senate and temple and the festive throng
Of eager citizens, to whose glad fields
The golden harvest bounteous Ceres yields,
With russet pears and apples rosy-ripe,
Soft-bleating lambs, the shepherd's tuneful pipe,
The singing vintagers, the rustic dance,
Sweet spell of wooing words and amorous glance.
Then rang a wilder strain, and wind and wave
Hurled the wrecked sailor to a watery grave,

As the song shifted to the caverned seas
Cleft by swift bands of white-limbed naiades
Who steer the monstrous horses of the deep
Past Tenedos toward Ilium's wave-washed steep.
It told of Stygian shores and regions fell
And demigods in meads of asphodel
And the unnumbered dead, some smit with eld
And some ere life's first opening buds had swelled,
Frail infants from their cradles snatched away
And maidens dying on their wedding day.
Next, O ye woods and hills and fountains clear,
With what half-hidden laughter did ye hear
How in the isle of Lemnos Vulcan's hands
On his huge anvil forged those viewless bands,
Fine as the tenuous web Arachne spins,
Which prisoned Mars and Venus in their gins!
How grieved ye at the never-dying moan
Of queenly Niobe transfixed in stone,
And the sad tale of her who madly slew
Her loved son Itylus and thenceforth flew
A lonely nightingale in the dark woods,
Singing her sorrows to the heedless floods;
How wondered at the magic power that lurks
In sweet nepenthe, anodyne that works
Forgetfulness of woe and mortal care,
With moly that lays heavenly secrets bare,
And lotus, opiate draught, whose poisoned taste
Veils the dim past and makes time leaden-paced
Move in the compass of one endless day,
Blotting all thoughts of home and love away! . . .
     Thus the old bard's melodious rhapsody
With magic tints from many a land and sea
Gladdened the listener's heart. The shepherd
     swains

Marvelled to hear those more than human strains,
Those wingèd words the learned Muse instils,
Like snowflakes dropping on the greening hills.
From every side, with dances and with song,
Flocked to the shore an ever-swelling throng,
Virgins and warriors, flower of all the land,
Crying: "Upon this hospitable strand
Thou find'st a lasting home. Be one of us,
O prophet bard, O voice melodious,
Guest of the gods at their ambrosial feasts
And lord among their poets and their priests.
Amid these woods and hills, by this still sea,
With epic song and joyous minstrelsy,
White-stoled procession and quinquennial game,
Shall Scyros greet the day great Homer came."

The Death of Heracles

O SOARING Oeta, whose ennobled height
Shone like a beacon-fire on that dread night
When Heracles took from his jealous mate
The fatal tunic, gift of Nessus' hate—
That vengeful Centaur whom his hand laid low—
Thy forests fall beneath his shattering blow,
And thy vast summit, wrapped in mist and gloom,
Is heaped heaven-high with aromatic bloom
Of verdant pines plucked from the mountain-side.
He flings his torch amid them, and with stride
Imperial mounts the pile where, wide outspread,
The heroic lion-skin serves for a bed.
His face uplifted, clasping his great mace,
He waits to take among the gods his place.
The wild winds swell and roar. The funeral pyre

Shines round Alcides, and its climbing fire
Lights the broad heavens, while in the Olympian
  dome
That mighty soul mounts to its deathless home.

The Flute-Player

EVER THOSE far-off days come back to me
When to his flute that old man smilingly
Fitted my lips and bade me mime his art,
Perched on his knee and nestling 'gainst his heart.
Kindly he feigned, even when I played most ill,
That I did rival, yea, surpass his skill.
He trained my infant piping, all unsure,
To shape the liquid notes more clear and pure,
And his deft hands my tiny fingers moved
Now up, now down, till he at last approved,
And I had learned with touches grown less rude
To close each stop along the sounding wood.

Epilogue

SUCH WERE the songs my fountain-loving Muse
Sang to the nymphs of sacred Arethuse
Where by the portal of their rocky shrine
The ivy and acanthus intertwine.
There from his leafy screen did vine-crowned Love
Come forth to hail her Siren of the grove,
And on her lovely forehead golden-tressed
A wreath of hyacinth and myrtle pressed:
"For your smooth lays," he cried, "are dear to me
As clover-bloom is to the honey-bee."

The Young Captive

"The golden corn its silken tassels twines
All summer long, and the fruit-laden vines
      Ungarnered hang on high;
And I, who am as fresh and fair as they,
Though only ravaged roses strew my way,
      I am too young to die.

"Let hearts more brave than mine make light of
      death;
I weep, yet hope. Bowed by the north wind's
      breath,
      The roses rise again.
Some hours are dark, yet some most lovely be;
What honey's purely sweet, what placid sea
      Knows never cloud nor rain?

"From these dark prison walls my thoughts take
      flight,
And my heart dances when the sun shines bright;
      Hope lends me its white wings;
Thus, disentangled from the fowler's snare,
Through heaven's blue fields, more blithe, more
      debonair,
      Sweet Philomela sings.

"And must I die? No guilt my spirit blights,
No spectre haunts my quiet days and nights,
      My peace has no alloy;
My welcome to the dawn shines in all eyes,
My smile in this dark house of tears and sighs
      Brings back a gleam of joy.

"I have but entered life's enchanted realms,
And now I go, when of the wayside elms

I scarce have passed the first.
The feast invites, the golden goblets shine,
But not for me is poured the ruddy wine,
    I go my way athirst.

"I scarce have seen life's spring, its budding hour,
O for a vision of the full-blown flower,
    And the completed year!
O hapless rose, from broken branches torn,
So newly opened to the dewy morn,
    So soon to disappear!

"Spare me, O cruel Death! and fly away
To comfort hearts where guilt and shame hold
  sway,
    Or grief stands ever nigh!
Me the green garden lures, the twittering bird,
The dream of love, the song I never heard—
    I am too young to die."

O plaintive maid! thus did my mournful lyre
Echo thy grief, thy hope, thy fond desire,
    While I too sat ensnared,
And half forgot, locked in the selfsame cage,
Poor captive bird, I could not long assuage
    The sorrows that I shared.

ANTOINE ARNAULT
1766–1834

Autumn Leaf

"Poor wandering withered leaf,
O whither are you faring?"
"Unknowing and uncaring,
Across the earth, athwart the air,
I wander here, I wander there.
The storm wind and the thunder-stroke
Have flung to earth the giant oak
And snapped my natal bough.
Birdlike, unfearing, unsorrowing now,
From mountain-top to shady valley,
Down crystal stream and grassy alley,
I float with every breeze that blows,
I flee where all things flee,
The petal of the dying rose
And leaf of laurel tree."

CHARLES-HUBERT MILLEVOYE
1782–1816

Falling Leaves

No blossoms oped to drink the dew,
No leaf hung on the barren bough,
The woodland wore a somber hue,
The nightingale was voiceless now,
When languidly, with laboring breath,
Pausing at each familiar tree,
A youth, foredoomed to early death,
Paced the bare meadows restlessly.
  "Loved forest, hear my last farewell;
These slowly fading leaves portend,
Like the sad dirge of Philomel,
My own inevitable end.
Once more I see the yellowing leaves,
See Autumn gathering in her sheaves;
Once more I see October's showers
Tear the last petals from the flowers;
Once more I read my coming doom,
And 'mong these yew trees spy my tomb.
For well I know, ere Winter pass,
Ere Spring revive the withered grass,
Ere purple vines festoon the hill,
I shall no longer wander here,
No longer feel the season's thrill,
No longer greet the opening year.
Pale Autumn, messenger of Death,
Has chilled me with her icy breath;
My Winter looms; my race is run,
Although my Spring had scarce begun—

Frail plant that only lived a day
Ere its pale petals dropped away,
Leaving upon the languid stem
No sheen of Spring's bright diadem,
No seed beside the sheltering rock,
No slip to graft the parent stock.
Fall, fall to earth, fast-fading leaf,
Cover the pathway to my grave,
O'er which the chilly north winds rave,
And hide it from a mother's grief.
Yet, if to this deserted spot
My loved one come at close of day,
To mourn a lover unforgot,
Up this lone avenue let her stray
And to my waking spirit bring
A gleam of joy, a touch of spring."
        Thus spoke the youth—and came no more!
When Autumn stripped the frosted bough,
The last flowers from the garden's store
Were wreathed around his pallid brow;
And love and life, so sweet, so brief,
Lay withered with the last brown leaf.
The pathway to his silent tomb
By love's light foot was never trod;
Only the shepherd of the dale
Led homeward through the moonlight pale
His bleating lambs across the sod.

PIERRE-JEAN BÉRANGER
1780–1857

The King of Yvetot

IN YVETOT once there lived a king,
　　Unknown in song or story;
All day he'd drink, or sleep, or sing;
　　He had no thirst for glory;
His crown a cotton bonnet—
His mistress helped him don it,
　　　　My oath upon it!
　　　　Ha, ha! Ho, ho!
　　A jolly little king, heigh ho!
　　　　Heigh ho!

Four times a day he'd eat his fill,
　　Then from his hut he'd ride
Upon his ass, uphill, downhill,
　　A mastiff at his side.
Without a care he'd onward jog,
He had no guard, this good King Log,
　　　　Except his dog.
　　　　Ha, ha! Ho, ho!
　　A jolly little king, heigh ho!
　　　　Heigh ho!

He did not waste, he did not wive,
　　Though always drinking like a sieve,
For if his happy subjects thrive
　　A king must also live.
So in the tavern he would squat
And levy on each cask a pot,
　　　　Downed on the spot.

Ha, ha! Ho, ho!
A jolly little king, heigh ho!
Heigh ho!

Of every home he went the rounds
Where gentle maidens gather;
A hundred subjects had good grounds
To call the King their father.
He kept no wanton soldiery,
But four times yearly, maybe three,
He practiced archery.
Ha, ha! Ho, ho!
A jolly little king, heigh ho!
Heigh ho!

He did not try to swell his states,
As most kings think they've got to;
He was the cream of potentates,
And pleasure was his motto.
He was at kingship so inept
That only when in death he slept
His people wept.
Ha, ha! Ho, ho!
A jolly little king, heigh ho!
Heigh ho!

This scion of a royal line
You still may see portrayed
Upon a swinging tavern sign
With right and left a maid;
And crowds at every drinking bout
On holidays still sing and shout,
Sipping their stout:
Ha, ha! Ho, ho!
A jolly little king, heigh ho!
Heigh ho!

My Old Coat

MY BOSOM FRIEND, my long-loved coat,
You're growing old and so am I;
Ten years you've clung round breast and throat;
Ten years I've made the dust-specks fly.
Upon your sadly thinning stuff,
That lies less heavy on my heart,
May time now lay a hand less rough;
Old bosom friend, ne'er let us part.

I well recall—'tis an old story—
The day when first I put you on:
My friends convened to sing our glory;
Who else so fine a coat could don?
Though all your charm has taken wing,
Your threadbare glow still warms my heart;
Our friends still come, and still they sing:
Old bosom friend, ne'er let us part.

Down your lapel there runs a seam:
It was my sweet Lisette who sewed it,
Lisette, my idol and my dream.
That tear, to her I likewise owed it,
So hard she tugged my coat, when I,
To test the metal of her heart,
Feigned that I spoke a last good-bye.
Old bosom friend, ne'er let us part.

You've never smelled of musk and amber,
Never paraded through the town
To haunt a gilded antichamber
And to some haughty lord bow down.
Let others flatter and cajole
And wear red ribbons on their heart,

A wild-flower decks your buttonhole;
Old bosom friend, ne'er let us part.

Let's face the wear and tear of life,
Its days of pleasure and of pain;
We've shared the glory and the strife,
Together trudged in sun and rain.
But soon I'll sleep beneath the heather,
With you tight-buttoned round my heart.
It won't be long; let's die together;
Old bosom friend, ne'er let us part.

MADAME DESBORDES-VALMORE
1786–1859

The Roses of Saadi

What time the golden gates of dawn unclose,
I culled for you full many a dewy rose;
I fixed them in my girdle till the bands
Let fall my spoils. I stood with empty hands
And watched my blossoms floating on the sea
That bore them from me never to return.
On the blue waves the crimson petals burn:
Only their haunting odor clings to me—
Come breathe its incense from the emptied urn.

Elegy

Some day, perhaps, my loved one's tender voice
Will speak my name beneath these cypress trees;
O silent valley, shall I not rejoice
To hear revived the old-time memories?

I'll watch him slow descending this lone hill,
Thinking his labor lost, his hope grown vain;
At his warm tears I'll waken from death's chill
And, lying at his feet, forget my pain.

I will no longer fear, no longer start,
Nor seem to shrink from those thrice-welcome
   showers,
And my shy words, sweet traitors to my heart,
Will woo him in the perfume of the flowers.

Here a wan rose shall hang, withering alone;
Let him inhale its fragrance and exclaim:
"Here is her heart, that heart I did not claim,
Whose fragrance shall forever fill my own.

"Scarce one brief day it blossomed on this bank
And glassed its tender green in this bright stream;
Then in the fleeting wave its petals sank,
Each lighted deathward by a pale moonbeam."

Ah, then perhaps, then will the slumbering swal-
    low,
Roused by the sigh that echoes love's despair,
Rise on the wing out of this leafy hollow
And bear to heaven his dear and dirge-like prayer.

Then weary of the world and penitent
Of love's delay, will he not love me dead,
And fondly twine round my low monument
The laurel wreath that girds his glorious head?

Then—then I were content to bide alway,
Consoled at last, here in my lonely home!
Loved valley, let me wend toward you today
And wait for him—O God, should he not come!

ALPHONSE DE LAMARTINE
1790–1869

The Lake

FOREVER BORNE toward some untrodden shore,
Still darkly drifting on our fated way,
Why on time's ocean may we nevermore
     Cast anchor for a day?

O lovely lake! Though scarce a year has passed,
In this dear spot, love's promised trysting-place,
I walk alone, here where I looked my last
     On my belovèd's face.

Thus moaned your waves 'neath the o'erhanging
  dome
Of rifted rocks, thus did its walls repeat
The wild wind's song, thus curled the crested foam
     Like garlands at her feet.

One moonlit night, sacred to lovers' pleasure,
We floated where the rippling water laves
The silent bank, and heard in cadenced measure
     The music of the waves.

With sweeter strains than earth had ever known
She poured her voice upon the silent night,
Till the charmed shores caught up the silver tone
     With answering delight:

"O Time, suspend your flight! O happy hours,
     Speed not so fast away;
Let us enjoy the season's scented flowers—
     They live but for a day.

"Too many mourners count the lagging hours,
    For them more swiftly move,
And lull their woes with your restoring powers,
    But pause for us who love!

"Yet all in vain I bid the moments linger,
    I cannot stop their flight;
Love's tryst must end, for lo! Dawn's rosy finger
    Is blotting out the night.

"Haste then to taste love's sweets, for we disport
    Like shadows on a glass;
We have no goal, time bears us to no port;
    It passes, and we pass."

O rock-rimmed lake, dim grots, and woodlands
    steep,
Time spares your splendors and renews your prime;
Then of this night, fair nature, keep, oh keep,
    The thought to after-time.

Speak it in your repose or in your storms,
O lovely lake, and in your sunny hills,
In your dark pines and rocks whose pendent forms
    Shadow your laughing rills.

Breathe it to the soft zephyrs stealing past,
Let bank to bank the happy tale recite,
And sing it to those silver stars that cast
    Such radiance on the night.

Let balmy garden scents, let all the choir
Of piping winds to vocal music moved,
Let all we hear, or gaze on, or respire,
    All whisper: They have loved!

Love Song

WHERE SILVER streams steal down the grassy hill
Through clumps of violet and daffodil
  That dot the sea of green,
Where sunbeams dance all day upon the slope
Or through the intertangled branches grope
  That o'er the waters lean,

There a wild vine two ancient oaks embraces
And round their trunks its amorous tendrils laces,
  Then from their tops descending
Paints with its paler tints their somber green
And hangs its garlands like a fairy screen,
  Vine-leaf with oak-leaf blending.

There in the shadow of a jutting rock
A mossy hollow lures the vagrant flock;
  There hides the lovelorn dove;
There many a verdant bough doth wave on high
Its odorous fronds, through which the azure sky
  Gleams scantly from above.

There pallid violets, fresh from winter's sleep,
A longer time their tender colors keep,
  And in this cool retreat,
Out of the veined recesses of the mountain,
Stealing through beds of moss, a crystal fountain
  Makes music soft and sweet.

There every sense is lulled, and the pleased eye
Views through a leafy veil the cloudless sky,
  Or from the wave-washed steep
Watches the fisher's bark, whose shining sail
Skims birdlike the blue lake, where never gale
  Breaks the still waters' sleep.

There no sound echoes but the lapping waves
Winding past ivied banks and shallow caves;
    There soothing zephyrs rove;
There the sad music of the nightingale,
Blending with the soft sighs that we exhale,
    Will mingle love with love.

    In this shadowed arbor hiding,
    We'll beguile the wingèd hours
    Till the late sun, westward gliding,
    Kisses shut the drooping flowers.
    Seek no ampler sky, my star,
    Than this grotto's vine-clad ceiling.
    Brighter than pale Dian's car,
    Through the moonlit heavens wheeling,
    Is the lustre of those eyes
    That like shining Pleiads rise.
    On this mossy bank recline,
    Where the loitering day reposes,
    While the breeze-blown eglantine
    Decks your couch with thousand roses,
    Or with hand laid warm in mine
    Let us by this flowery bed
    Pace the fountained watershed.
    Brighter gleams the dewy grass
    Which your feet so softly tread;
    And the blossoms where you pass
    Blush a more vermilion red,
    Hoping that your lips, O bliss!
    Like the bee will light and kiss.

Ischia

To OTHER WORLDS the sun has borne his light,
High on the bare horizon rides the moon,
Casting from airy spaces star-bestrewn
A gauzy veil across the brow of night.

From lofty mountain-tops its quivering beams
Steal in a glimmering torrent down the steep,
Glide o'er the slopes, and in the valleys sleep,
Or flash in radiance from the crystal streams.

Now faintly through the growing shadow wanes
The blue penumbra of its filmy rays,
While far away across the heavenly plains
The pale horizon swims in silver haze.

The orange-trees embalm the terraced steeps,
The myrtle blooms, the peaceful landscape smiles,
And in his garland of encircling isles
The ocean, like a happy lover, sleeps.

Is it the daedal earth that breathes of love?
Does Venus' star rule o'er this southern sea?
Is it the night that like a plaining dove
Sighs, as we sigh, from pure felicity?

Why gleams on yonder hill that flickering light?
Is there some maiden in the darkness roaming,
Carrying her smoky torch into the night
And waiting breathless for her lover's coming?

Trembling she stands in restless ecstasy,
Lost in sweet dreams that through her spirit sing,
Her fingers o'er the lute-strings wandering,
Thrilling the air with dulcet melody:

"Silence, too fond to measure time and space,
Hangs o'er the sea. When will my lover come,
Cleaving the tossing billows that efface
The whitening sail that brings the fisher home?

"I saw at dawn your frail bark seaward move,
And all the livelong day with anxious eye
I watched your lessening sail, as the fond dove
Watches her mate's wing whiten in the sky.

"I saw your dancing boat that left the land,
And heard across the waves your distant song,
Which the soft zephyrs breathing on the strand
In my fond ear through all the day prolong.

"When the loud billows thundered on the shore
I lit my lamp to guide the evening star,
And my low prayers, recited o'er and o'er,
Smoothed the rough seas and drove the winds afar.

"Now all is love and peace, all sounds are dying,
Wave ripples after wave in endless numbers,
The flower sleeps on its stem, and, softly sighing,
Reposeful Nature, like her children, slumbers.

"For us the moss has carpeted the valley,
The creeping ivy and the sinuous vine
Curl round our feet, and down each perfumed alley
Above our heads the orange-blossoms twine.

"Here, hand in hand, from the far world with-
    drawn,
We'll sing together, 'neath the jasmine seated,
Until the moon, its nightly round completed,
Grows pale and paler in the fires of dawn."

So sings the maid. Her lute's rich music married
To swelling strains fills all the leafy hollows,

Then feebler on the lazy breezes carried
Dwindles to dying sighs—then silence follows.

He who, his heart aglow with love's bright fire,
In this rapt hour, 'neath the enchanted moon,
Should feel his mistress in his arms suspire,
And on his bosom sink in amorous swoon;

Who, while o'erhead the bending branches meet,
And sapphire-lighted waters murmur nigh,
In bedded moss kneels at his lady's feet,
Knowing no other language than a sigh;

Who, by her beauty tranced, feels her warm breath
Kindle his cheek, while the rash breeze unfurls
Her flag of golden hair and weaves a wreath
That blinds his willing eyes in perfumed curls;

Who, all oblivious of the fleeting hours,
Love's captive, lying on this flowery sod,
Heeds only Venus' spell and Eros' power—
Is he a mortal, or is he a god?

And we, my love, who tread this paradise,
We too have known what these high raptures are,
We too have walked beneath Elysian skies
In the dim radiance of the evening star.

We too, mid nature's pomp and nature's glory,
A little while have drawn our happy breath,
Forgetting that this world is transitory
And love itself must yield at last to death.

The Nightingale

WHEN YOUR celestial notes prelude
     The silence of the starry night,
Sweet charmer of my solitude,
     I hear you, although hid from sight.

You know not how my ravished ear,
    That on your melting music dwells,
From some enchanted thicket near
    Listens delighted to your spells,

Nor how, with notes more faint and fleeting,
    A rival poet sings his love,
In his thrice-happy heart repeating
    Your nocturne in the silent grove.

Yet if the wan moon, earthward gliding,
    Pause on the hill to hear your notes,
From branch to branch you flutter, hiding
    In shadows where no moonbeam floats.

And if the brook, whose current tosses
    Its foamy spray around the stones,
But raise its voice among the mosses,
    You silence all your dulcet tones.

That music so sublimely ringing,
    So pregnant with unearthly fire,
Those heavenly sounds, that wondrous singing,
    Were destined for an angel choir.

Your warbling notes, your murmurous trills,
    In subtle blendings harmonize
The undertones of seas and hills
    With spheral music of the skies.

All unawares, your silver staves,
    To the blue firmament upleaping,
Soar over trees and vocal caves
    And valleys in the shadows sleeping.

Your mingled music interweaves
    The cadence of the sighing sea,

The tuneful rustling of the leaves,
    The dying echo's threnody,

The crystal fountains, ever dripping
    From barren rocks on babbling streams,
And from dim caverns softly slipping
    Beneath the moonlight's bluish beams,

The plaintive sound of amorous quiring
    That floats by night o'er dewy meads,
And songs of moaning seas expiring
    Among the sand-dunes and the reeds—

Of all these tones you form your spell,
    That sovran compound of delight,
That sacred song, O Philomel!
    That holy choral to the night.

Oh, mingle with my own that strain:
    The same ear hears your song and mine,
But yours, more free from earthly stain,
    Soars sooner up to heaven's shrine.

Isolation

ALONE AND PENSIVE in the evening shadows,
How often, seated on the green hillside,
I sadly watch the sunset gild the meadows
And through the reeds the shallow streamlet glide.

Yonder the noisy river heaves and billows,
And in dark thickets vanishes from view.
Here the calm lake reflects through waving willows
The evening star that rises in the blue.

Glassed in the sleeping waters, the dark trees
Crowning the summit catch the sun's last beams,
And riding low near the pale Pleiades
The white moon on the far horizon gleams.

The solemn music of the chiming bell
Arrests the listening traveller on his way,
And the faint tones that far off rise and swell
Lend holy grandeur to the dying day.

Alas! I feel no spell; no orison
Falls from my lips; for me the charm is fled;
I am but as a wandering shade; the sun
Shines on the living, not upon the dead.

Suns rise and set, and rise and set again,
And emptily the days succeed the days;
Earth's beauty has no balm to cancel pain,
And death and sorrow walk in nature's ways.

In all the orbit of the circling sun
Only the desert and the void I see;
Of all earth's proffered gifts I ask not one,
The universe holds not a hope for me.

But can it be that in remoter spheres
Where other suns illumine other skies,
Unstained by mortal hopes and mortal fears,
I yet may find a heavenly paradise?

There would I drink at fountains of pure joy,
There would I find again my hopes, my love,
And that ideal bliss that cannot cloy
And bears no name save in the realms above.

Why cannot I, borne on Aurora's car,
Vague object of my vows, attain to thee?

Why, mournful exile, view thee from afar?
There is no bond between the world and me.

As gusty Autumn whirls the withered leaf
Far from the tossing branch to which it clings,
So from this earthly sphere of death and grief
Bear me away, wild storm-winds, on your wings!

Autumn

HAIL, BARREN TREES, crowned with a few last
   leaves,
Hail, yellow foliage, scattered o'er the plain;
These last fair days, when fainting nature grieves,
Fit my sad soul and medicine my pain.

Down these lone avenues, lost in my dreams,
I walk for the last time, in pensive mood,
And view the pallid sun, whose fitful beams
Scarce pierce the darkness of the circling wood.

In these autumnal days when nature dies,
She has a charm I never knew before,
A fond farewell, a smile that sanctifies
The lips death comes to seal forevermore.

O earth, O sun, O loved and flowery vale,
Shall I no more see these familiar skies,
Morn's balmy air, cool evening's star-sprent veil,
And the warm sun, so dear to dying eyes?

I long to empty to the very lees
This cup which mingled sweet and bitter fill;
Perhaps 'twill bring oblivion or heartsease;
Perhaps a drop of honey lingers still;

Perhaps the future yet may hold in store
Some happy moment that I shall not see;
Perhaps, somewhere, some soul I know not of
Waited to hear my cry and answer me.

The floweret, fainting on the perfumed air,
Exhales its last farewell in odorous breath,
And, like a strain of music, my despair
Would still the grief of my too early death.

The Valley

ALL MY DESIRES, all hopes, all dreams have per-
    ished;
I draw in weariness my mortal breath;
O, lend me, lovely valley once so cherished,
A still retreat where I may wait for death.

Two silver streams that through the meadows glide
Make mingled music in their pebbly bed,
Wedding their waters on the green hillside
Beneath the trees that rustle overhead.

Like them the current of my life has run
Nameless and silent toward that shoreless sea
Where all things tend; but the resplendent sun
Gilded their course; it has not shone on me.

'Neath this green canopy I lie hour-long,
In the cool shadows, nursing dream on dream,
And, like a child lulled by the evensong,
Hear slumberously the murmurs of the stream.

I ask naught else; give me this leafy pale,
These low horizons that appease the eye;
Here let me bide, and in this lonely vale
For sole companions keep the streams and sky.

Too much have I beheld, and felt, and loved;
Still living, let me find in this fair spot
A silent Lethe, and abide unmoved,
The world forgetting, by the world forgot.

Now my lost days shine like a melting mist
That fades into the blue and leaves no trace;
Love only and love's memory subsist,
And the dear image of my loved one's face.

Here dwell, my soul, here find thy last retreat,
Like the tired wanderer at the city gate,
Who rests outstretched upon some vine-clad seat,
Breathing the air like a sweet opiate.

Our lives are short and dark as autumn days,
And wane like shadows on the sloping hills;
Our friends desert us, the cold world betrays,
And each, alone, his lonely doom fulfills.

But nature loves us and invites us still,
Still bids her children to her bosom flee;
She greets us always from the same green hill,
And the same sun still rises from the sea.

She garments us with shadow and with light,
She wakes for us the music of the spheres,
And hangs her glittering stars aloft the night
To dwarf this transient life of hopes and fears.

Follow the light in heaven, the shadows here;
Fly with the wingèd winds through airy space;
Glide on the moonbeam's shafts in swift career
Through this dim vale to your last resting-place.

The Crucifix

O SACRED SYMBOL, blessed by dying lips
Of one who sleeps beneath the mouldering sod,
Relic at once of earth's sweet fellowships
   And token of my God.

How many tears have washed those feet of thine
Since this memorial of my loved one's death
Passed from her tremulous fingers into mine,
   Still warm with her last breath.

The holy candles cast a flickering light;
The priest was chanting verses for the dead,
Like those soft strains that mothers sing at night
     Above an infant's bed.

Her pious hope was written on her brow
And in the solemn radiance of her face;
Death had bestowed immortal beauty now
     And a diviner grace.

The breeze that played among her loosened
  tresses
Half hid her white cheek and revealed it half,
As the quick-shifting cypress shade caresses
     A marble cenotaph.

One arm hung down from her funereal bed,
The other on her breast groped for the adored
And blessed image of the Saviour dead,
     The image of her Lord.

Her lips, half-parted, seemed to kiss it still,
Though in that holy kiss her soul had fled
Like the faint perfume which the flames distil
     From rose-leaves lately shed.

Now silence slept upon her icy lips,
Her quiet limbs, her slumbering heart reposed,
Her sightless eyes had passed into eclipse,
     Her eyelids lay half closed.

And I, who harkened to that failing breath,
Awe-struck, hung back from her I loved so much,
As if the sacred majesty of death
     Forbade all human touch.

I stood apart, but the priest, coming near,
Said, speaking now for my belovèd one,

"Here is remembrance, heavenly hope is here,
    Bear both away, my son."

We shall not part. Above her nameless tomb
The tree I planted on the grassy hill
Seven times on her has shed its leafy bloom:
    I bear thee with me still.

Thy sacred image time shall not efface;
Rest on this heart whose hope is all in thee.
My frequent tears have left a lasting trace
    On the pale ivory.

Last confidant of the departing soul,
Tell me those words which I could not divine
When through her lips her voice so faintly stole
    It reached no ear but thine.

In that dark hour in which the soul retires
Behind the veil, when death the spirit quells,
Which momently to mortal things expires,
    Deaf to the last farewells,

When the low chant melts into plaintive sobs,
When, monitory of the coming end,
The ebbing pulse-beat still more faintly throbs,
    O thou, our only friend,

Celestial witness of this mournful scene,
Thou whose blest face our dying glances seek,
Divine consoler on whose heart we lean,
    What message dost thou speak?

Thou knowest death! Under the olive tree,
Through that long night when thou didst pray
    in vain,
In the lone garden of Gethsemane,
    Thy tears dropped down like rain.

And from the cross thy dying eyes surveyed
A mother weeping and a world in gloom,
When thou didst leave the loving friends who laid
     Thy body in the tomb.

I pray thee by thy holy death that I
May on thy breast exhale my latest breath.
May I still feel thy spirit hover nigh,
     O thou who knowest death!

May I still find the imprint of fond lips
Upon this cross, and may its silver ray
Lead my bewildered soul through death's
   eclipse
     To God's eternal day.

O grant that by my bed of mortal pain
Love's pious hand, still faithful to the last,
May from my lifeless lips take up again
     This relic of my past.

Sustain the faltering steps, soothe the last hour,
Dear pledge of love and hope, of her who stands
Beside my couch, and with thy holy power
     Make life and death join hands,

Until a voice from out the clouded sky,
Where livid lightnings flash and tempests toss,
Summon the dead who in the shadow lie
     Of the eternal cross.

ALFRED DE VIGNY
1797–1863

The Shepherd's Wain

If, wearied by the heavy load of life,
Like me you suffer and like me you languish;
If, like a wounded eagle, in your anguish
You call on death to end your hopeless strife;
If your heart, chilled by an untimely blight,
Sees love from its horizon vanished quite,
Sweet love that was the wellspring of your life;

If, your arm chained unto the oar like mine,
Like me you spurn your jailers' bitter bread,
And o'er the somber galley lean your head
And shed your mournful tears into the brine,
Tracing strange routes across uncharted seas,
An outcast victim of man's cruelties
That evermore the world incarnadine;

If in your heart some secret passion burns,
Some love for aught but solitude too sweet,
Some tender love that palpitantly yearns
To hide its flame in a profound retreat
Where beauty may be free to steer its feet
Far from the idle worldling's shameless stare
And poisoned words that wound it unaware;

Then flee courageously the haunts of men,
Nor stain your white robe in this miry land,
For there is nothing pure or fair or grand
That lives 'neath such a slavish regimen.
The wildwood lures, the golden meadow smiles,
And quiet hovers o'er the sea-girt isles:
Walk through the fields a flower in your hand.

Come to the realms where solemn Nature dwells,
Where to the mist-veiled earth at evening
The lingering sun exhales his last farewells,
While lily-flowers like silver censers swing
In forests through whose darkling colonnades
Far mountains loom and in whose fountained
    glades
The willow branches weave reposeful cells.

There friendly twilight lulls the slumbering val-
    ley,
Painting with golden hues the grassy bowers
And dreaming woods where lonely streamlets
    dally
Down reedy channels worn by summer showers;
There casting on the bank her mantle grey
And kissing to new life each drooping spray,
She speeds the budding of the sleeping flowers.

Come to my mountain-side, where the tall
    heather
Scarce yields a footing to the roving swain,
There will we lie in the wind-blown grass to-
    gether
And sing of love and love's delicious pain;
But if for dearer privacy you sigh,
More closely screened from the world's peeping
    eye,
Then mount with me the shepherd's tented wain.

We'll ride afar to many a wonderland
Where unknown stars look down from tropic
    skies,
Or where dim night on the Antarctic strand
Chariots the wind-blown snow that ceaseless
    flies.

I care not where we roam or where abide;
What boots the world if you are by my side?
All lands are lovely, mirrored in your eyes.

O come! The heavens are but your aureole,
Their stainless blue your bluer eyes repeat;
What are the hills but temples for your soul?
The birds that sip the honeyed meadowsweet
Sing but for you, through you all things are fair,
For you the nodding flower embalms the air,
And earth is but a carpet for your feet.

You absent, Nature has no human charms;
I see her only through your dreamful eyes;
Her radiant landscapes and her peaceful skies,
Her colors, music, scents, eternalize
Only the raptures of your circling arms.
Then let me ne'er alone with Nature dwell,
I know her cruelty too well, too well.

She cries: "I am the passive theatre
Whose emerald stairs and alabaster halls,
Hung by the gods on soaring capitals,
Ne'er felt the foot of human actor stir.
Calmly I view the petty tragedies
Where mortal to immortal vainly calls,
Seeking spectators in the empty skies.

"Unmoved I bury in my ruthless course
Whole tribes and nations, dead without a name;
I make no choice of better or of worse,
Ant-hill and palace are for me the same.
Man calls me mother, and I am his tomb.
I use his death to fructify my womb,
And my green springs wave greener o'er his
    corse.

"Before man was, in perfumed beauty dressed,
I rode the wind, and with loose-flowing hair
Sped on my customed pathway through the air,
Moved by the impulse that the gods impressed:
Serene and silent, after man is gone,
Through the vast spaces I shall fare alone,
Cleaving the heavens with scornful brow and
    breast."

So speaks that awful voice, and, thrilled with
    pain,
Where sleep my dead I smell the taint of blood,
And drop the gathered rose or crimson bud
That on my fingers leaves a telltale stain.
My heart, avert thee from these poisoned
    charms;
Seek hope and easeful rest in human arms,
And love what, dead, you ne'er shall see again.

Not twice shall I behold your tenderness,
Your angel grace, your beauty, my beloved!
Ne'er feel a second time your soft caress,
Never again be thus profoundly moved,
Nor read your answering love in languorous eyes
And drooping head, and softly murmured sighs,
And that dear smile that speaks love's blessed-
    ness.

Live, then, fell Nature, soulless deity!
Disdaining man that should have been your king,
And, bearing his dead dust upon your wing,
Traverse your barren heavens eternally.
More than your gorgeous pomps and hollow
    shows
I love the majesty of human woes;
You shall not win one cry of love from me.

Come then, my sweet consoler, come, and bend
Those tender eyes on me, and lay your head
In shelter of my heart. So may we blend
Our thoughts in happy visions tenanted
By the same dreams that many a lover dead
Once nursed like us while his warm fancy sped
Down these same silent lanes of green that never
    end.

Wandering from clime to clime, only our shadow
The Stygian earth shall grasp at, while beneath
The swaying boughs in a far Asian meadow,
Mid twilight glooms, forlorn, with quick-drawn
    breath,
To some bright fountain in the wilds you move,
A weeping naiad, trembling for your love,
Your silent love, that dreads the touch of Death.

Moses

O'ER ISRAEL'S waving tents, with fitful gleams,
The slanting sun, scattering his dazzling beams,
Hangs on the far horizon, redly grand,
Before he plunges in the desert sand.
Earth clothes itself in a purpureal light,
And all the sky like burnished gold is bright
With rainbow hues and radiance opaline.
    And now on lofty Nebo's rock-strewn side
God's servant Moses, void of joy and pride,
With weary eyes surveys the glorious scene:
Here, girt with fig-trees, fruitful Pisgah shines,
There, past the mountain barriers, Gilead,
And Ephraim in verdant beauty clad,
And rich Manasseh all festooned with vines;
Towards the hot south lies Judah's desert land,

Whose plains slope down unto the foaming strand;
Next Nephthali in evening's fading glow
Gleams mid its olive groves, then Jericho
Magnificent, outspread in dreamy calm
Among her flowers, the city of the palm;
In Peor's bounds and down the watershed
Of Zoar, groves of green lentiscus spread;
Fair Canaan, too, he sees, the promised land
From which, in life and death, he still is banned.
He pauses, gazes, lifts his hands to pray,
Then toward the mountain-top resumes his lonely
    way.
        Darkening the fields of Moab with their
            numbers,
The tribes of Israel, spreading far and wide
Like stalks of wheat wind-wakened from their
    slumbers,
Swarmed countless near the holy mountain-side.
What time the dew moistens the golden sands
And on the maple hangs its glistering pearls,
The centenary prophet, with clasped hands,
And head round which the bright flames wreathed
    like curls,
Had stood, high-stationed under Nebo's top,
Waiting for converse with the Lord of Hosts
'Mong drifting clouds that know no let nor stop
And lightnings that illume the farthest coasts.
The offerings on a thousand altars burned,
Spikenard and myrrh and smoking frankincense
By the sun's rays to golden mist were turned,
And all the assembled multitude immense,
Bowed to the dust, intoned in solemn chant
The deathless glories of God's covenant,
While Levi's sons exalted high, as stand
The cypress trees above the rolling sand,

Seizing their harps, smote loud the golden strings,
Extolling to the heavens the King of Kings.
    Wrapped in dark clouds which veil that awful
        place,
The prophet and the Lord stood face to face,
And Moses spake: "O Lord, is there no end?
To what new land must now my footsteps tend?
Must I yet carry out some new command?
Thy chosen people, whom my cares protect,
Rest on the border of the promised land.
What have I done to be the Lord's elect?
Kingly in power, yet lonely from my birth,
O let me sleep the peaceful sleep of earth!
    "Choose some new leader for thy work, O
        God!
Of Israel's courser let him hold the reins
And guide its steps across Judea's plains.
I give to him my book and brazen rod.
Why cancel from my life all pleasing hope?
Why give its little span such mighty scope?
'Tween Horeb's wilds and Nebo's barren crown
Where shall I find my tomb, where lay me down?
I wander homeless toward thy people's home,
Waiting for restful hours that never come.
Alas! Thou gavest my youthful spirit wings,
Authority to guide thy wandering flock,
Power to invoke fire on the head of kings,
Wisdom to write thy laws on granite rock;
The tombs of ancient dead I can unlock,
And bid them speak yet unaccomplished things;
My feet rest heavy on the heads of nations;
I make and unmake tribes and generations.
Clothed with thy power, yet lonely from my birth,
O let me sleep the peaceful sleep of earth.
    "Alas! I sound the secrets of the skies

And read the future with prophetic eyes;
I can command the night to rend its veil
Or make the swiftly gliding planets sail
Whither I would; when I lift up my voice
Calm breeze or stormy winds wait on my choice;
I bury cities 'neath engulfing sand,
Lay low high mountains, flood the deep morass;
I stride from mountain-peak to mountain-peak
And move with tireless feet from land to land;
I make the waters part to let me pass,
And the loud seas are silent when I speak.
When Israel suffers, when bewilderment
Reigns in her counsels, when in dark eclipse
Earth trembles and the sun stands hesitant,
When archangelic and angelic hosts
In silent wonderment take up their posts
Beside their Lord—then thou anoint'st my lips
To speak new laws and bring new blessedness.
Yet I alone am reft of happiness—
Weary of power and lonely from my birth,
O let me sleep the peaceful sleep of earth.
          "Seeing my brow with heavenly glory blaze,
Men shun me as a stranger to their ways
And from my glance of flame avert their eyes,
Awe-struck by these supernal mysteries.
I have seen love die out and friendship perish,
And there is none to comfort me or cherish.
The virgins veil their face and hush their breath
And turn them from me as in fear of death.
Hid in thy column of dark smoke I move
Alone before the tribes with somber brow,
And my heart cries: What can I wish for now?
My mission banishes all human love;
My weary head that longs for easeful rest
Is all too heavy for a woman's breast;

My touch breeds terror where I lay my hand;
My voice is thunder, lightnings wreathe my lip,
And I know naught of human fellowship;
When I would speak, men's timid glances freeze,
And when I spread my arms, they clasp my knees.
Weary of power and lonely from my birth,
O let me sleep the peaceful sleep of earth."
     The tribes stood anxious. Fearful of his rod,
They bowed in prayer before their jealous God,
Lowering their heads. From out the blackening
   cloud,
Peal upon peal, the thunder echoed loud,
And lightning flashes, blinding every eye,
Rent the dark spaces of the midmost sky.
Then stillness followed and returning light,
And the great mountain loomed again in sight,
But the grim prophet was no longer there.
They mourned his death. Then, grasping Moses'
   rod,
Joshua stood forth, pale and with awe-struck air,
For he was now the chosen one of God.

The Wrath of Samson

THE TENT STANDS lonely in the desert sand.
What daring shepherd set it in this land
Where tawny lions roam? No cool twilight
Divides the flaming day and torrid night.
In the hot air an intermittent gust
Makes a faint ripple in the floating dust
And softly sways the whitely gleaming tent.
The flickering lamplight where it dimly falls
On the blank curtain of the canvas walls
Paints two weird figures. One, magnificent,

Of godlike bulk. 'Tis Samson. At his feet
A woman couchant, with looks honey-sweet,
Clasping the hero's knees. He, young and grave,
Through love's fell charm is slave unto this slave.
Delilah like a fawning leopard lies
Before him, and with loosened locks entwines
His giant limbs. In her perfidious eyes
A mingled gleam of lust and hatred shines.
Her finely molded arms are warm and moist,
Her shapely feet voluptuously crossed.
Her legs, more slender than the swift gazelle's,
Ringed round by bracelets hung with tinkling bells
And all with amber and pale gold embossed,
Are dyed like bronze by Hazor's burning sun.
Smooth as the wind-blown sand, each rounded
    breast,
Heavy with ancient amulets, is pressed
By veiling folds of Syrian dye, fine-spun.
Her head reposes on his sinewy knees,
Colossal as a god's. She lies at ease,
Her dainty neck by his huge fingers spanned,
That toy, half-hid, with an escaping strand,
The while he mutters a low plaintive song
In Hebrew words she cannot understand,
And her light head is lulled to sleep ere long.

    "In all times and all lands war without truce
Is waged between man's truth and woman's ruse.
Man ever yearns for dalliance and for love;
He learns this craving at his mother's breast
When, cradled in her arms, he sinks to rest,
As in the nest the tender turtle-dove.
In the world's press, as in his restless bed,
He ever longs to pillow his tired head
On that soft bosom, and he still will dream
Of music floating on the air of night,

Of parting kisses when the dawn grows bright,
Of tangled tresses that around him gleam
And hold him captive to a wanton's whim,
Whose image through the long day follows him.
Sly courtesans will pluck his garment's hem,
And fondly amorous he will yield to them—
For the best-born most easily are misled,
And love most quickly conquers the most brave,
As nobler streams flow with a wilder wave
And more compulsive current down their bed.
When by God's will unwillingly we scan
A foe in nature and our fellow man,
We find relief in tears, and fragile bliss
In a warm bosom and a passioned kiss.
But the fell ordeal is not ended yet;
Another foe, more traitorous, must be met,
Secret and base; for woman in man's heart
Plays always, more or less, Delilah's part.
Smiling she mocks and, secretly unmoved,
Disdains to love though eager to be loved.
      "O God omnipotent! Know that my soul
Fed on no food except this woman's love:
She was my strength, my star, my aureole,
And in her only did I live and move.
Judge then between us. At my feet she lies;
Thrice has she sold the secret of my strength,
Thrice bathed me with false tears; but now at
    length
I read the hidden malice in her eyes,
And in my grief I falter. Now, alas!
My giant body and my massive head,
That once upheld the city-gates of brass,
Are bowed to earth; my spirit is of lead.
Must I still let this gilded serpent twine
Its coils around me, idly watch it shine

Out of the mire, and feel it slyly creep
About my heart to sting me in my sleep?
Must I still cling to my ill-chosen bride,
Still keep this impure creature at my side,
And day by day hide the consuming rage
That fills my fainting soul? Why must I wage
This endless war against myself, and keep
My lips from speaking and my eyes from sleep?
In sooth, it is too much! Have I not told
My secret? Yet I knew it would be sold.
How beautiful the feet that run toward me
To work my doom! For what must be, must be."
    He ceased and slept beside her till the hour
When his foes, creeping through the hero's house,
Clipped the long hair that held such wondrous
    power,
Poured their heaped gold before his treacherous
    spouse,
And tied his hands, and burned out his two eyes,
And dragged away in chains their bleeding prize—
Then set him up to make their people sport,
Fronting their god, their Dagon, in his fane.
Twice did the idol groan, twice on its base
It wheeled about, the while, like souls in pain,
His priests ecstatic stared with pallid face
On fallen Samson, bound like some wild beast.
They kindled incense flames, and made a feast:
The Hebrews on the distant mountains heard
And wept. Their foes a snow-white heifer slew
In honor of their god, and at his side
They placed the harlot, Samson's traitorous bride.
She sits on high, enthroned in public view,
A diadem on her lascivious brow,
And trembling cries, "He cannot see me now!"
    But evil days await Philistia's town:

Jehovah holds aloft his vengeful rod,
And Samson, clothed anew with godlike might,
Hurls at one stroke their gilded columns down,
And in their ruins buries in one night
Three thousand foes, their temples, and their god.

The Wolf

Black clouds pursued the flying moon, red-
    tinged
Like trailing smoke that streaks a moving fire,
While frowning woods the dark horizon fringed.
Silent we crept, now through the yielding mire,
Now through deep heather or bleak moorland
    waste,
Till suddenly, as we advanced slow-paced,
Beneath some pines we spied the winding trail
Of roaming wolves athwart the twilight pale.
We listened with suspended breath; no sound
Rose from the silent woods or the dank ground;
Only the weather vane sent its drear cry
With toneless echoes through the somber sky,
For the wind, blowing where the cloud-wrack
    lowers,
Scarce touched the top of solitary towers,
While far below the oak trees seemed to sleep,
Leaning their heads against the rocky steep.
Then in the stillness, peering with keen eye,
The oldest huntsman sought again to spy
The footprints in the sand, and suddenly
He pointed out what all had failed to see,
The half-hid tracks imprinted by the claws
Of two large wolves and of their tender young
That still as nurselings to their mother clung.

Intent upon the prey, each hunter draws
His keen-edged blade and hides his shining gun,
Pushing aside the branches one by one
And stealing silent on. With swift surprise
Between the trees I saw two flaming eyes
And, farther off, four shapes that danced together
In the dim twilight on the brownish heather,
As merrily as leaping hounds rejoice
At the glad summons of their master's voice.
Such was their aspect, such their frolic dance;
But the young wolves played silently, aware
That man, their foe, with sleepless vigilance,
Lay ambushed near to slay them or to snare.
The wolf stood watchful, while beside a tree
His mate lay, like that marble deity,
The gaunt she-wolf, who in her caverned home
Reared the twin founders of imperial Rome.
The huge wolf crouched, plunging his crooked
      claws
Deep in the sand. He guessed his doom because
By watchful foes each forest path was blocked.
In his red jaws he seized the panting throat
Of the most forward hound, and ne'er unlocked
His deadly teeth, although his shaggy coat
Was riddled by repeated fusillades
And torn by stab on stab of our sharp blades
That in his fainting flesh crossed and recrossed,
While ever to his helpless prey he clung
That from his bloody mouth inertly hung,
Till the dead carcass at his feet he tossed.
But well he knew his savage battle lost:
Our pointed guns faced him from every side,
And our long knives were buried to the hilt,
Pinning him to the soil on which he spilt
His steaming blood that poured in crimson tide.

He stretched his quivering limbs upon the ground
And licked with parching tongue each gaping
    wound,
Then glowered upon us all defiantly,
And closed his eyes and died without a cry.

Resting my head against my smoking gun,
I fell to thinking, for my heart was wrung
Too much to slay the she-wolf and her young
That hesitantly fled. The widowed one,
Somber but beautiful, had surely stayed
Beside her mate, had she not been afraid
To leave her tender whelps. These she must save
To teach them hunger's gnawing pangs to brave,
To shun all contact with man's cruel race
And never set foot in his dwelling-place,
Where servile beasts, to eat and drink their fill,
Join him in hunting down in deadly chase
The first inhabitants of wood and hill.
Alas! I mused, how base a thing is man,
That deems himself the darling child of time!
Life's woes to scorn, its cruelty to scan
Unmoved, ye only know, ye brutes sublime.
So slight our action and so vain our thought,
Silence alone is great, all else is naught!
O savage rover, well you played your part,
And your last look is graven in my heart.
This was your message: May your spirit reach,
With wisdom and slow patience for your guide,
Unto that lofty pitch of stoic pride
That to the beasts the winds and waters teach.
To groan, to weep, to pray, is cowardly;
Do with stout heart your long and dreary task,
No respite look for and no mercy ask,
And in unbroken silence die like me.

The Horn

SWEET SOUNDS the horn at evening in the wood,
Echoing the plaintive outcries of the hind,
Or huntsman's call that mid the foaming flood
Swells through the leafage on the northern wind.

How oft, when Midnight walks his ghostly round
In the lone groves, is heard the mournful sound
Of those prophetic strains that ushered in
The doom of ancient king or paladin.

O mountains that in azure melt away,
High-cliffed Frazona, stony Marborée,
Wild cascades of the snowy Pyrenees,
Springs, fountains, torrents, and rock-rooted
    trees!

Here Winter reigns, with Summer for his queen,
Throned on white peaks while all below lies
    green;
Here oft I sit and drink in the forlorn
And tender echoes of the hunting horn.

Here oft the shepherd, when the air is still,
Makes his wild music leap from hill to hill,
While ever through the lengthened cadence
    swells
The tinkling of his lambs' melodious bells.

The listening doe, entranced, forgets to hide
And hangs immobile on the mountain-side,
Where the white cascade in its thunderous fall
Flings its loud song against the caverned wall.

O knights of old! Do you still haunt this ground,
Still summon us with the horn's mournful sound?

O Roncevaux! does your dark valley hold
Great Roland's shade, still wandering uncon-
  soled?

Symetha

"O swift-winged galley, hung with wreathèd
  flowers,
Thy rose-crowned prow above the blue sea
  towers
Through tossing spray! Blow softly, Aeolus!
Shine, kindly stars! and, tides impetuous,
Guide swift and safe the bark to Lesbos' shore,
And grant the boon these dying lips implore—
For death awaits me! On the perilous seas
Symetha sails! Forgot thy olive trees,
O Attica! Forgot the crystal springs
Of cool Ilyssus where the swallow sings.
Forgot the groves, blest haunt of nymph and god,
And cadenced dances on the flowery sod,
White-stoled processional of chosen maids
In stately march through marble colonnades,
And hilly steep crowned by the Parthenon!
From these loved sites you are forever gone;
No more will you invoke Athena's name,
No more will your long golden tresses flame
Through clustered asphodel, no more your hand
To the blithe gods who rule this Attic land
Will lift the sacred veil and silver vase
Or purple webs that on your distaff blaze.
        "O Lesbian virgin, may your isle abhorred
Sink fathoms deep in sea-caves unexplored
Before your ship graze Lesbos' pebbly strand!
What would you there? What spell, what wonder-
  land,

Allures your truant feet? What would you there,
Sweet Lesbian maid? Can Lesbos still seem fair?
Three jocund springs have seen your beauties' bud
In Hellas' garden grow to womanhood;
Three summers warm have seen the flowery stem
Lift high in air its queenly diadem.
The Attic Muse smiled on this tender flower;
Here seas sleep calm, here tempests never lower,
Here nightingales from fountained Helicon
Intone their hymns round the white Parthenon.
'Twas here I saw you first, 'twas here I loved,
And here I sometimes dreamed your heart was
    moved,
Symetha! Could I think my love was doomed,
When in your steps a thousand roses bloomed,
When like a breeze-tossed rose your virgin heart
Would at my amorous pleading seem to start,
When your lips smiled, sweet as the daystar's rise,
While lights Elysian danced in your bright eyes?
But now by wave on wave your bark is tossed,
And my fond fears deem my Symetha lost!
Ah, lost to me, indeed, to me denied!
May Venus pardon you her power defied,
And crown a later love! Depart, forget!
Yet some day near this spot where first we met
Your random foot may tread the Grecian soil
Where your dead lover shed his mortal spoil."
        O sweet lament of love and love's despair,
That died unheard on Sunium's perfumed air!
The lovely Lesbian at the galley's side
Watched the dipped oars and the receding tide,
Then, leaning from the stern in childish glee,
Smiled at her image dancing on the sea
And flung down scattered flowers and garlands gay.

Laughing to see them fall and float away,
Or, lapped in languorous dreams, with half-closed
eyes,
Heard on the breeze the lute-strings' plaintive sighs.

VICTOR HUGO
1802–1885

Olympio

THE FIELDS were sunlit, with no cloud in view,
And fathomless o'erhead the vaulted blue
  Over the world was spread;
All earth was perfumed, every meadow green,
When he revisited the lonely scene
  Where once his heart had bled.

Brown autumn smiled; the hills that crowned the
 plain
Shone through tall trees scarce yellowed by the
 rain,
  The skies were all of gold,
And chirping birds that through the grasses ran,
Those winged messengers 'tween God and man,
  Were singing as of old.

He longed to see again the stream, the fountain,
The battered hut that nestled 'gainst the moun-
 tain,
  The bent ash near the spot
Where in deep thickets meant for lovers' bliss
Their hearts had mingled once in love's first kiss,
  All mortal cares forgot.

Behind the iron gate, 'mong clustered trees,
Dim paths and winding ways and flowery leas
  And purple orchards lay,
And yon the lonely house and garden-close:
At every step a thousand memories rose
  Of that departed day.

His listening ear through the familiar trees
Caught the mysterious music of the breeze
    That wakes our mortal loves,
That pulses in the oak and sways the rose,
And through the universe flows and reflows
    And never-resting moves.

The fallen leaves that strewed the lonesome wood
Rose at his step with sudden hardihood
    And fluttered in the air:
So our sad thoughts, oblivious of time's stings,
Oft rise a moment on their wounded wings,
    Then sink in dull despair.

All day he roamed among the vast domains
Where nature dwells, through the pacific plains,
    The mountains, the morass,
The wild ravines that climb with sinuous grace,
Viewing by turns the sky, celestial face,
    The lake, celestial glass.

His spirit wandered through his vanished past,
Too sweet for blotting out, too sweet to last;
    His thoughts cut like sharp swords;
Somber he stood and viewed with alien eyes
The unscaled walls of that green Paradise,
    Then spoke these mournful words:

"O love! O grief! My passioned soul has sought
To taste again the joy of yesteryear,
To learn if this fair valley holdeth aught
Of the rich treasure I abandoned here.

"Our leafy boughs are grown to forests now,
The tree on which we carved our name is gone,
And time has ravaged many a rosy bough
Whose blossoms love once loved to slumber on.

"By the walled fountain, in the noontide hour,
In caverned nooks where shadowy silence lingers,
Sportive she drank, and tossed a glittering shower
Of liquid pearls out of her fairy fingers.

"The ancient milestone where so many a day
She waited for me in the pale twilight,
By clashing wheels is almost worn away
Of the great creaking carts that rumble home at
    night.

"Must then our lives end in oblivious sleep,
All our vain cries be stilled, our love forgot?
The birds sing in the branches while I weep,
My house beholds me and it knows me not.

"Others will have our woods, our fields, our bowers,
Lovers unknown will wander by our streams,
Strange feet will tread the paths that once were
    ours,
And strangers here will dream the selfsame dreams.

"Of all our hopes and ardors and desires
No relic shall survive, no thought remain;
The heart that burns, the spirit that aspires,
Relentless nature takes them all again.

"Speak, ye ravines, cool streams, and trellised
    slopes,
Nest-laden boughs, dark grots, and soaring hills,
Shall others bid you echo their sweet hopes?
Shall others hear your songs by these fresh rills?

"Tell me, green valley, tell me, solitude,
Tell me, O Nature! when our life is fled,
Will you in this fair spot forget to brood
Compassionate above the voiceless dead?

"Will you, unmoved, behold my loved one stand,
A bloodless ghost, forlorn as a lost child,
Mournfully beckoning me with trembling hand,
Toward some lone fountain sobbing in the wild?

"If somewhere through these shadowy thickets
    rove
Two happy lovers, blossom-garlanded,
Will you not whisper: Ye that live and love,
O give one passing thought unto the dead!

"God gives us for a day these silver fountains,
These whispering woods, these dells, this flowery
    plain,
These azure skies, and these mysterious mountains
To hide our love—then takes them back again.

"So let it be—forget us—we are shadows,
House, garden, greensward, hawthorn dewy wet!
Sing, flitting bird! Flow, streams! Bloom, fertile
    meadows!
Though you forget us, we will not forget.

"Age chills our hearts, our waning passions fly,
Like strolling actors singing through the land
With mask and dagger till their straggling band
Pass the next hill and vanish from the eye.

"But age can never alter thee, O love!
Thy hopes, thy joys, thy sorrows undergone,
In memory's dim chancel live and move,
Grown ever holier as the years wear on."

Love Notes

LET US, love, with fancy play,
Dream we mount on wingèd steeds,
Dream we take the forest way
Where the birds swing on the reeds.

Guide us, Cupid, Venus' boy;
Come, the skies grow dim above;
I will mount the palfrey Joy,
You shall mount the palfrey Love.

We will ride them neck to neck
Past the hills and precipices;
They shall feel no spur nor check,
They shall feed on songs and kisses.

Come, our magic coursers seem
Eager from the earth to rise,
Mine to soar where soars my dream,
Yours to pace the starry skies.

For our baggage we will take
Only kisses and caresses,
Only love's delicious ache
And the blossom in your tresses.

Come, the dusk embrowns the oak,
And the twittering sparrows sing,
Mocking at the foolish folk
Wounded by love's honeyed sting.

Through the starlit woods we'll ride,
Where the timid turtle-dove,
As we journey side by side,
Shall rehearse our carolled love.

Turn on me your tender eyes
In this thicket wet with dew,
Where the startled butterflies
Spread their wings to follow you,

Where the envious owlet turns
On your charms his blinking eye,
Where the nymphs with brimming urn
Stop to gaze as we ride by.

Sweet their song so clear and shrill:
"Watch no more these lovers kiss
Lest our crystal lymph we spill—
That's Leander, Hero this!"

Come, my love, let us away!
Soon the dawn will gild your brow.
Life shall all be holiday;
Love shall ever bloom as now.

Through green meads, through skies all blue,
And by Paradisal founts,
Let us canter, me and you,
On our wingèd fairy mounts.

Love's Symphony

WHY listen so long
To the wildwood bird,
When a sweeter song
In your voice is heard?

Though in heaven afar
A million stars rise,
The most beautiful star
Is the star in your eyes.

Though April embower
The fields with her art,
Yet the loveliest flower
Is the flower in your heart.

That bird in its flight,
That bright star above,
That flower snow-white,
Form the blossom called love.

If You Have Naught to Tell Me

IF YOU HAVE naught to tell me,
    Why sit beside me here,
With lips that smile so tenderly
    A king would hold them dear?
If you have naught to tell me,
    Why sit beside me here?

If you've no secret to confess,
    Why press my hand so sweetly,
It almost seems a stray caress
    That hints of love discreetly?
If you've no secret to confess,
    Why press my hand so sweetly?

If you would fain that I depart,
    Why do you walk this way,
Knowing full well that to my heart
    You usher in the day?
If you would fain that I depart,
    Why do you walk this way?

Expectation

CLIMB, SQUIRREL, climb the tall oak-tree,
Where the branches highest be,
Where the green tips weave a bower;
Stork, mount from your airy perch
On mossy-steepled church—
For a wider look-out search
Than belfry top or beacon tower.

Old eagle, soar into your airy
Nest on mountain centenary
Where eternal snowdrifts lie;
And you, who drive away the dark,
Nature's tuneful hierarch,
Fly up, fly up, warbling lark,
Warbling lark, into the sky!

Now from out the topmost tree,
From mass of marble masonry,
From mighty mount and flaming sky,
From mist in cloudland floating by,
Do you not see a plume wave high?
On foaming steed do you not see
My lover riding home to me?

The Past

IT IS A GREAT chateau, moss-clad and old,
Of Louis Thirteenth's day. The sunset light,
On wall and window falling manifold,
Drowns all things in a sea of liquid gold
Till roofs and battlements are lost to sight.

Its ancient splendor gone, the ruined park
Is threaded by an intertangled maze

Of grass-grown paths o'errun with ivy dark,
That clothes a shivering statue near a vase
In which a cluster of red poppies blaze.

The fountain sleeps, and sleeps the lonely pool,
A greenish Neptune mouldering on its edge;
The lazy tide is smothered in the sedge,
And gaunt trees stand in darkling shadows cool
Where Boileau hunted rhymes along the hedge.

Shy deer come wandering toward the silver
    stream
Where huntsmen come no more. Fall'n in decay,
Wan statues which the stunted trees upstay
Whiten the meads where, lovely as a dream,
Queen Venus smiled on Gabrielle d'Estrée.

In these dusk thickets and moss-coated caves,
With eyes downcast and palpitating breast,
Oft fair Caussade or gay Candale would rest
Beside her prince, rehearsing amorous staves,
Like some fond bird within its downy nest.

Then as today, for Candale and Caussade
The fleecy clouds sailed through the azure skies,
And bee-tossed hairbells, as in glad surprise,
Laughed to the sunbeams on the bright façade
And tinkled tremulous 'tween lovers' sighs.

Then as today, two hearts in unison,
In these green woods where love held holiday,
Roamed down the paths or strayed where path
    was none,
Singing soft strains till evening shades grew dun
And stars lit up the heavens, then as today.

O happy times of old that could beget
Those soaring notes that chimed on blending lips,

Echoing the shepherd's distant flageolet!
O vanished days! O splendors in eclipse!
O suns beyond the dim horizon set!

In a Garden

IN THIS OLD GARDEN down whose winding ways
The sunshine through the veiling lindens plays
So chastely that methinks each argent flower,
Like a swung censer, warns the passing hour
To print the movement of its creeping pace
In shadowy records on the marble vase
That mirrors now the sunbeam, now the tree—
With what fond joy, as in a waking dream,
I saw the rosy light of daybreak gleam
While the birds twittered on the swaying bough!
What happy fancies smoothed my wrinkled brow
While the glad child who drew me by the hand
Urged my slow steps across the level sand
Toward the dim grot where ivy tangles nod
And hang a green beard on the river-god.

My Two Daughters

IN GOLDEN GLORY of the twilight hour,
One like a swan, the other like a dove,
Two sisters sported in a shady grove,
Running with eager feet from flower to flower,
Or leaning breathless on the mouldering wall.

They watched the fragile-stemmed carnations fall
In wind-swept clusters from their marble urn,
And fluttering hang in the sun's rosy light,
Like wheeling butterflies that make sojourn
In sudden ecstasy at some glad sight.

Dreamland

IN HIS curtained room
The infant blue-eyed
Lies asleep in the gloom
By his fond mother's side;
And while he reposes,
His lids, like the roses
That morning discloses,
To heaven open wide.

O sweet are his dreams
On the bosom of night:
Of the sea-sand that gleams,
Of the moon shining white,
Of the sunset's red flames,
Or of beautiful dames
With melodious names,
Lovely angels of light.

O visions enchanting!
Bright rivers he sees,
And white mermaids haunting
The depths of the seas;
'Tween waking and sleeping
He hears a voice sing
Like a lark on the wing
Lulling him in soft ease.

He sees fairy flowers,
White lilies, red roses,
Bedewed by spring showers
In green garden-closes,
And by the wayside
Silver streams on whose tide

Fishes lazily glide
Where the dragonfly dozes.

O child, dream on still,
Mortal sorrows foregoing
While, free from all ill,
Life's currents are flowing;
Like dead seaweed drifting
On waves unuplifting,
Yet ever more shifting,
You slumber unknowing.

Drawn round in a ring,
The angels of bliss,
Who descend on swift wing
From God's world into this,
Seeing him so unarmed,
Unafraid, unalarmed,
Bend over him charmed
And his dainty hands kiss.

Then, standing anear,
They sing "Hushaby"
Till, bedewed by a tear,
He wakes with a cry;
But with seraph hands swaying
His couch and allaying
His fears, softly praying
They soar to the sky;

While his mother, aroused
By his infantine cry,
Is afraid she has drowsed
While some evil drew nigh;
And with witching wiles
She sweetly beguiles
Her babe till he smiles
'Tween her kiss and her sigh.

Night in June

O BALMY NIGHTS, when thousand flowers distil
Sweet odors that our slumbering senses steep,
While with closed eyes we feel their witching
     thrill,
Lying half-wakeful in transparent sleep!

The stars shine with a more entrancing power;
Vague lights, not yet of day, the shadows tinge;
And the dawn, waiting her accustomed hour,
Seems all night long to wander on heaven's
     fringe.

Ecstasy

I WANDERED by the lonely shore,
The stars shone overhead,
No sail the glancing waters bore,
No mists through cloudland sped.
My eyes outstripped the bounds of space
And spinning planets' track,
Where sentry-stars forever pace
The golden zodiac,
And, whirling in eternal round,
Forever with commingling sound
About the orbèd moon
Still chant their mystic rune.

The legionary hosts of stars
Arrayed in glittering gold,
Like shining tips of scimitars,
Pierced every wood and wold.
Bending their glowing crowns of fire,
Loud or low-voiced they sang,

And from the ocean's billowy choir
An answering anthem rang,
Rolling along their crested white
And skyward borne and blown
Through avenues of celestial light
Up to the sapphire throne,
Still singing in divine accord,
Hail, our Creator, hail, our Lord!

Revery

THE DIM HORIZON, wreathed in circling mist,
Tints all the clouds with pearl and amethyst,
Clustering around the crimson daystar's setting.
The yellow leaves gild every shining hill,
And Autumn in the woodland lingers still,
The windswept trees with russet splendors
    fretting.

O for some magic touch that at one stroke,
While I sit musing in the growing dusk,
Out of the mystic cloudland might evoke
A Moorish city rising up with brusque
Fantasmal rocket-flight that silhouettes
In glowing fires its soaring minarets,

And lure my Muse, with odorous lotus-flowers,
Far from this clime and its autumnal hues,
To roam where faery palaces and towers
Their shadowy tints and dying echoes fuse
Mid thousand shining pinnacles that rise
Through climbing mists into the violet skies.

Sunrise

IT WAS THE HOUR when Phoebus' trampling
    steeds
Rise from the caverned deep. The new light
    speeds
Past cloudy turrets, while the golden doors
Of day burst open, and the white dawn pours
Her silver torrents on the shining world.
Across empurpled fields the car was hurled;
High waved the arm of the directing god,
And the four horses, governed by his nod,
Fronted the whirling winds with flame-girt
    breast
And bristling manes that floated golden-tressed.
Between the tenebrous and fiery zones
They bounded, shedding myriad gemmy stones,
Diamonds and pearls, bright onyx, sapphires
    pure,
That in the trackless seas found sepulture.
The first three horses from their nostrils threw,
Down level shafts of light, like drops of dew,
Their orient showers. The last one in his flight
Flung back a train of stars into the night.

The Spinning-Wheel of Omphale

IN THE HIGH ATRIUM stands the ivory wheel,
White-rimmed, with distaff black, of ebony
Incrusted with blue lapis lazuli
And rich inlaid with many a jeweled seal.
An Aeginetan sculptor on the plinth
Had carved Europa borne by the white bull

Through the blue seas: like a pale hyacinth
She droops down, wan and faint yet beautiful,
Feebly lamenting while her frightened eyes
See round her rosy feet the billows rise.
Miletus yarns of purple streaked with gold
And splendorous with Oriental dyes,
Gemmed caskets, thread and needles manifold,
And subtile fabrics wrought in cunning wise
Lie by the wheel—strange marvels to behold.

Meanwhile foul phantoms, veiled as in a mist,
With muffled tread through the dim palace
    steal,
And monstrous, blood-bedabbled, cicatriced,
Prowl furtively around the moveless wheel.
The Nemean lion, Lerna's hydra-spawn,
The cavern-haunting Cacus, son of night,
The triple Geryon, Typhon whilom drawn
By subject winds that reed-like moan all night—
All bear the mark of the Herculean mace
On their scarred fronts, and with averted face,
Reluctant eyes, and terror-stricken frown,
View the fine thread that spins its silky down
Round the black distaff, and with shamefaced air
Upon the idle wheel obliquely stare.

The Cow

NEAR THE WHITE farmhouse, in the noonday heat,
An old man loiters on his sun-warmed seat,
Flanked by shrill-clucking hens with blood-red
    crests.
The kenneled mastiff barks with heaving breast
In answer to the cock's loud clarion,
Who struts, tall, varnished, shining in the sun.

Near by a cow stands in the golden light,
Superb, huge, reddish-brown, with spots of white.
As with its fawns a gentle hind is seen,
Leading them slowly through the pastures green,
So patiently she let a noisy group
Of urchins round her pendent udders troop,
With teeth like marble and with unkempt hair
That tossed in tangled skeins on shoulders bare.
With lusty interchange of clamorous cries,
They swarmed around her like a cloud of flies.
Some heedless milkmaid, absent to her cost,
Found all too late her evening garner lost.
A dozen greedy mouths and ruffian hands
Circled the foamy nipples like hooped bands,
Making the warm milk spurt to every side.
Meanwhile she watched them unperturbed, big-
    eyed;
And, fecund nurse, licking her glossy coat,
She let them riot, seeming not to note
Their clamors and rude touch. Her silken flank
Scarce quivered, and her dewlaps rose and sank
In pulsing quiet. Her calm gaze, distraught,
Wandered remote in regions void of thought.

Oceano Nox

Now MANY mariners from this gray land
Have steered light-hearted toward some luring
    strand,
Only to die, far from the beckoning shore,
Tossed on rude billows, like a floating spar,
Where the long moonless night broods evermore
On blank horizons bare of any star.

None knows in what far stretches of the sea
Your bodies roll with multitudinous shocks,

Striking your dead brows on uncharted rocks,
While daily your old parents on the quay
Wait, even as death stands waiting for them-
    selves,
For you, whose bones lie strewn on ocean's sandy
    shelves.

Seated on rusty anchors near the shore,
The merry friends you reveled with of yore
Mingle your names, grown shadowy with time,
In their gay songs or tales of ancient deeds,
Or court your old-time loves in tender rhyme
While you sleep silent in the green seaweeds.

Wondering they ask if in some tropic isle
You harvest ampler fields where warmer suns
From the unclouded blue forever smile.
Then in their minds your image fades away,
As fade 'mong coral caves your skeletons
In ebon gulfs o'er which the wild waves play.

All trace, all memory of you disappears;
One has his plow, another has his bark.
Only your widowed mate, bent low with years
And lassitude that haunting hopes impart,
Murmurs your name while stirring in the dark
The ashes on her hearthstone and her heart.

And when at last she sleeps in holy ground
None speaks your name; not even a humble stone
Records with hers its once familiar sound.
Nor leafless willows sighing in the breeze,
Nor beggars chanting in low monotone,
Repeat it in their plaintive melodies.

Where rest the sailors whelmed in stormy seas?
O waves! what somber mysteries you hide
From wailing mothers on their bended knees!

You sing them as you climb the rising tide
In those wild notes repeated o'er and o'er
While all night long you moan upon the shore.

The Bagpiper's Song

THE FOG HANGS chill, and gray is the heather
Where the lowing kine come down to drink.
The moon and the clouds are bringing foul
    weather,
And the pale beams fade on the river's brink.

> I know not why and I know not where
> Old Yvon is piping a doleful air.

The wayfarer hastens, the frothy seas shimmer,
Black shadows precede him, a black shadow fol-
    lows.
The east is all white; in the west a red glimmer
Sets the hillsides aflame; all black lie the hollows.

> I know not why and I know not where
> Old Yvon is piping a doleful air.

By the roadside old witches they mumble and
    lisp;
The spiders are spinning webs downward and up;
And a goblin darts from a will-o'-the-wisp
Like a pistil of gold from the tulip's cup.

> I know not why and I know not where
> Old Yvon is piping a doleful air.

Rough billows are plashing the floating buoy,
And a bark with torn rigging and yard-arms all
    bare
In the ocean's trough is tossed like a toy,
While the wild waves ring with cries of despair.

I know not why and I know not where
Old Yvon is piping a doleful air.

The stagecoach driver who posts to Avranches
Cracks his whip till it whirls like a lightning
    flash;
The twilight hangs dismal on bush and on
    branch;
And tall pines in the grove topple down with a
    crash.

I know not why and I know not where
Old Yvon is piping a doleful air.

The waters swirl on the silver sand,
The osprey flits where the clay-banks rise,
And the shepherd sees from the wind-swept land
Wild flights of demons that furrow the skies.

I know not why and I know not where
Old Yvon is piping a doleful air.

Gray smoke-plumes curl from the chimney tops;
The wood-chopper, laden with faggots, limps by;
And yon, where the water plashes and plops,
The wind-lopped branches gurgle and sigh.

I know not why and I know not where
Old Yvon is piping a doleful air.

The wild wolves howl at the skies overcast;
The river rushes, the clouds scud past;
Through the window-pane where the lamplight
    glows
The faces of children shine like a rose.

I know not why and I know not where
Old Yvon is piping a doleful air.

Adam and Eve

IN THE FIRST DAYS of earth the new-born clouds
Wrapped land and ocean in their golden shrouds,
For rising evil had not yet dispelled
Heaven's blessèd airs, and man's eyes yet beheld
The lingering light of the lost Paradise
Hover all night upon the starlit skies
Till waking dawn strewed roses on the sea.
The unborn years were ripening on time's tree,
And stillness brooded upon pathless wastes
Of sea-green pampas, haunt of tawny beasts,
And beetling crags, where giant cedars leaned
Over vast caverns in rich frondage screened.
Here 'mong gray rocks, their roofless habitat,
Naked, august, and gloom-enshrouded, sat
Our white-haired mother Eve, pale and forlorn,
And, near her, Adam, with long labors worn
And painful thought, his terror-haunted eyes
Still dazzled by the fire of wrathful skies.
There under stars that wander without rest
Over the snow-crowned mountains' towering
    crest,
On the bare hillside, with averted gaze
From lights that in forbidden heavens blaze,
They sat. All nature seemed a barren tomb,
And Paradise itself a place of doom.
No word fell from their lips, no human sound
Soothed their sad hearts, but on the stony
    ground
Stone-like they stared, each seeming unaware
Of all companionship except despair.
They crouched immobile as the voiceless dead;
Only from hour to hour each heavy head

Sank ever lower, doomed by fell decree
Of limitless and nameless Deity,
They and their race, to watch in dateless sorrow
The slow days die and nights melt into morrow,
Till in the footsteps of returning night
The gradual constellations lift their light
And the blithe halcyon's nest floats on the sea
Toward the blue shorelines of infinity,
Rocked on calm tides o'er which soft zephyrs
    blow
And stars uncounted flash with golden glow
Into the heavens like flowers from an urn,
Far-glancing fires that on heaven's threshold
    burn.
Meantime they lingered, lost in somber thought,
Blinded with grief, with horror overwrought.
Unheedful of the billows' lulling song,
Among the gliding shadows all night long
They shed salt tears, Adam for Abel slain,
His latest-born; but Eve mourned over Cain.

Boaz

BOAZ, WITH heavy weariness oppressed,
After the long day's toil in summer's heat,
Lay down in his accustomed place of rest
And slept beside his bushels filled with wheat.

The aged man had many a bursting sack
Of wheat and barley carefully upstored,
Yet kind he was, and let no poor man lack
A needed pittance from his swelling hoard.

With beard as silvery as an April brook,
He moved exultant 'mong his yellow sheaves,

And many stalks he takes and many leaves,
Dropped for the gleaners from the reaping-hook.

Thus Boaz slept in peace, and, all around,
The harvesters beside the stacks of hay
In shadowy groups lay scattered on the ground,
As was men's wont in that primeval day.

A judge ruled the nomadic folk of God,
Who dwelt in tents, fearing the trail of blood
And the fresh print of giant feet that trod
The earth still wet and miry from the Flood.

As Jacob slept, as Judith slept, so lay
Boaz in sleep, the clear heavens overhead,
When lo! a dream came down the dim pathway
That leads from star to star. On his green bed

He saw an oak-tree shoot out of his breast
Past sun and moon into the utmost sky;
A whole race up its million branches pressed,
A king sang at its base, a God expired on high.

And Boaz cried, as one whose heart is sore:
"How may this come to pass? It cannot be.
The number of my years exceeds four score,
I have no son, no wife—God mocketh me!

"How then should I beget a future race?
How from my loins be born a line of kings?
Youth holds high festival of strength and grace
And waits the budding of uncounted springs,

"But age is like the birch whose ravaged bloom
Shakes in the wintry wind. My brow is cool
With the death-damp; my soul leans toward the
    tomb
As thirsting oxen bend above the pool."

Thus Boaz spake, and sorrow dimmed his face.
His golden dream seemed all a fond conceit.
Cedars see not the roses at their base,
Nor he a woman sleeping at his feet.

While Boaz slumbered, Ruth, the Moabite,
Bare-bosomed by his couch had laid her down,
Led by some heaven-sent vision through the
    night,
Some secret hope which dawning day should
    crown.

Boaz knew not there was a woman there,
His destined bride. The clouds were silver-
    white,
Bright clumps of asphodel perfumed the air,
And Galgala basked in the balmy night.

The shadows hung, nuptial, august, divine;
White angels trooped like nuns at vesper-bell,
And in the blue one saw pale glimmers shine
That seemed to fall from wings invisible.

The breath of Boaz in his sleep is blent
With murmurs of the stream among the moss;
The shining hilltops are with lilies sprent,
And thousand flowers each bending branch
    emboss.

Ruth dreams, and Boaz sleeps. The grass gleams
    black;
The tinkling sheep-bell's echoes rise and sink;
The blue sky smiles above the cloudy wrack.
'Tis the hushed hour when lions come to drink.

In Ur and Jerimadeth all is still,
Bright stars enamel the abysmal sky,
And the new moon that lights each jutting hill

Shines in the west, while Ruth asks wonder-
   ingly,

Seeing that fine and splendent crescent hung
High on the far horizon's pearly bars,
What god, what heavenly harvester, has flung
His golden sickle in the field of stars.

The Infanta's Rose

A LITTLE child in her duenna's care
Walks in the royal park. She holds a rose,
Round which her tiny fingers tightly close.
She gazes dreamily into the air—
At what? She knows not. At the fount, may be,
That sings in the shadows—at some rustling
   tree,
Tall pine or birch—or may be at the swans,
As snowy as the snowdrifts on her brow,
Floating white-winged past many a whispering
   bough
Down the vast gardens and receding lawns.
Deep in the grove the palace, aureoled
In sunset splendor, shines like molten gold,
Girdled by lucid waters at whose brink
The dappled deer come tremblingly to drink,
And tall star-spangled peacocks wander wide
In shady thickets by the fountain-side.
     How sweet the pureness of that angel face,
Set in its tremulous bloom of clustered grace!
The grass waves greener where her foot has trod,
Rubies and diamonds glitter in the sod,
And sapphires trickle from the dolphin's jaws.
Beside the fountain still her footsteps pause,

She holds the red rose still, and still she dreams.
Her flower illumes the point-lace of her dress,
Whose floating folds of shimmering silk caress
An arabesque that through the gold-thread
    gleams.
The full-blown rose, the sweet child's sole con-
    cern,
Rising from its green bud as from an urn,
O'erflows the dainty compass of her hand.
Such royal pomp dwells in that splendid flower
And in its color such purpureal power
That when the Infanta lifts it to her lips
Her damask cheeks are hidden in eclipse,
And he who views her flower and her in turn,
Like one that dreaming walks in fairyland,
In sweet perplexity awhile will stand,
With wondering eyes that gazing scarce discern
Whether above the rose her face be scanned
Or if before her face the petals burn.
She is all joyousness and perfumed charm,
For all in her is lovely, all is fair,
Her azure eyes, brown curls, and dimpled arm.
How pure her glance, how musical her name,
Echoing the Virgin's like a murmured prayer
That stills all strife and banishes all harm.
        Radiant she lingers in the sunset flame,
And vaguely conscious of her princely blood,
Usurps the foreground of the brilliant scene,
Girt by the firmament that pours its flood
Of burnished gold, the shifting light and shade,
The softly flowing streams that sing unseen,
And nature's self, eternal and serene.
She gazes round her gravely, like a queen.
Is she not greeted upon bended knee,
Will she not soon be duchess of Brabant?

Hold Flanders or Sardinia in fee?
Such hopes make little princes arrogant
Beyond their tender years. Round their white
    brow
Strange shadows hover, and their wavering gait
Mimicks the royal stride. Contented now
With her red rose, soon she will crave a state.
       O happy, happy child! whose fingers close
Round the warm stem of her resplendent rose,
Content to live, to count the enchanted hours,
To gaze upon the skies, the trees, the flowers.
The day expires, the songbirds faintly twitter,
On every branch the slanting sunbeams glitter,
The marble nymphs amid the verdure blush,
Feeling the night descend; all noises hush,
All light is gone; the caverned deep receives
The sinking sun; the birds sleep in the leaves.
      Thus, flowerlike, the princess holds her
      flower.
Meanwhile, within the donjon's somber tower,
A death-pale figure at the window looms,
Ghostly, like one who gropes in churchyard
    glooms,
So full of fear, so vaguely menacing,
That if it be not Death—it is the King!
The dreaded King, whose nod makes Europe
    tremble.
If you could look in that fantasmal eye,
While it forgot its terrors to dissemble,
What spectral images would you espy
That from those tenebrous abysses mount?
Oh not the child, the lawn, the crystal fount
Picturing cloudless skies and golden light,
Nor groves, nor birds that sing their sweet good-
    night!

Not these he views; no such fair visions rise
To cheer his sight; but in his glassy eyes,
Those fatal orbs no human gaze can sound,
Those eyeballs like the ocean waste profound,
Moves, like a moving mist, a white-sailed fleet,
Whose wind-borne galleons through the water
     sweep,
Cutting in scornful flight the silver sheet
Of foam-flecked billows while the evening star
Mirrors its light on every wave-drenched spar,
And on the line where sky and ocean meet
Looms in the clouds, resplendent from afar,
A verdant isle that from its sea-washed steep
Hears those loud thunders roll across the
     deep.
     And still the King dreams of his battleships,
Still the Infanta by the fountain lingers,
Fondling her rose between her dainty fingers,
Or kissing its soft leaves with crimson lips,
When sudden, from the far horizon blowing,
A gusty wind, racing o'er flood and fell,
Shakes the tall trees and bends the lithe reeds
     growing
Mid banks of myrtle and white asphodel.
Of what avail her rank and princely power?
One moment, and the cruel wind has shorn
The hundred petals of her royal flower:
Her rose is gone, she only holds a thorn.
Amazed, above the marbles that enclose
The eddying pool o'er which the wreckage drifts,
She counts each angry wavelet that uplifts
On scornful swells the petals of her rose.
     The pool, so silver-bright, is darkened now,
Its quiet waters turned to boiling waves.

The rose-leaves dance like foam churned by the
    prow
This way and that, then sink in watery graves,
And vanish like ships whelmed below the tide.
"Madame," the grim duenna, hollow-eyed,
Cries to the child, who stares with knitted brow,
"Only the tempests are undisciplined,
And kings can govern all things, save the wind."

ALFRED DE MUSSET
1810–1838

Night of May

The Muse

ONE KISS, O poet, ere you lift your lute
To greet the new-born spring! The sultry breeze
Kisses the trembling buds of eglantine,
And happy birdlings 'mong the leafy trees
Sit shrilly piping on the first green vine,
Waiting the dawn that makes their music mute.

The Poet

What shadow dims this sylvan copse?
Whence comes that phantom form that
    soars
So lightly past the dark tree-tops
Where through the mead the fountain
    pours?
Its feet scarce sway the flowery grass,
And like a mist upon a glass
Its ghostly garments gleam and pass.

The Muse

O poet, take your lute, the darkness settles
Upon the greensward; in its odorous veil
Night swathes the zephyr; and the jealous rose,
Still virgin, feels its crimson life-blood fail,
While, buried deep within its perfumed petals,
All heedless though they round him close,
The little wandering, wanton bee
Dies in a careless ecstasy.
How still the night! How softly from above

The shadows fall! How sweet the thought of love,
Its trysts, its long farewells, its tender sighs,
Its roamings in this perfumed paradise
Where all things bloom, all things sweet vigil
    keep,
With murmurous plaints and blended harmonies,
On beds of odorous flowers where lovers sleep.

The Poet

What makes my heart so wildly beat?
What spirit lures my restless feet?
I fear, as ne'er I feared before,
This spectral rapping at my door.
Why does my lamp that burned so low
Dazzle me now with sudden glow?
Great God! I look up shudderingly.
Who comes? Who calls? No voice replies;
I am alone. The night-watch cries.
O solitude, O poverty!

The Muse

O poet, take your lute. Youth's ruddy wine
Fills mortals and immortals with desire.
The spring's warm winds have set my lips on fire,
And my pulse throbs with ecstasy divine.
Thou listless child, time has not stol'n my
    charms!
Have you forgot our rapturous first kiss
When, all in tears, you fell into my arms
And wan despair waxed paler at such bliss?
Did not my white wings brush your grief away?
Too young were you to die for love's sweet sake,
As now I fain would die of sweet heartache,
Unless you bid me live to a new day.

The Poet

Whence this voice I hear, unseeing?
Pensive Muse, 'tis thine, 'tis thine!
Blossom-crowned immortal being,
In whose eyes a love divine
Still for me doth chastely shine.
Still thou comest; still befriendest;
Still thy soul with mine thou blendest;
Thou alone art loyal still.
In the mist that wreathes me round,
In the darkness so profound,
From thy golden-gleaming dress
Shimmering splendors flash and thrill,
Lighting up my deep distress
With strange sense of blessedness!

The Muse

'Tis I, your heaven-born Muse. Take up your lute,
O poet. Let not the sad strings hang mute.
Like the wild bird that hears its wailing brood,
I come to share your mournful solitude.
Some hidden grief has fallen to your lot,
Some blighted love is moaning in your heart,
Some dream of bliss that will not be forgot,
Yet finds on earth no heavenly counterpart.
God gave the poet song: sing then your sorrows,
Your happy yesterdays, your blithe tomorrows.
Let dulcet music with its melting tone
That tells of faith, of fame, of lovers' folly,
Bear us on downy wing to worlds unknown
Where dwells no semblance of earth's melancholy,
To some far region where oblivious ease
Soothes the sad heart 'neath shady laurel-trees.
Green Scotia here, there brown Italia lies,

There Hellas, home of Venus and the Loves,
Argos and Ptelion, where white temples rise,
And holy Messa, haunt of brooding doves;
There looms the brow of cloud-girt Pelion,
There Titaresus by the silver sea
That mirrors, whiter than its whitest swan,
Camyra to white Oloossone.
What golden lay shall lull our griefs to sleep
Or dry our tears if haply we should weep?
When rosy dawn had ushered in the day,
What pensive seraph, leaning o'er your bed,
Shook out the dewy lilacs of mid-May
From his light robe upon your slumbering head,
And talked of love to drive your cares away?
Wouldst sing of death, of wedding-bells, sweet-
   chiming,
Of barren fields where valiant warriors bleed,
Of lovers on a silken ladder climbing,
Of the wild gallop of a foaming steed?
Or shall we tell of Tarquin's fatal hour,
Or of the million orbs high-hung above
Our circling globe by that celestial power
That feeds their flame of life and deathless love?
Wouldst join the shepherds by the dancing rills
Calling their flocks with plaintive melodies,
Or dive for pearls beneath the sounding seas,
Or track the huntsman on the barren hills?
Lo! the struck deer looks up with mournful eye
Towards its green heath and new-born fawns so
   nigh—
In vain—in vain. The butcher stoops and kills
And flings her warm heart to the yelping pack.
Or shall we paint a maid with damask cheek,
Wending to mass, a page behind her back,
Her mother at her side; with glance oblique

All tremulous she notes the clanking spur
Of the bold knight who stands in wait for her
Behind a pillar, while her holy prayer
Dies half unuttered on the heavy air?
Or shall we strew pale elegiac flowers
Upon the grass-grown tomb of Bonaparte,
Where God's avenging angel with his wings
Laid low that pride that mocked at earthly kings,
And crossed those iron hands upon his heart?
Or shall we sharpen satire's deadly sting?
O poet, take your lute! My restless wing
Is lifted heavenward on the air of spring.
Give me one tear! God calls. 'Tis time to sing.

The Poet

If you ask, my cherished Muse,
From fond lips a farewell kiss,
'Tis not I that could refuse,
Who would fain give more than this.
If you leave me now to mount
Heavenward to the holy fount
Of sweet song, shall you not miss,
Even as I, our old-time bliss?
Yet I cannot hymn love's blisses,
Ardent hopes and honeyed kisses,
Or its tears when lovers part.
When the soul is in eclipse,
Silence sits on pallid lips
And listens to the wailing heart.

The Muse

Fear not that, like the parching autumn wind,
I would dry up those burning tears you shed.
A parting kiss! nor deem the Muse unkind
That lures your feet toward Hellas' fountainhead.

I would not ban your heartache: let it live!
But spurn this apathy, this sterile weed,
That stifles lofty dream and noble deed
And the fine impulse fecund sorrows give.
Naught renders us so great as a great grief,
But let not grieving make your passion mute.
Lift up your heart, O poet! Snatch your lute
And find in timely song a sad relief.
For sweetest are the strains that tell of sorrow,
And only sad songs live beyond tomorrow.
When through the mists that veil the reed-rimmed
    shore
The pelican at dusk returns heartsore,
Cleaving lone tracts of sky on weary wing,
He grieves to see his callow young once more,
With gaping beaks that noisily implore,
Run o'er the salt sea-sands a-hungering.
Gaining with halting steps a rock's high crest,
He gathers close his brood; then his sad eyes
Stare long into the dull, unanswering skies.
Slowly the blood streams from his wounded
    breast;
In vain has he explored the ocean-caves
And barren shores and yet more barren waves:
No food, no food, save this fast-ebbing flood!
Silent and somber, prostrate on the stone,
Sublime officiant at this funeral feast,
He stills with tender love his dying moan
And offers shudderingly his bleeding breast.
Or haply, mad with pain and love and grief,
Longing for death, in his divine despair,
To make his savage agony more brief,
He cleaves with sudden flight the startled air
And utters to the night so wild a cry
That all the sea-birds quit the drifted sand,

And the belated traveler on the strand
Crosses himself and feels death hovering nigh.
Poet, 'tis thus impassioned poets do:
Not for the carefree children of the hour
Do they invoke the Muses' sacred power,
But, wearing crowns of cypress or of yew,
They sing strange songs that tell of hopes long
    dead,
Of blighted love and hearts untenanted
That languish in oblivious solitude.
And evermore their stream of golden words,
That flash athwart the air like wheeling swords,
Is darkened by a crimson drop of blood.

The Poet

O cruel Muse! too much you ask:
When storm-winds blow across the land,
Man writes no message in the sand;
I have no spirit for such task.
There was a magic hour when youth
Forever on my lips was heard,
As musical as any bird,
And sang as sweet, in very truth.
But time has made my heartstrings bleed
With dole so deep, that should I sing,
My lyre with such wild notes would ring
It would be shattered like a reed.

Night of August

The Muse

SINCE TO THE Southland Sol has borne his flame,
My ancient bliss is gone. In vain I wait
To hear my heedless lover call my name.
Blank silence reigns. His house stands desolate.
Gone is my loved one, gone the joys of yore.
Veiled and alone I seek his empty room
And lean my burning brow against his door,
Like a lone mother at an infant's tomb.

The Poet

Hail, Muse! my glory and my love!
Whene'er my footsteps homeward wend,
Thou still, o'er all the rest, dost prove
My surest hope, my dearest friend.
A little while on feeble wing
I followed fame's seductive lure;
I found the world an empty thing,
I find thee only kind and pure.
Give me one kiss and I will sing.

The Muse

Speak, restless heart, so barren of all hope,
So swift to flee, so languidly returning;
In what dark world of passion do you grope?
Whence come these grievous wounds so hotly burn-
    ing?
Where do your footsteps wander in the night,
In the pale wake of what ill-boding star?
Why barter for a semblance of delight
A love too pure for time and change to mar?

While at your dusty window-ledge, distraught,
I view these garden walls, these untrod alleys,
I, hapless Muse, am banished from your thought,
And in some spot unblessed your spirit dallies.
See this untended basil, once so cherished,
Whose creeping tendrils in those happy hours
Fed on your dropping tears—lo! it has perished!
Its withered petals, like this love of ours,
Droop and decay through your forgetfulness.
So in your heart perchance affection dies;
For may not love, too, perish like this flower,
Whose fragrance, wafted bird-like to the skies,
Fades as, in you, our sacred memories?

The Poet

When roaming at the twilight hour
'Tween hedgerows decked with trailing vine,
I spied a trembling, faded flower
Upon a spray of eglantine.
A green bud sprouted at its side
And danced upon the swaying bough.
What cared it if the wild rose died?
It was its turn to blossom now.
Indifferent thus to false or true,
Man ever turns to what is new.

The Muse

Life in all times and climes is but a game;
Vows made today are broken on the morrow;
Man lives, desires, and dreams without an aim,
And finds naught true except the truth of sorrow,
Alas! fond child, why do the silent strings
Hang tuneless now on your abandoned lute?
Is there no song that in your spirit sings?
Has sad experience made your music mute?

Do you not know that love takes cruel toll
And melts in idle tears the riches of your soul?

The Poet

Strolling at daybreak through the wood,
I heard a bird sing on its nest,
Though in the night its little brood
Had died beneath its quivering breast.
How loud it sang to greet the dawn!
O pensive Muse! let fall no tear;
God still remains when all is gone,
God dwells on high, and hope lives here.

The Muse

Who will await your coming when at last
You turn again toward this deserted spot,
To dwell among the ruins of your past
In this lone refuge you had half forgot?
Think you forgetting is an easy art,
That things proved false can e'er again seem true?
It is not you who sing; it is your heart:
If you foreswear it, will it answer you?
Will not love shatter it, and fatal passion—
And the cold world impart its cynic fashion?
Poor child! we had no fear of fortune's spite
When in the sylvan dells we roamed at eve,
Under green chestnut trees and poplars white,
Pensive yet gay, down paths that wind and weave.
I was young then, and the fair dryades
Parted the boughs to spy my roseate face;
And our too happy tears dried in the breeze
Or fell in crystal founts and left no trace.
How have you used the glory of your youth?
Where lie the fruits of my enchanted tree?
Time has devoured them all with greedy tooth.

Your blooming cheeks that pleased the deity
Who in her hands brings gifts of strength and grace
Are pale with ceaseless tears that bathe your face.
Ah! must I too leave you to your despair?
And how, thus lonely, will my loved one fare?

The Poet

Since the wild bird sings on the swaying
    bough
Beside the nest in which its eggs lie broken;
Since the frail flower that bloomed so fair but
    now
Gives place to lustier buds, and fades heart-
    broken,
Yet asks not, dying, what these things be-
    token;
Since, under the dark forest's high-hung ceil-
    ing,
The dead branch crackles 'neath the wander-
    er's tread;
Since, through the pathless wastes of nature
    stealing,
Man finds no precious anodyne for healing
The ancient griefs that he so vainly fled;
Since rock-ribbed hills their granite substance
    shed;
Since men but die to yield the living room;
Since battlefields where mighty hosts have
    bled
Behold, upshooting from the grass-grown
    tomb,
The sacred grain that gives the children bread—
O Muse! what matter life and death to me?
I love, and for a kiss I give my soul in fee!
I love, and pray that like the dropping rain

My tears shall flow and ever flow again.
Banish the pride that withers and devours;
O bitter heart, pour out thy richest store;
Love, and your heart shall bud like summer
    flowers!
What though love grieve in bitter after-hours?
Who once has loved must love forevermore.

Night of October

SHAME BE THINE, who taught me first
All the ugliness of treason,
Till the wrathful tempest burst,
Till I turned my back on reason.

Shame be thine, O lustrous-eyed!
Whose sweet glance I took for truth,
Cursèd charmer, vampire bride,
Blighting all my budding youth!

That loved voice, that lovely smile,
And those false eyes fathomless,
Taught my sick soul to revile
Every dream of happiness.

Sullied beauty that endears,
Cruel heart that shattered mine,
If I mock at woman's tears
'Tis because I witnessed thine.

Shame be thine, for I was yet
Simple-hearted as a child,
As a blossom dewy-wet
When the new-born day has smiled.

My fond heart had no defence,
Thou couldst play on it at will;

Yet to spare its innocence,
That had been more easy still.

Shame be thine, O thrice-accursed
Fountainhead of griefs and fears,
Thou, the dearest and the first
Source of ever-flowing tears!

Days will come and days will go,
Still that sorrow will endure;
Thou hast wrought a bitter woe,
Such as time can never cure.

Yet I hope this fount of tears
May at last wash clean from me
Memory of the poisoned years
That united me to thee.

Souvenir

I come to weep the woes fond hearts endure,
Returning to this ever sacred spot,
This grave, the dearest and the most obscure,
    Where love sleeps unforgot.

Why seek to wean me from this solitude?
Why bid me tarry when such willing feet,
Such rooted custom and long-cherished mood,
    Lead to this green retreat?

Here smiles the hillside, here the flowery heath;
Here ran her footsteps in the silver sand,
And here the petals of her rosy wreath
    Fell from her snow-white hand.

Here tower the dark and melancholy pines;
Here lies the gorge that led down winding ways

To the cool fount that in the wildwood shines,
    Haunt of my happy days!

From this white hawthorn, like a mating bird,
I flung wild music to each vale and hill—
Sweet spot, where last my loved one's voice was
   heard,
    Sweet spot that lures me still!

Then let them flow, these ever welcome tears
That from the founts of sorrow fall so fast,
These sad reminders of once happy years,
    That were too sweet to last.

Calm nature cannot share the soul's alarms;
Why then to her deaf ear my woes impart?
Proud is this forest in its tranquil charm,
    But proud, too, is my heart.

Let his sick soul in sorrow find relief
Who mourns a love that moulders in the tomb;
Here all is beauty; the dark flower of grief
    Springs not from nature's womb.

See, the moon rises from yon somber copse!
How thy torch trembles, radiant queen of night,
Till, soaring high above the black tree-tops,
    Thou turn'st the gloom to light!

As from the rain-drenched earth the new buds start
And fill the ambient air with rich perfume,
So calm, so pure, in my grief-laden heart
    Love rises from its tomb.

Where art thou fled, my grief so shadowy pale?
What anodyne has soothed my old-time pain?
What gentle air, breathed in this lovely vale,
    Makes me a child again?

O witchery of time! O wingèd years!
You blot away the record of our woes,
Yet spare the flowers we sprinkled with our tears,
    Nor ravage youth's last rose.

I had not dreamed of this blest solace found
When swooning love lay vanquished by despair,
Nor had I dreamed time's touch could cure this
   wound
    And make it sweet to bear.

Hence idle words, delusive thoughts, away,
Ye customary cheats of vulgar sorrow,
Suborned to comfort love that weeps today
    And blooms anew tomorrow!

Why, Dante, say there is no greater woe
Than happy days recalled in days of grief?
From what strange sorrow did such mockery grow,
    What joy too bitter-brief?

Though dark the day, shall we deny the light?
And was thy soul, torn from thy Beatrice,
Who trod God's mansions, vested all in white,
    So scornful of our bliss?

Nay, by those stars that gild night's coronal,
Thy bitter tongue was traitor to thy thought,
For of those vanished joys that we recall
    Our truest bliss is wrought.

Why mock us if we seek a random spark
In the spent embers where our dead joys sleep,
Or bear a glimmering torch into the dark,
    Lit at this ashen heap?

What though our hearts cling to this vanished past,
This radiant mirror where we glass our dreams!

Why scorn this joy because it cannot last
     And is not what it seems?

To thy Francesca, angel glorified,
How couldst thou lend a speech so harsh as this,
To her whose lips, red with love's crimson tide,
     Were warm still from a kiss?

Alas! of what avail our anxious thought?
Why seek a barren truth past finding out,
Since joy and grief alike melt into naught
     And all things end in doubt?

O wayward mortals on delusion fed,
Who laugh, and sing, and walk your carefree ways,
Your minds by no high vision tenanted,
     No hope of deathless praise!

If by mischance your wandering steps are led
Toward some low monument of love forgot,
You pass the spot where once your heart has bled,
     As if you knew it not.

Aye, life's a dream in which we vainly clasp
Fantasmal joys banned by returning day,
Pale fading flowers that drop from our loose grasp,
     Borne on the winds away.

Vain the first kisses, vain the first fond vows
With which earth's primal couple sealed their trust,
Under some barren tree's wild-tossing boughs,
     On rocks dissolved in dust.

They took for witness of their solemn oath
The cloudy skies that every moment change,
And nameless stars shone on their plighted troth
     That through blank heavens range.

All round them spoke of death: the leaf-hid bird,
The transitory flower, the trampled worm,
The fountain in whose depth sank sepulchred
     Their own fast-fading form.

Beings of clay, they longed by love's decrees
On beds of flowers to draw their blissful breath
In timeless faery-lands of sweet heartsease
     That nothing know of death.

If this be madness, 'tis a happy folly.
What timid love holds lodgement in your breast
If nature's changes feed your melancholy,
     If wild winds break your rest?

I have seen fairer things in ruin laid
Than autumn's beauty drenched by icy rain,
Than drooping roses that too long outstayed
     The lingering woodbird's strain.

I have seen sights more tragic than blue-veined
Immobile Juliet in her marble tomb,
More awful than the chalice Romeo drained
     To seal love's double doom.

She that stood centered in my deathless love
Is turned into a whited sepulchre,
A living tomb where never life doth move
     Nor ghostly memory stir.

That mournful love is slain, sweet Eros' child,
That once lay cradled on my pulsing breast;
No more in dreamland shall it wander wild—
     Here is it laid to rest.

How fair my loved one seemed, more heavenly fair
Than in old days—with softer smile, meseems,
And gentler voice, and that same gracious air
     That haunts me in my dreams.

But ah! that voice, those eyes, that tender grace,
Lived not for me; they all were alien grown:
With heart still full of her, I saw her face
    Shine blankly on my own.

And yet I fain had clasped that faithless one
And kissed her pulseless heart and held her fast
And cried: O cruel love, what hast thou done,
    What done with our dead past?

She seemed a statue carved in lifeless clay,
A ghostly thing dowered with that voice, those
    eyes;
I let this icy phantom glide away,
    Pale 'neath the pallid skies.

O smiling farewell, climax of all woe!
O love that toward my own turned spectral chill!
O nature, in mortality's last throe
    Shall I not feel it still?

Now let heaven's thunder break upon my head!
I turn to this dead memory evermore
As the wrecked mariner, storm-buffeted,
    Looks toward the shining shore.

What matter if the springtide fade or bloom,
If time's fell touch dissolve this mortal clay,
Or if the sundered heavens proclaim the doom
    Of all that lives today!

I only cry: Here was my being's goal!
I loved, and I was loved, and she was fair!
I shrine this hallowed image in my soul
    And keep it deathless there!

To La Malibran

SINGER DIVINE! when bard and painter die
They leave undying heritors behind;
Death shoots his shaft—it hurtles idly by—
It cannot conquer the immortal mind.
Time cannot spoil the work by genius wrought;
The body dies, but not the deathless thought.

The sculptor hews his dream in lasting stone;
The poet sings it in his golden strain,
And quiring angels make his words their own.
Upon his canvas Raphael lives again,
Hallowed by what all hearts hold loveliest,
A child asleep upon its mother's breast.

Unscathed the Phidian Pallas lives and glows
Like a bright lamp in the high Parthenon,
And Aphrodite, whiter than the snows
That feed the streams of fountained Helicon,
Undimmed by age, by chance and change un-
    harmed,
Smiles on the centuries her spells have charmed.

Time touches beauty with renewing power,
Giving dead glories an eternal span.
The voice of genius is not of the hour,
It is the voice of universal man.
Yet thou, so lately dead—O heavy loss—
Hast no memorial but a little cross.

A cross, and night, and chill forgetfulness!
I hear thy voice—was it the moaning sea,
Or some lone sailor chanting his distress,
That thrilled the night with sudden melody?

O plaintive song, sweet as Apollo's lyre!
Stilled is that voice and quenched that heavenly
    fire!

Ah, why, Ninette, dear muse, must death eclipse
Those tones, all love, all charm, all tragic power,
That flitted nightly on your siren lips
Like the light perfume of the hawthorn flower?
Tell me in what far world that music rings,
So vibrant yesterday on your heart-strings.

Was it not yesterday, madcap Corilla,
You flitted toward the footlights in wild dance,
Or, pert Rosina, fluttering your mantilla,
Sang amorous roulades with provoking glance,
Or in your Willow-song breathed love's farewell,
Pale Desdemona, while your warm tears fell?

Was it not yesterday, *madonna bella*,
You charmed all Europe with your melodies,
And danced 'neath Naples' sky the tarantella,
Or sported, naiad-like, in foaming seas,
Angelical yet brave, O woodbird wild!
Now high-souled artist and now laughing child?

What secret hurt made your proud spirit bleed?
Was it your tropic heart's too fiery bloom
That bent your beauteous body like a reed,
Its bright flame quenched, its light hid in the
    tomb?
It was a god, the cruel Muse it was,
That bowed your head to death's relentless laws.

Did you not know such passion left you weak,
That those wild cries, that fever in the blood,
Deepened the pallor on your fading cheek
And nipped the rose of beauty in the bud,

Blasting the root and drying up the leaf?
'Tis tempting God to fall in love with grief.

Did you not know the trancing charm of youth
Fed that rich stream of too impassioned tears
That gave your moving voice such mournful truth?
Still witnessing our ever anxious fears,
Did you not know, frail singing bird, that now
Death sat beside you on the swaying bough?

Death in Life

SHE WAS divinely fair, if Night,
In her dim Medicean shrine
Sleeping in marble semblance white,
Is beautiful and is divine.

And she was good, if goodness be
To lavish gold with liberal hand;
If alms unblest by charity
Be not a building set in sand.

Sweet were her thoughts, if the vain sound
Of speeches sweetly syllabled
To hold an idle ear spellbound,
A proof of kindly thought be held.

She prayed, if that a lustrous eye
That now is lowered to the earth,
Now lifted upward to the sky,
Can to a Christian prayer give birth.

She might have smiled, if the red bud,
Still sheathed in its green coverlets,
Could feel the springtime warm its blood
And know the rapture life begets.

She might have loved, if barren pride,
That girt her in an aureole
Like lamps placed by the coffin's side,
Had not burned in her sterile soul.

No love, no hate, her being shook;
She has not lived who now lies dead;
Her listless hands have dropped the book
Where not a page was ever read.

Pépita

PÉPA, when it's time for bed,
When your mother cries goodnight,
When, bare-kneed, with heavy head,
You say your prayers by candlelight,

At the hour when spirits roam
And in darkness stalk benighted,
When you undo braid and comb,
And peep beneath your bed affrighted,

When with eyelids slumber-laden
You begin to nod and blink,
O Pépita, charming maiden,
Tell me, tell me, what you think!

Do you dream of heroines,
Victims of some sad romance?
Do guitars and mandolins
Lead your soul in airy dance?

Do you dream of mighty mountains,
Fairy castles, ruby crowns,
Spanish knights by Moorish fountains,
Lollipops, or wedding gowns?

Do you dream of lovers' speeches
Tender as your childish thought,
Or of Breton bathing beaches,
Perhaps of me—perhaps of naught?

Song of Venice

At Saint Blaise, at La Zuecca,
Ah, how happy were our days,
    At Saint Blaise,
At Saint Blaise, at La Zuecca,
Floating in our gondola.

Do you still remember them
With a throb of pain?
Do you still remember them?
Will you come again

To Saint Blaise, to La Zuecca,
Where the sea shines like a gem,
To Saint Blaise, to La Zuecca,
Floating in our gondola?

Fortunio's Song

So sweet my love, her face so fair,
    So pure her fame,
Not for a kingdom would I dare
    To tell her name.

We'll sing our loves, each lover his,
    And I'll sing mine,
How blithe she is, how blond she is,
    How blue her eyne.

Whate'er she asks me, I will give
   Without a sigh;
It is for her alone I live,
   For her I'd die.

Though love that worships unconfessed
   Is grievous woe,
Yet will I hide mine in my breast
   And fain die so.

Too fond am I my love to tell
   Lest I should shame
Her whom I love and love too well
   To breathe her name.

Barberine's Song

BOLD KNIGHT a-faring to the war,
   Why ride so far,
     So far from here?
Full fast the evening shadows fall
   And cover all
     In darkness drear.

Did you then love but to forget?
   Does no regret
     Dwell in your heart?
Oh, why should love of martial fame
   And vain acclaim
     Make lovers part?

Bold knight a-faring to the war,
   Why ride so far,
     So far from here?
And why so grievously beguile
   Poor me, whose smile
     Once seemed so dear?

When Lovers Have Parted

WHEN LOVERS have parted,
Nigh broken-hearted,
With murmured farewells,
What charms melancholy?
Sweet music solely
And beauty's spells.

There dwells more grace
In a lovely face
Than in armored might;
And we banish pain
With a tender strain
That was once our delight.

To His Reader

THIS BOOK records my wayward youth—
    I took no pains to fetter it.
A foolish book! In very truth
    I had been wise to better it.
Yet all things change without redress;
        Then why amend my past? Ah, no!
        Go, little bird of passage, go!
Go, if God will, to thy address.

And you who read, whoe'er you be,
O do not think too ill of me,
        Read what you will, read what you can;
My earliest rhymes reveal the child,
The next betray the stripling wild,
        The last scarce savor of the man.

Sadness

My LITTLE LIFE I've lived in vain,
Friendship has fled and gaiety,
And pride can never bloom again
That once the Muses woke in me.

When Truth unveiled her shining face,
I thought to find in her a friend;
But day by day she lost her grace,
I grew to hate her in the end.

Yet Truth is an immortal thing,
And none without her tutoring
In the world's way can be adept.

Truth is God's voice; I must respond,
Even though I find no joy beyond
This one—that I have sometimes wept.

GEORGE SAND
1804–1876

Love's Choice

THERE WERE three shepherds loved a lass,
 In tender passion vying;
They let their lambkins nip the grass
 And roamed the meads a-sighing,
 And roamed the meads, tra-la!

The youngest in a dewy dell
 Had plucked a spray of roses.
 He sang: "The love I dare not tell,
 My blooming wreath discloses,
 My blooming wreath, tra-la!"

The second sang: "For thee I twine
 This chain of purple heather,
And by this rite I make thee mine,
 And bind our hearts together,
 And bind our hearts, tra-la!"

The third bore lilies white and fine;
 He kissed them tenderly,
And sang: "Sweet maid, if thou wert mine,
 I'd do the like to thee,
 I'd do the like, tra-la!"

The maiden sang: "I'm not for you,
 O bringer of red roses;
The dainty flower that's fed on dew
 Soon fades and soon upcloses,
 Soon fades, soon fades, tra-la!

"Nor you who sport the heather-flower
    Shall never be my master;
Love does not bow to tyrant power,
    It only flees the faster,
    It only flees, tra-la!

"But unto you, my shepherd true,
    That kissed your flowers so sweetly,
This heart you sue I give to you,
    I give to you full featly,
    I give to you, tra-la!"

FÉLIX ARVERS
1806–1850

The Poet's Secret

A SECRET LOVE lies hidden in my heart,
A thought eternal in a moment born,
A silent grief I never dared impart,
And she I worship knows not why I mourn.
I shall have passed unnoticed at her side,
Though she dwells ever in my constant thought;
My lonely heart shall to the end abide,
Not daring ask and not receiving aught.
Though God has clothed her soul in gentleness,
She goes her way, divining not nor seeing
The passion that from her derives its being
And murmurs round her footsteps comfortless.
"Who is this woman?" she will ask in reading
These lines, all hers, and turn the page unheeding.

GÉRARD DE NERVAL
1808–1855

Fantasy

THERE IS AN AIR that makes my soul more glad
Than Mozart's or Rossini's sweetest tone,
An old-time ditty, languorous and sad,
And full of hidden charm for me alone.
For whensoe'er I hear that plaintive strain
My soul grows younger full two hundred years.
I live in Louis Thirteenth's reign. Again
A green hillside in golden haze appears;
A red brick castle takes the sunset glow
On crimson panes that burn in frowning towers,
And through vast lawns cool silver streamlets flow,
Washing its walls athwart a rim of flowers.
Framed in the oriel stands a lady fair,
Blond, with black eyes, and with a snow-white
    brow,
Whom I mayhap in bygone days saw there
And dimly do remember even now.

Happy Birdland

How GAY the coming of the spring
In this green solitude!
How softly swell, how blithely ring,
The bird's songs in the wood!

In summer, constant to its mate,
It rears its fledgling brood.

How joyous, how inviolate,
The bird's nest in the wood!

Then autumn comes, and chilly showers
The bough and nest denude;
And yet how blest compared with ours
The bird's death in the wood!

Myrto

WHENCE COME YOU, Myrto, from what land of
    dreams,
To greet the dawn on high Posilipo?
On your white brow what Orient splendors glow?
Your golden hair through clustered vine leaves
    gleams.
Drawn by your smile toward fountained Helicon,
From your fresh cup a draught divine I drank
And prostrate at Iacchus' feet I sank,
For Hellas' Muse had claimed me for her son.
Why do these flames from cleft Vesuvius rise?
You grazed its top with flying foot yestreen,
And straight the ashes darkened all the skies!
Parthenope bows to the Nazarene,
And Virgil's laurel evermore allies
The pale hortensia to the myrtle's green.

Delphica

KNOW YOU NOT, Daphne, that enchanting strain
Sung in old days 'neath shining laurel trees
And myrtle bloom, that song of sweet heartsease
Which evermore young love begins again?
Know you the pillared temple's solitude,

Its golden lemon-trees that lure the eye,
The fatal grotto with death hovering nigh,
Where sleep the vanquished dragon and his brood?
They will come back, those gods for whom you
    weep;
Revolving time will speed their blest return,
And earth will tremble at the prophet's breath:
Meanwhile the Latian Sibyl lies asleep,
The arch of Constantine o'erhangs her urn,
And still the antique world lies bound in death.

El Desdichado

I AM THE widowed spirit, pale and mute,
The Prince of Aquitaine; low lies my tower,
My star is dead and stilled my stellar lute;
Here Melancholy paints her somber flower.
Thou who didst soothe my sorrow by the tomb,
Bring back Posilipo and the blue brine,
Restore the promontory and its bloom
Where trellised vines and roses intertwine!
Phoebus am I? or love-god libertine?
My brow still burns with kisses of the queen,
And I have dreamed in caves where sirens swim.
Twice have I crossed the somber Acheron,
Playing on Orpheus' lyre a heavenly hymn
While saint and fairy sang in unison.

THÉOPHILE GAUTIER
1811–1872

Art

THE FAIREST things are wrought
With most expense of time
      And thought,
Gem, painting, marble, rhyme.

No false rules countenance,
But like a stately god
      Advance
In tight cothurnus shod.

Fie on cheap artistries,
Like to a shoe outworn,
      Whose ease
A shapely foot will scorn.

Shun, sculptor, the soft clay
Shaped while the spirit floats
      Away
On tide of alien thoughts.

Carve with unflagging care
Carrara, Parian pure
      And rare,
That hold the sharp contour.

Borrow from Syracuse
Its bronze and in it trace
      The Muse
In her immortal grace.

With wonder-working hand
In agate stone imbed
    The grand
Apollo's golden head.

Shun watery tints that faint
And swiftly fade again,
    And paint
On the hard porcelain

Blue sirens lily-pale,
Twisting circumfluent
    Their tail,
Heraldic blazonment.

In nimbus triple-lobed
Show Virgin and Christ-child
    Englobed
In radiance undefiled.

Time turns all else to dust,
Art only keeps its crown;
    The bust
Outlives the ruined town.

The graven medal found
Where the plowshares displace
    The ground
Reveals a Caesar's face.

Jove and Jehovah fade;
The sovran verse alone
    Is made
To outlast brass and stone.

Carve, polish, mold your dream,
And the bright forms unlock
    That gleam
In the resistant block.

Noel

DARK IS THE night, all white the earth;
Chime low, ye bells, chime soft and mild;
Madonna, glad at Jesu's birth,
Leans her sweet face above the child.

No curtains rich festoon his bed
And fold around him like a gown,
Only the cobwebs overhead
From the bare rafters hanging down.

Cold straw heaves on each rounded rib
And quivers on each dainty limb;
To warm the infant in his crib,
The ass, the ox, they breathe on him.

But in the snowy heavens the fire
Of one bright star illumes the morn,
And, all in white, an angel choir
Sings to the shepherds: Christ is born!

Caerulei Oculi

WHENCE CAME this mermaid that I see
Steal down the white sea-sand,
All loveliness, all mystery,
From what dim magic land?

She bears the blue sky in her eyes,
Yet in their liquid deep
What tender pearl-gray tints arise
Such as in sea-caves sleep!

Veiled in their languorous sheen one marks
A melancholy grace,

And tears that flash like lambent sparks
Gleam on her starlit face.

Their lashes rise like wingèd gulls
That haunt the halcyon seas
Or sink upon the tide that lulls
Pale sea-anemones.

I see in those unfathomed eyes,
As from its ocean-cave,
The cup of Thule's monarch rise
Out of the azure wave.

Through lucent tides that softly swirl
I spy mid seaweeds dun,
Near Cleopatra's rosy pearl,
The ring of Solomon.

I find in that profound abyss
The fabled crown of gold,
The guerdon of a lady's kiss,
Still splendent as of old.

Her lingering glance allures my soul
Those soundless seas to brave
From out whose emerald caverns stole
This daughter of the wave.

Her bosom on the rose-strewn tide
Heaves with the billows' swell,
And singing sirens white-limbed glide
While Nereus tunes his shell:

"Come on my pearly couch to lie
In green translucent bowers,
Where waveless seas move softly by
Through beds of floating flowers.

"Like anchored ships with sails upfurled,
Screened from the storms above,

Here in our silent watery world
We'll dream of only love."

Tell Me, Dainty Maiden

"TELL ME, dainty maiden,
Whither shall we go
In our bark light-laden
While the zephyrs blow?

"The ivory oars are tipped with gold,
Their shining silk the flags unfold,
Our shallop is a pretty toy:
An orange serves for ballasting,
Our sail is a white angel's wing,
A seraph plays the cabin-boy.

"Tell me, dainty maiden,
Whither shall we go
In our bark light-laden
While the zephyrs blow?

"Shall we cleave the Baltic wave
Toward shores that Polar oceans lave,
And pluck the mystic fairy flowers
In some rock-girt and unexplored
Snow-tapestried Norwegian fjord,
Or sail where high-cliffed Java lowers?

"Tell me, dainty maiden,
Whither shall we go
In our bark light-laden
While the zephyrs blow?"

"Bear me," she cries, "to some far isle
Where changeless skies forever smile

And lovers always love!"
"Alas, my sweet, in all earth's round
This perfect bliss was never found
In lands where lovers rove."

Night Walk

LIKE PEARLS the rounded dewdrops shine,
Upon the pointed grass blades hung,
And near the wind-tossed eglantine
The finch and blackbird vie in song.

The daisies in their new frocks dight
Border the pathway's verdant edge,
The jasmine bloom entwines its white
With honeysuckle in the hedge.

The moon, an agate vessel, sails
Past shorelines bathed in lunar blue,
And far away it wanes and pales
Where unplumbed seas heave into view.

Night never decked her floating robe
With brighter galaxies of stars
Nor let our far-flung vision probe
So deep beyond her cloudy bars.

Love, take my hand, and through the wood
We'll roam where silver fountains gleam,
Or in the flowery solitude
On mossy banks lie down and dream,

And watch the ever-babbling brook,
Whose rhythmic music never hushes,
Steal past us in our shady nook,
Soft whispering to the nodding rushes.

O Plaintive Turtle-Dove

O PLAINTIVE turtle-dove,
Cease, cease to sing,
And lend thy downy wing
To serve my love.

Sad bird, dost thou too weep
A mate torn from thy breast,
Who far away doth sleep
By her lone nest?

Fly to my love, oh, fly!
Light not on tree or tower:
See how for her I sigh
Each weary hour!

Sink not with drooping head
Where clustered palm-trees grow,
Nor where shy ring-doves shed
Their down like snow.

Her window clamorously
Beat with thy wing,
And, kissing amorously,
Thy message bring.

Bear my heart on thy breast,
Like a red rose,
And make her own a nest
For thy repose.

The Last Leaf

TODAY IN THIS bare garden-plot
No flower blooms, no song is heard,

But on the branch, by time forgot,
Is one dead leaf, is one reft bird.

My song is mute, my joys depart,
Slow pales my lingering dream of love,
And down the lone aisles of my heart
The autumn winds forlornly move.

The brown leaf falls, the bird takes wing,
And love lies dead! O plaintive wren!
Return by my low grave to sing
When wakening woods turn green again.

Satiety

SATIETY DWELLS in those slumbrous eyes,
Submerging all desires, all hopes, all love,
Sunk in their lucid depths, as the pale skies
In the refractive ocean dimly move.
You share with the tired gods their lassitude,
And in your soul a chill despair is glassed;
Fulfilment dogs desire sans interlude,
And things to be wear semblance of things past.
Your eyes are weaned from thoughts of mortal
    things,
In their calm deep no human hope is seen,
And love, disheartened, folds his drooping wings,
The while, disdainful, with Olympian mien,
Like some marmoreal deity you seem
Forever sunk in your unfathomed dream.

The Pot of Flowers

PLUCKING a flowret of exotic strain,
A child, enchanted by its lively hue,

Planted it in a pot of porcelain
Decked with strange flowers and dragons red and
  blue.

The child runs off—the green plant grows amain,
Shoots high and higher its aspiring bloom,
And shatters the confining porcelain,
Scorning to blossom in so little room.

The child comes back—he sees with wondering
  eyes
The towering plant sprung from a tiny seed;
He plucks at it in vain with angry cries,
And on its prickly darts his fingers bleed.

So love one day in my young heart awaking,
Love that I took but for a springtime flower,
Has proved a giant aloe that is breaking
The bright-hued vessel with its fatal power.

The Doves

ON THE GREEN slope above the scattered tombs
The gentle doves at evening flock together,
Hiding in stately palms whose waving plumes
Shelter their nests from rain and windy weather.

But at daybreak, from their aerial home,
Like pearls dropped from a broken string, all white,
Through the translucent blue of heaven's dome,
Down to some mossy roof they bend their flight.

My soul is such a tree, where every night
White galaxies of visionary dreams
From the blue sky with fluttering wings alight
Only to scatter at the sun's first beams.

Chinese Interlude

IT IS NOT YOU I love, Madame, not you,
Nor you, sweet Juliet, so heavenly fair,
Ophelia, no, nor Beatrice I woo,
Nor you, blond Laura with the golden hair.

She now I love lives far across the main,
Where yellow Yangtze rolls through fields of rice,
In a tall tower of finest porcelain—
Black cormorants perch in this paradise.

Her little foot would hardly fill your hand,
Her cheek shines clearer than a copper lamp,
Her slanting eyes by slanting brows are spanned,
And her long nails with crimson paint are damp.

Through trellised roses I behold her head
Where sportive swallows spray the leaves in show-
    ers,
And like young poets, when the day is dead,
Sing of lithe willows and of peach-tree flowers.

Pastel

I LOVE TO SEE you in your oval frames,
Time-yellowed portraits of fair ladies dead,
Clasping pale roses that once lit their flames
On budding breasts whose beauty time has shed.

The April breeze that once so softly fanned
The lilies and carnations of your cheek
Has yielded place to wintry winds, whose band
Among your faded charms plays hide-and-seek.

'Tis gone, that golden age of ladies fair:
Sweet Parabère and Pompadour are dead;
No amorous pilgrims to their shrine repair,
And love sleeps with them in their grassy bed.

Yet in these faded portraits still they gaze
Forever on their pale and scentless flowers,
And, sadly smiling, dream of bygone days
And beaux that wooed them in their rosy bowers.

The First Smile of Spring

WHILE FOOLISH man lays waste his powers
With toil that ends in sorrowing,
March smilingly defies the showers
And slyly ushers in the Spring.

Enamored of the daisies' grace,
While slumber lies on young and old,
He weaves them broideries of lace
And carves them buttons all of gold.

'Twixt apple-bough and hawthorn-bush
He steals along in impish glee,
To powder with his swan's-down brush
The snowy-fronded almond-tree.

While Nature in her bed reposes,
He through her garden glides unseen,
To lace the buds of blushing roses
In velvet corsets all of green.

Then softly singing in the shadows,
While listening blackbirds note his spells,
He scatters snowdrops in the meadows
And violets in mossy dells.

Where sleeps the pool mid tangled cresses,
Where drinks the stag with ears pricked up,
He stoops to clothe in nun-like dresses
The white bells of the lily-cup.

From out of grasses emerald green
He bids the crimson berries peep
Or garlands round with leafy screen
The shepherd where he lies asleep.

At last, when wild winds are disbanding
And pinks and marigolds appear,
On April's flowery threshold standing,
He cries: "Come, Spring, and crown the year!"

The Swallows

THE GARDEN BEDS are bleak and shorn,
The paths with yellow leaves are strown,
Cool breezes blow at eve and morn,
Alas! the summer days are flown.

Lorn Autumn, walking her sad round,
Counts her last flowers into her lap,
Kissing the dahlia petal-crowned
And marigold with yellow cap.

The raindrops in the fountain bubble;
The swallows tardy council hold:
"Winter is nigh and winter's trouble—
Where shall we fly to 'scape the cold?"

A thousand strong they veer and flit
And answer to each other's call.
One says: "Next month I hope to sit
Upon a high Athenian wall.

"My nest fits like a carven bowl
'Mong Parthenonian metopes;
A cannon ball once made the hole
In which I yearly lie at ease."

The next replies: "My pathway leads
To Smyrna, to a great café;
There Hadjis count their amber beads
In doorways where the sunbeams play.

"I flutter in and out amid
The smoke that all around me spreads,
And in the vaporous cloud half-hid
I graze in flight their turbaned heads."

The third one cries: "In far Baalbec,
Above a temple's white façade,
I hang in air, like a dark speck,
And sing all day my gay roulade."

The fourth bird speaks: "I always steer
To Rhodes, where dwell the Templar Knights;
'Tis there I'll pitch my tent this year,
High as the pillared eremites."

An older bird: "I plan to halt a-
While, if so far I still can go,
At the white terraces of Malta—
Blue skies above, blue seas below."

Then says the sixth: "I'll wing my way
To Cairo's tallest minaret;
There, in a nest of moistened clay,
I'll lie secure from winter's threat."

"Beyond the Second Cataract,"
Another cries, "in desert dust

I'll build my home—to be exact,
In some old Pharaoh's granite bust."

Then sing all seven: "O swift-winged breeze,
Blow us across the watery floor
To sunny lands and azure seas
Where palm-trees line the tropic shore."

With twitterings loud and beating wings,
From their high cornice looking down,
The chorus of dark swallows sings
When autumn woods turn rusty brown.

I hear their songs, I comprehend,
For what's a poet but a bird?
But in my cage I sit close-penned
And cannot act on what I've heard.

O for the swallow's daring flight!
O for the swallow's tireless wing,
To cleave the heavens in one short night
Toward regions of eternal spring!

The Obelisk of the Place de la Concorde

WHAT BOREDOM, in this Paris square,
To watch, a mateless obelisk,
While rain and snow and icy air
Paint my red granite toneless bisque!

My stele, glowing red, somehow
Shedding each day its sunburnt hue,
Contracts nostalgic pallors now
Where skies are never truly blue.

Where Egypt's gods, sublimely grand,
Adorn the pylons of Luxor,
With my twin pillar I would stand,
Guarding the temple's corridor.

There where the cloudless blue expands,
My soaring pyramidion
Should cast its shadow on the sands,
Numbering the footsteps of the sun.

Lo, Ramses! thy columnar mass
Which time eterne could not destroy,
Is plucked up like a blade of grass
And shipped to Paris for a toy.

Lone sentinel, whose towering peak
Made the astonished gazer tremble,
I stand 'tween temple pseudo-Greek
And hall where deputies assemble.

Here where a king did lately bleed,
I rise, unmeaning monolith,
Recording what no man can read,
Five thousand years of deed and myth.

The shameless sparrows stain my crown,
On which, before the world grew old,
Pink ibises and hawks flew down
With plumage white and claws of gold.

The Seine, all thick with slime and mud
Churned from the sewer's labyrinth,
Befouls my base, which Nilus' flood
Laved swelling high above my plinth.

With lotus crowned and sprays of fern,
The god, round these white peristyles,

Poured from his overflowing urn
Not gudgeons but huge crocodiles.

Slow-marching priests with fillets crowned
Of old, before my antique shaft,
Carried the mystic bari round,
With holy symbols pictographed.

Now, far from stoled ecclesiast,
Between two spurting fountains placed,
I watch gay courtesans roll past
In their barouches, brazen-faced.

From fall to spring, from spring to fall,
I view these dull automata,
Pale Solons strutting to their hall,
Young lovers hieing to the *Bois*.

Here in a hundred years each corpse
Must needs decay, sans bands or veils,
Unshielded from damp air that warps
Their coffins pegged with iron nails.

Here is no rock-built hypogeum
Where side by side the dead may sleep
So never mortal eye may see 'em,
And where, embalmed, they're sure to keep.

In Luxor mid scrawls hieroglyphic
And men in garb pontifical
Weird sphinxes whetted claws horrific
On coping of my pedestal,

While underfoot the silent crypt
Gave harborage to bat and hawk—
Ah! why was I from Egypt shipped
To this mad land of dance and talk!

The Obelisk of Luxor

How DULL, a mateless sentinel,
Set in this mass of masonry,
Day after day alone to dwell
In converse with eternity!

Sterile and mute and infinite,
Where through the void the sky expands,
By incandescent suns uplit,
The desert rolls its yellow sands.

The earth lies barren to the sky,
Stretching with achromatic hue
Where never cloud comes floating by
Across the inexorable blue.

The Nile's broad waters stagnant lie
Thick-coated with a leaden sheet,
Where oily hippopotomi
Roll restless in the tropic heat.

The crocodiles with tearful face
Behold all nature blaze and burn,
And parboiled in their carapace,
Swooning and sobbing, toss and turn.

The ibis on his thin legs perches
And droops his head upon his wings
Or vaguely on my pillar searches
The records of primeval kings.

Hyenas laugh and jackals mew,
While caracoling through the air
Esurient hawks sail into view,
Black commas in the solar glare.

In the reverberant solitude
The weary sphinxes blink and yawn,
Transfixed in the same attitude
Since Egypt's immemorial dawn,

Calcined by ever-burning sands
And suns the West has never seen—
O horror of these lotus-lands!
O luminous Oriental spleen!

This same ennui funereal
Made kings of old forswear their crown
And prostrate on the terrace fall.
O how it weighs my spirit down!

'Tis this dread phantom bodiless
Makes revelers shun the banquet-hall,
And Time's own self for weariness
Lean on the crumbling palace wall.

While other lands fleet-footed move
Down flowery paths of truancy,
Old Egypt in her ancient groove
Lies fixed in immobility.

Unmet, unmated, unsalaamed,
My only agapemones
Are held with mummy maids embalmed
In days of Ptah or Rameses.

What greets my eyes? A pillar leaning,
A Hyksos king (without a nose),
A white-sailed bark mayhap careening
Where through mud flats old Nilus flows.

Ah, could I, like my fellow column,
Enjoy a zestful change of air

And lead a life less staid and solemn,
Like him set in a Paris square!

He sees the busy gadabout
Trying, between tobacco whiffs,
To work the cross-word puzzle out
That lurks in his hieroglyphs.

Sprayed by cool fountains left and right,
He shines like a Parisienne,
And, clothed in iridescent light,
All rosy-hued, grows young again.

Alas! carved from the selfsame stone
In pink Syene's granite bed,
He's à la mode, I mope alone;
He is alive, and I am dead!

CHARLES BAUDELAIRE
1821–1867

Invitation

My loved one, my sweeting,
Oh heed my entreating,
Hand in hand let us wander away,
Among blossoms to lie
And to live and to die
In a land where the pallid noonday,
And the sun and the showers
And the cloud-drift that lowers,
Have the changeful mysterious charms
And the smiling disguise
Of your traitorous eyes
When you nestle wet-cheeked in my arms.

There order and beauty we'll treasure,
And splendor, and quiet, and pleasure.

Antique table and chair,
All agleam with long wear,
Shall lend a rich glow to our chamber,
And flowers most rare
Shall perfume the air
And load it with odors of amber;
Rosy nymphs on the ceiling,
By tall mirrors kneeling,
Crowned with lotus from Orient lands,
Shall the wonders unroll
Of our secretest soul
That love, only love, understands.

There order and beauty we'll treasure,
And splendor, and quiet, and pleasure.

In the sluggish lagoon
Sleep, sunken in swoon,
Strange galleons with streamers upfurled,
Bringing robes of spun gold
And bright gems manifold
From far isles in the tropical world.
Lo! the westering orb
In its light doth absorb
Fields, canals, and the city entire,
Which in glory enfolden,
Hyacinthine and golden,
Lies asleep in the lambent fire.

There order and beauty we'll treasure,
And splendor, and quiet, and pleasure.

The Fountain

YOUR EYELIDS droop with weariness,
Sweet mistress mine; ah! let them close;
Too indolent for love's caress,
Half-slumbrously let them repose.
The fountain whose faint systole
Is never still by day or night
Begets the swooning ecstasy
That love drinks from the pale moonlight.

On mossy towers,
On garden-bed,
A thousand flowers
Their petals shed
In tearful showers
Round your loved head.

Even so, uplit by visitings
Of love's unconquerable fire,

You soar aloft on flashing wings
Toward some far land of heart's desire;
Then, wrought on by pale melancholy,
On languid pinions you decline,
And all love's tears and tender folly
Steal from your spirit into mine.

On mossy towers,
On garden-bed,
A thousand flowers
Their petals shed
In tearful showers
Round your loved head.

O pallid blossom of the night,
Its frailest and its loveliest,
O luring fountain of delight
Whose sobs make music in my breast!
O moon! O night! O singing stream!
O rustling leaves that faintly move!
Your melancholy soothes my dream
And is the mirror of my love.

On mossy towers,
On garden-bed,
A thousand flowers
Their petals shed
In tearful showers
Round your loved head.

Altogether

THE DEVIL on his wings of flame
In at my attic window blew;
And, bent on putting me to shame,
He bade me tell him, if I knew,

What spell of lissom limbs, what grace
Of spirit crowns my lady's charms—
Her ebon hair? Her rosy face?
Or the white rondure of her arms?

Which is most lovely? O my soul!
How shall I choose the daintiest?
In her each part adorns the whole,
No single charm outvies the rest.

Her every glance, her breath light-drawn,
Her speech, her silence, all delight;
She thrills me like the joy of dawn,
She soothes me like the quiet night.

Lured by her beauty's subtle spells,
I stand as by a fountain's brink,
Mid lily-buds and asphodels,
And gaze till I forget to drink.

O mystic metamorphosis
Of severed senses strangely blent,
The fountain's song throbs in her kiss,
Her words exhale the lily's scent.

Dark Vigil

O TOILSOME load! O weary life!
O futile Sisyphaean sport!
How vain the poet's passioned strife,
Since Art is long and Time is short!
Far lie the tombs where glory sleeps;
My soul a darker vigil keeps;
By muffled drums my march is led.
Full many a gem is rolled unseen
In curtained caverns submarine

Where never spade or pick resounds;
Full many a flower is doomed to vent
Its sweet yet all unheeded scent
In some lone desert's pathless bounds.

Don Juan in Hades

WHEN JUAN in the murky underworld
Had paid his obol into Charon's hand,
A proud-eyed beggar with swift oar-blade hurled
The stagnant ooze against the Stygian strand.

Beneath that starless cope, with pendent breast
And gaping robes, a band of women thronged
Toward their betrayer, clamorous hosts unblest,
Cursing the hour when trusting love was wronged.

His jesting valet claimed his unpaid wage;
His sire, from the sad ranks that lined the shore,
Pointed a finger tremulous with age
At the base son who mocked him and forswore.

Black-stoled Elvira, fain to reconcile
Her faithless lover and her almost spouse,
Still begged from love-in-death a last fond smile,
Stored with the sweetness of his earliest vows.

Erect and moveless, a tall man of stone
Stood at the helm, where seething waters rise,
While o'er his rapier bent, Juan alone
Stared silent on the tide with cold, calm eyes.

The Cat

THE STUDENT grave, the young voluptuary,
Cherish with equal love this fecund beast,
This tigrine thing that loves to sleep and feast,
Chill-blooded like themselves and sedentary,
Friendly to musing or to amorous sport,
Avid of silence and nocturnal gloom,
And fit to chariot Pluto from the tomb,
Could he subdue its pride and royal port.
O feline tribe, your drowsy attitudes
Mimic the granite sphinxes that lie stretched
In lonely sands where breathless silence broods.
What secret dream is on your eyeballs etched?
In what strange deeps is lit the magic spark
That from your gravid breasts leaps through the
    dark?

Beauty

MORE LOVELY than a dream in carven stone,
With breasts round which men's yearning lips
    have curled,
In poets' hearts a passion I enthrone
Mute and eternal as the changeless world.
I tower in azure, sphinx-like and divine,
With soul white as a marble cenotaph;
I shun the movement that deflects the line,
And never do I weep and never laugh.
The poets by my faultless grandeur awed,
In homage to my monumental air,
Shall in their dedicated music laud
These subtle spells they find so heavenly fair,
These mirrors making all things doubly bright,
My eyes, my lustrous eyes, those wells of light.

The Secret

I'VE LIVED long years under the caverned vault
Of ocean grottos that illumed the brine
With thousand-tinted radiance vespertine
Flashing from towering pillars of basalt.
The furrowed seas that tossed reflected skies
Fused in majestic ever-swelling round
Their solemn anthems of euphonious sound
With sunset gleams shot from my dazzled eyes.
Through slow-paced aeons of voluptuous calm
I watched those azure waters fall and rise
While bare-limbed slaves, impregnate with rich
    balm,
Refreshed my face with fans of pliant palm,
Having no wish save only to surprise
The secret dolor of my languorous eyes.

Exotic Perfume

WHEN, WITH closed eyes, on warm autumnal
    nights
I breathe the perfume of your throbbing breast,
I see strange lands lit by fantastic lights
Of pale suns floating in the golden west,
Green island realms where swooning lotus flowers
And waving palm-trees, bent with luscious fruits,
Lure happy men and maids toward magic bowers
Mid glowworm lamps and sound of silver flutes.
Your beauty's perfume conjures up dim shores
And quiet havens where white sails upfurled,
Still tremulous from the tempestuous world,
Sleep in the shadow of the tamarind trees
That open on blue tides their emerald doors
While sailors sing far off on moaning seas.

Love in Death

O DEATH! LET odorous beds of ease be ours,
Beds downy soft and deep-shelved as a tomb;
Crown our faint heads with wreaths of alien flowers
Which tropic skies have warmed to languorous
    bloom;
Let our linked hearts exhale their vital heat
Like wedded torches that across the night
Cast doubled sheen of intermingled light
On mirrors where our swooning spirits meet.
In twilight glow, all rose and mystic blue,
We will depart at sound of vesper bells,
Breathing low sobs surcharged with sad farewells,
And there shall come an angel to renew
In our twinned souls, all purged of earthly shame,
The tarnished mirror and the faded flame.

Love Sanctified

WHAT WILL YOU say tonight, poor lonely soul,
What will you say, my heart, pale faded flower,
To her, most fair, most good, most dear, whose
    power
Has crowned me with a golden aureole?
Shall I not honor her with holy rite
Whose angel grace and spiritual flesh
Perfume my thoughts and my spent soul refresh
And robe me in a dress of living light?
When lonely night and leaden-winged despair
Drive me down peopled streets, though fain to hide,
Like a bright torch she dances at my side;
"Am I not fair?" a voice rings on the air—
"Then if you love me, love but what is fair:
I am your guide, your Muse, your heavenly bride!"

Death

Tis Death that comforts us and bids us live;
It is our being's goal, our kindly light;
It is the philter that alone can give
Us strength to walk until the fall of night.
Through frost and snow and through the tempest's
    din,
Star-like it shines on the horizon's gloom.
It is the dear, the long-awaited inn
Of still repose locked in a little room.
It is an angel whose blest hands invoke
Soft sleep on weary lids, and silent dreams,
To smooth the bed of wretched pauper folk.
It is God's gift that gladdens and redeems,
The beggar's purse, the wanderer's fatherland,
A house of peace too deep to understand.

Night

Be still, my grief, and find surcease from pain.
You longed for night, and lo! the night descends;
A veil of darkness shrouds the world again,
And some sick hearts it wounds, but some it mends.
The human herd lies stretched on pleasure's rack,
And seeks for comfort where no comforts be,
Laying remorseful burdens on its back.
Come, Sorrow, take my hand and wend with me.
Wend far away! Behold, the dying Years
In faded garb lean from heaven's balconies,
Whence, smiling, through the bitter water steers
Wan-eyed Regret, while through starred tapestries
Peers the pale Twilight, and adown the sky
The trailing robes of Night sweep softly by.

Exaltation

Above the lonely tarns and shelving steeps,
The cloud-girt ocean and the mountain meres,
Beyond the sun and the ethereal deeps,
Beyond the confines of the starry spheres,
Rise up, my spirit, on impetuous wing,
Stout swimmer breasting the aerial sea
In swooning rapture, gaily furrowing
The vasty reaches of eternity.
Fly far away from this miasmic world,
To mount white-winged those azure thoroughfares
And from the clouds drink drops of dew impearled
With roseate fires shot from the wandering stars.
Thrice blest the mortal scorning mortal doom
Who ever higher in his conquering flight
Soars from this misty world of sullen gloom
To those ethereal fields of ample light;
Thrice blest whose thought, like to the mounting
    lark,
Is lifted up on happy morning wings
To hover easeful in the heavens and mark
The mystic speech of flowers and voiceless things.

LECONTE DE LISLE
1818–1894

The Showmen

LIKE SOME GAUNT beast, bruised, beaten, mud-be-
　　sprent,
Chained, howling, in the torrid summer heat,
Let him who will show in your gaping street
His sorrows for the mob's divertissement.
To wake in your dull souls a fire long spent,
To be your clown, your piteous parasite,
Let whoso will put off his robe of light
And seal his own disgrace with his consent.
Nay, rather will I in proud solitude
In an inglorious grave forever rest;
I will not court your plaudits or contest
For honors on a stage where art grown lewd,
And beauty vile, can find no partisans
Save histrions and sullied courtesans.

The Supreme Illusion

WHEN MAN HAS SCALED the summits whence his
　　way
Winds downward through your shade, O somber
　　skies!
The dawning splendors of his primal day
Shine through the mist on his enchanted eyes.

Nothing has vanished of that bygone time,
His native hills, the aged tamarind trees,
And the dear dead who loved him in his prime
And now repose beside those sandy seas.

There mid tall lilacs, haunt of buzzing bees,
The peaceful cot peeps through the flowering thorn
And tangled vines and vermeil fruits that tease
The bluebirds perched upon the tasseled corn.

The cascades fling their sheets of jeweled spray
From the high mountain in a shower of snow,
And the light skiffs that cleave the azure bay
Dip their beaked prows where foaming currents
   flow.

Then all is wrapped in slumber. The still moon
Hangs like a white pearl on the brow of night,
And on its silver waters the lagoon
Rolls the pale planets in their wheeling flight.

A balmy incense from each bush respires
Where golden glowworms make the darkness
   bright;
And on the distant hills the hunters' fires
Flame through the shining azure of the night.

You too relive, O fair and fleeting shade
Of her I loved in youth's first blossoming,
Sweet floweret gathered ere the sun could fade
The odorous beauty of your transient spring!

O vision unforgot! you still impart
From your sepulchral bed on that far shore
A sad auroral radiance to a heart
Where grief and darkness dwell forevermore.

Time has not altered your immortal grace,
The grave is guardian of your loveliness,
It has not marred the wonder of that face
Nor dimmed those eyes whose glance was a caress.

Yet time hides all to which it once gave birth:
What after-age will know how once you bloomed

And with your beauty gladdened all the earth,
Sweet visitant, to chill oblivion doomed?

O golden days in season of heartsease,
O dazzling nights, whose glowing stars illume
With fleeting glory all the silver seas!
You bear off dream and dreamer to the tomb.

We are time's sport; youth, love, and joy, and
   thought,
The song of seas and woods, the holy past,
So rich in promise, all shall come to naught,
All love of mortal things that cannot last.

Then let the wild winds whirl this human dust
Whither they will; vain is our passioned strife,
The worlds we fashion, and the gods we trust;
Better death's dreamless sleep than mortal life!

Night

THE SIGHING BREEZE that haunts the shadowy
   valleys
Lulls with its slumberous spell the nodding trees;
No bird-notes echo through the silent alleys;
The rising stars have silvered all the seas.

On the wild slope below the somber pines,
The winding paths in veiling mist have vanished;
The pensive moon through the black foliage shines;
And every sound of human life is banished.

Far off the seas their ancient chant prolong;
The towering forest sighs with answering notes;
And through the moonlit night melodious floats
The ocean's music with the woodland's song.

Swell, sacred hymns, more pure than human speech,
Symphonious harmony of earth and sky!
Mount to the stars and ask if we shall reach
Those happy worlds for which we vainly sigh.

Noon

Noon, LORD OF SUMMER, overspreads the plains,
Falling in sheets of silver from the sky;
The hushed air stagnates on the dusty lanes,
And wrapped in robes of flame the moorlands lie.

The sky looms vast, the fields are shadowless,
The springs are dry where drank the roving flocks,
The yellow woods, yielding to summer's stress,
Sleep motionless above the arid rocks.

Only the wheat stalks, like a golden sea,
Roll o'er the plain and ceaselessly lift up
Their shining heads in wakeful jubilee
To drain the torrid sunshine's brimming cup.

Yet sometimes from their burning soul exhales
A low majestic music like a sigh,
Moves down dense rows of swaying stems, then
    pales
Till its faint echoes in the distance die.

Near by, white oxen dot the parching grass,
Clotting their dewlaps with down-dripping foam,
While in their proud and languorous eyes they glass
The unending dream which is their spirit's home.

Klearista

FAIR KLEARISTA through the wheat-field passes,
Gold-filleted, dark-browed, and starry-eyed,
The loveliest of Sicilia's shepherd lasses;
Milk-white her neck, and in her tresses set,
Milesian roses kindle, crimson-dyed,
With here and there a violet.

The roseate dawn on the horizon glimmers,
The joyous lark floats on the morning air,
The blackbird whistles, and the sunlight shimmers
On dewy grass where limps the trembling hare,
Whose anxious leaps bring down in eddying swirls
A sudden shower of liquid pearls.

Does beauty less divinely shine in thee,
O dreamy-eyed, soft-smiling shepherdess,
Than in the dawn that gilds the misty sea?
Who knows if this same star, sweet sorceress,
That fills the world with light and loveliness
Feed not love's fount of ecstasy?

From Hybla's summit, where his rams are grazing,
The shepherd sees this fairy vision gleam
Over the fields like an embodied dream,
And cries aloud, in amorous rapture gazing,
" 'Twas night, and lo, the morn!" and in his heart
Beholds dawn's rosy counterpart.

The Elves

WITH MARJORAM and wild thyme crowned,
The merry elves all dance in round.

Through the greenwood aisles where the brown
    deer stray
A knight on his steed is winding his way.
All of gold are his spurs that gleam in the night,
And when he rides into the moon's pallid light
One sees the white sheen intermittently shed
From the helmet of silver that circles his head.

    With marjoram and wild thyme crowned,
    The merry elves all dance in round.

The elves wind about him, a light-footed band,
Diaphanous children of bright fairyland.
"Whither ride you so late through the boskage
    green,
Bold wayfaring knight?" cries the elfin queen.
"Evil spirits are roaming the woodland ways,
Come dance on the mead where the moonlight
    plays."

    With marjoram and wild thyme crowned,
    The merry elves all dance in round.

"Nay, a mortal maiden with soft blue eyes
Is waiting to wed when the daystar shall rise.
Loose your hold, nor so wildly your white arms
    toss,
Blithe fairies that foot it in flowery moss;
Keep me not from my love, it is time to be gone;
Already I see the first glimmer of dawn."

    With marjoram and wild thyme crowned,
    The merry elves all dance in round.

"Stay, knight, and I'll give you to have and to
    hold
My magical opal, my circlet of gold,
And more rich than a crown with diamonds strewn

My dress that was spun in the light of the moon."
"Nay, nay, I must go." "Go then, let us part!"
And the queen of the elves lays her hand on his
   heart.

    With marjoram and wild thyme crowned,
    The merry elves all dance in round.

'Neath his spur the black steed through the shad-
   ows flies on,
But the face of the knight has waxed haggard and
   wan.
With a shudder he leans o'er the neck of his horse,
For a shadowy form rises out of the gorse:
It advances, it beckons, it holds out its arms.
"Elf, demon, or sprite, cease thy magical charms!"

    With marjoram and wild thyme crowned,
    The merry elves all dance in round.

"Hence, specter! I hasten to join my fair bride,
My love so true-hearted, my love so blue-eyed."
"Lie down then, my lover, lie close by my side;
While awaiting your coming, your loved one has
   died."
And the elf queen's curse had such magical power
That the stricken knight died in the selfsame hour.

    With marjoram and wild thyme crowned,
    The merry elves all dance in round.

The Veranda

BY FOUNTAINS falling on red porphyry
The Iranian rose exhales its fragrant breath,
And drowsy ring-doves coo melodiously

While slender birds and wasps enwreathe
The laden branches of the gray fig-tree:
The Iranian rose exhales its fragrant breath
By fountains falling on red porphyry.

In the veranda's silver-trellised zone,
Fanned by warm airs, embalmed with jasmine scent
In which the daystar's rosy rays are blent,
The Persian queen thrones motionless, alone,
Her arms round her brown neck twined indolent,
Fanned by warm airs, embalmed with jasmine scent
In the veranda's silver-trellised zone.

Above its rim, in circling amber sheathed,
The crystal vase distils its faint perfume,
Whose mounting spirals, in white vapor wreathed,
Her crimson pillows, pranked with gold, illume,
While through the smoke from her curved hooka
    breathed
The crystal vase distils its faint perfume
Above the rim in circling amber sheathed.

Her secret ecstasy, unspoke, unseen,
Gleams in the half-veiled oval of her eyes
And in the blissful languor of her mien:
She seems oppressed by a so sweet surprise
That with her snowy bosom's fall and rise
Gleams in the half-veiled oval of her eyes
Her secret ecstasy, unspoke, unseen.

The fountain sleeps on the red porphyry,
The Iranian rose has spent its fragrant breath,
The doves forget to coo melodiously,
No longer do the birds and wasps enwreathe
The laden branches of the gray fig-tree,
The Iranian rose has spent its fragrant breath,
The fountain sleeps on the red porphyry.

The Sun-God

THE RADIANT GOD in floating Delos sprung,
The ever-beautiful, the ever-young,
In golden mantle clad, from the blue deep
Uplifts his head. The surging billows leap
Round his swift feet, and dimpling foam-drops shine
In rainbow splendors on his form divine.
To the huge axle his strong hands attach
Two gold-rimmed wheels, with brazen spokes to
    match.
The hubs are silver, silvern is his seat.
Four stallions snowy-white, with cloven feet,
He yokes with trailing reins to the long shaft,
Rebellious coursers that disdain the draught.
Foaming and bristling, with resounding jaws
They champ the bit, and ever without pause
Trample the deep. The air that they respire
From their broad nostrils shoots like roaring fire.
Their master, tightening the quadruple rein,
Bends their fierce necks down to the watery plain;
The sea-winds play through his ambrosial locks.
Selene pales, and from high-towering rocks
With moss embrowned, the rosy-fingered Dawn
Heralds his reign ere Night's last star is gone.
Loud shouts the god, and through the shoreless sky
The chariot and the immortal horses fly:
The rushing air is rife with sound and flame,
The ocean's heaving billows grow more tame
And sing more softly as his wheels roll past
With ordered motion, beautiful and fast,
While earth, mist-bound, sleeps in those placid seas
Like Panope girt by her naiades.

The Condor

PAST THE STEEP Andes towering ridge on ridge,
Beyond the murky clouds, the eagle's home,
Above the mist-clad mountains' utmost dome,
Where frightful rivers of red lava bridge
The chasms from peak to vale, high in the air,
With drooping pinions indolently spread
And mournful eyes in which all light seems dead,
The giant condor soars. With silent stare
He views the darkening continent and the sun
That sinks into illimitable space.
Night rolls up from the East, where one by one
The mountain chains unfold. Toward their broad
    base
The trackless pampas stretch a sea of grass.
The darkness mounts from every deep morass
And slowly steals round bays and curving shores
Till like a billowy ocean-swell it pours
Its heaving tides in whirling vortices
Past the pale skyline and the Western seas.
Alone and spectral, outlined on the peak,
Bathed in the sinking sun's empurpled light,
That reddens the white snow-fields vast and bleak,
He waits until the rising tide of night
In its black shadows hides the globe from sight,
Rolled through abysses of unfathomed air.
He rears on high his head, all red and bare,
And uttering a harsh exultant cry
That swells and echoes through the empty sky,
Shakes off the frozen snow that clogs his flight
And soars through sunless pathways of dim night
Where no winds blow and never sound is heard
Breaking the stillness: there the mighty bird,
Majestically floating overhead,
Sleeps in the icy air, his giant wings outspread.

Solvet Saeclum

Y ou shall be silenced one day, O sinister voice
    of creation!
Furious blasphemies rolled on the breast of the
    riotous winds,
Cries of horror and hate, delirious accents of rage,
Frightful clamors resounding over the wreck uni-
    versal,
Torments and crimes and remorse and multiplied
    sobs of despair,
Spirit and flesh of mankind, ye shall all be silenced
    one day!
All shall be silent, the gods and the kings and the
    woebegone rabble,
The raucous voice of the prison, the town's multi-
    tudinous murmur,
All the hosts of the living, the spawn of the land
    and the sea,
All that flies or leaps or crawls in this earthly in-
    ferno,
All that trembles and flees, and all that slays and
    devours,
All from the worm of the earth that is trampled
    into the mire
Up to the devious thunders that roll into outermost
    darkness.
This shall not be the repose that we dreamed in a
    realm beatific,
Bliss which the faint heart feigns in some far-away
    Garden of Eden,
Converse of Adam and Eve amid murmuring foun-
    tains and flowers,

Or sleep that lies upon lids long heavy with harrow-
    ing sorrow:
Then shall this mighty globe and all that inhabit
    upon it,
Sterile and tenebrous mass, from its circling orbit
    extruded,
Stupid and blind and bedazed with the sound of
    supreme lamentation,
Frenetic shrieks of despair waxing madder from
    moment to moment,
Shatter its cavernous shell, decaying in barren
    senescence,
'Gainst some mightier orb that bars its circuitous
    pathway.
Then from a thousand rifts shall flare its intestinal
    fires,
Piercing the floods oceanic and flinging in tortuous
    billows
All that once was the world to dissolve into ashes
    and dust,
Sown through the furrows of space where the in-
    choate worlds are fermenting.

THÉODORE DE BANVILLE
1823–1891

Precept

CHOOSE, SCULPTOR, if you court the envied bays,
A flawless marble for a lovely vase.
Shape it with patient art, and let there be
No amorous god, no marble deity,
Not Hercules with Nemean blood bedyed,
Nor Cypris rising from the rose-strewn tide,
Nor rebel Titan by Jove's might subdued,
Nor Bacchus drawn by harnessed lion brood,
With reins of purple grapevine in his hand,
Nor Leda sporting with her cygnet band
Where thick-set laurels gleam, nor Artemis
Whose snowy limbs the purling waters kiss.
Thy vase, too pure for Bacchic dances, twine
With green acanthus and with hawthorn fine;
Then through the clustering maze, in order due,
Lead a long train of virgins, two by two,
With white arms shining down their tunics' fold
And smooth brows filleted with ruddy gold.

The Strolling Players

THROUGH WOODS agleam with tufted goldenrods,
Spouting iambics to the empty air,
The strolling players come, robed in threadbare
Purple and gold, kings, queens, and demigods.
Grim Herod brandishes his gory blade,
Proud Cleopatra flaunts her broideries,

And petticoated in a bright brocade
Shines like a peacock gemmed with thousand eyes.
Flamboyant as translucent chrysolite
Dark-browed Adonis marches stately on
With gaunt Hippolytus in wolf-skin dight,
While sleek Pierrot clasps a huge demijohn—
And in their wake, across the trampled grass,
Plod dreamily the Poet and the Ass.

We'll to the Woods No More

WE'LL TO THE woods no more—the laurels all are
   cut:
The Cupids in the fount, the naiads' group,
Scan the low tides in voiceless basins shut,
Against whose edge the paling lilies droop.
The laurels all are cut—the trembling deer
Flees the loud horn—we'll to the woods no more.
No shrill-voiced urchins haunt the lonely mere,
Only wan Autumn from the silent shore
Views the smoke curling o'er the rustic hut.
We'll to the woods no more—the laurels all are cut.

A Song of Her That's Mine

THE FAR-FLUNG lakes of liquid blue
         Slumberously shine
With golden sunbeams filtering through,
Yet gladlier the bright eyes I view
         Of her that's mine.

The bird that sings on yonder bough
         So matutine,

Did never sing so sweet as now,
Yet sweeter is the voice, I vow,
      Of her that's mine.

The dewy drops the heavens shed
      Incarnadine
The autumnal rose's drooping head;
O tears from sweeter fountains fed
      Of her that's mine!

Time prints its cicatrice
      On all things fine;
Yet to forget all this
I ask but for a kiss
      Of her that's mine.

The rose that hot winds blight
      Drops from the vine;
Give me for rest tonight
The lily breast so white
      Of her that's mine.

Let faithless lovers rove
      From shrine to shrine;
I will more constant prove
And ever keep the love
      Of her that's mine.

Pierrot Among the Stars

PIERROT was a wondrous clown,
And wondrous too was his renown;
You'll find none such now he is dead.
It was indeed a cheerful sight,
His motley jacket, all of white,
Of green, of yellow, and of red.

Known as far as Madagascar,
Known to Sepoy and to Lascar,
Was this super-agile clown;
On a tight-rope he could caper,
He could leap through hoops of paper
And come bouncing nimbly down.

This divine equilibrist
Could have scaled through mire and mist
Spiral stairs of Piranesi
With no light save, round his head,
His long locks of flaming red
To illume those ladders crazy.

He could reach such giddy heights
In his green and yellow tights
That his rivals stared in wonder
As he shot up ever higher
Into cloudland, ever nigher
To the lightning and the thunder.

All the people yelled, "Huzza!
What a gorgeous clown, ha, ha!"
Meanwhile high in air he hung,
And with bare arms well anointed
Toward his old springboard he pointed,
Murmuring in exotic tongue:

"O my springboard, my beloved,
Fifty feet below me shoved,
How you thrill me with fantastic
Joy when from your tip I bound!
Heave me, lift me from the ground
To the heavens, my plank elastic!

"Toss me, toss me, frail machine,
Up where sun and stars careen!
Here I daily grow moroser,

Viewing these depressing black
Coats that hang upon the back
Of the lawyer and the grocer.

"Now, with some unwonted wonder,
In the lawless haunt of thunder
Let me cleave the azure air,
Where the planets and the suns,
Whirled in weird quaternions,
Blend their shocks of reddish hair;

"Up where starry nomads sound
Anthems on their nightly round,
Where the misty mirk enshrouds
Weary north winds while they rest
Breathless on the heaving breast
Of the pallid-bosomed clouds.

"High above this jail miasmal,
Lift me to the blue fantasmal
Nephelococcygian land,
To those Oriental spaces
Where Apollo palely paces
And Jove hurls his flaming brand.

"Farther! Higher! Still I see
Gold-rimmed glasses stare at me.
Free me from these horrid things,
Rhymster, spinster, ingenue!
Farther! Higher! In the blue!
Oh, for wings! for wings! for wings!"

From his plank into the sky
Leaped the clown so high, so high,
That he shattered bolts and bars
And, with blare of drum and horn
In ecstatic flight upborne,
Rolled and rattled past the stars.

SULLY PRUDHOMME
1839–1907

The Lost Cry

FROM THE abysm of immemorial time
A spirit rose and haunted me unbid,
Witness of Cheops' glory and his crime,
And toiler at his granite pyramid.
His knees shook, and his fragile body bent
With weight of stone and stress of torrid heat;
His muscles swelled, his fevered pulses beat,
And, like a tree the thunderbolt has rent,
He uttered a great cry. It shook the air;
It scaled the heavens; it shot beyond the stars,
Seeking that partial power that molds and mars,
Gives bliss to some and unto some despair.
Three thousand years that cry has pealed unheard,
And Cheops in his glory sleeps unstirred.

The Danaïdes

THEIR AMPHORS by their ivory arms upheld,
Callidia, Theano, Danaë,
Forever to their cruel task compelled,
Run with their leaking urns unceasingly.
The porous clay reddens their shoulders white;
Their slender arms grow weary of the load:
"Ah! why this futile labor day and night,
And wherefore pace this never-ending road?"
Their lagging feet give way, their spirits droop—
But younger, gayer, sweet Theano sings,
Till faith returning spreads her shining wings:

Thus our illusions fail but not our hope.
More young and gay, she sings her glad refrain
And cries: "Come, sisters, and begin again."

We Shall Forget

I LOVE YOU while I wait the immortal spouse
Who watches for me at the opening gate
Of blissful Eden, home of changeless vows,
Of fadeless flowers and bridals coronate.
There I shall see, in God's resplendent house,
Where lovers dead choose an eternal mate,
Your sisters gathered under olive boughs
Where I my earthly love will abdicate.
And you, not jealous, at some angel's call
Will leave me when you hear his blessèd voice
Name you of all the blest his heavenly choice.
We shall forget our old love's human thrall
As fellow-travellers at the parting way
Forget the frail bonds of a passing day.

Blue Eyes and Black

BLUE EYES and black, belovèd eyes,
Eyes numberless have seen the dawn,
Eyes closed by us in days bygone,
Yet each day brought a new sunrise,

And night more gentle than the day
Brought its sweet balm to eyes untold.
The stars still glisten as of old,
Though all these eyes are sealed with clay.

Are they then all amerced of sight?
Alas! we will not think them so!

They have but closed on mortal woe
To open in celestial light.

As firmamental stars grow dim
And disappear, yet haunt the sky
And shine below the ocean's rim,
So they, too, set but do not die.

Blue eyes and black, belovèd eyes,
The eyes we closed in days agone,
Reopening on a wider dawn
Behold a brighter day arise.

The Broken Vase

THE VASE that holds this dying rose,
Tapped lightly by a lady's fan,
Cracked at this slightest of all blows,
Though not an eye the flaw could scan.

And yet the line, so light, so slight,
Etched ever deeper on the bowl,
Spread to the left, spread to the right,
Until it circled round the whole.

The water sinks, the petals fall,
Yet none divines, no word is spoken;
The surface seems intact to all;
Ah! touch it not—the vase is broken.

Thus oft the heart is lightly bruised
By some slight word of those we cherished;
Yet through the wound our blood has oozed,
And lo! the flower of love has perished.

Though to the world our life seems whole,
The hidden wound is unforgot;
It grows and weeps within the soul:
The heart is broken—touch it not.

HENRI CAZALIS
1840–1906

Reminiscences

Vast worlds of thought not mine my spirit haunt,
Ancestral relics of aeonian life
Unrolled in murky caves and forests gaunt,
Hoar battlefields of bestial love and strife.

In wintry twilights, when the night looms chill,
Dead beasts and plants in me relive their pain;
In me Adonis bleeds on his cold hill,
And bygone springs in me grow green again.

In the primeval forest still I feel
The shuddering upsurge of wild life renewed;
Again nocturnal shadows darkly steal
With giant steps through the grim solitude.

We are the slaves of time and nature's thralls,
Bodied of mire and kindred to the clods;
Our souls are temples whose senescent walls
Reflect the fitful shadows of dead gods.

Too long my soul has slept in time's black womb,
With vague convulsions groping toward the day;
In this dim cell lives no unsullied bloom,
The old taint in the blood will not away.

Fain would I free my spirit from these chains
And slay a past that still disdains to die;
I would forget this bondage that remains
Of the long ages of my infamy.

O futile hope! Myself I am my past;
My groping thoughts, my reminiscent dreams,

Flow from the natal stream in which are glassed
These somber landscapes flashed in spectral gleams.

For I have traveled through uncounted forms,
Somber or shining shapes that darkling nurse
In my heart's core the selfsame soul that warms
The vital pulsing of the universe.

FRANÇOIS COPPÉE
1842–1908

Blithe April

Now BLITHE April dances toward us:
Darling, look, the spring returns!
Oh! what songs the nests afford us!
How earth's perfumed incense burns!
Now falls showering from above
Down of thrush and turtle-dove.

In the silver brooklet glass,
Fairy mine, those virgin charms,
Golden tresses, snowy arms;
Come and through the wildwood pass,
Where the hawthorn, as we go,
Pelts us with its petalled snow.

Let us fix our trysting-place
Where the wandering butterflies
Veer and flit in airy chase
'Mong the shining dragonflies,
By the pool upon whose brink
Shy gazelles stoop down to drink.

Autumn

ERE STREAMS are numbed by winter's sting,
Ere skies are canopied in gloom,
A last time hear the woodland sing
And see the last pale roses bloom.

October, when the year grows old,
Sheds silver mists on hills and springs;
Its crimson glow, its trees of gold,
Have all the charm of dying things.

But ah! this splendor cannot last
That robes the browning forest glades;
Yet for one flitting hour hold fast
The season's magic ere it fades.

Let Fancy still hold holiday
A little hour 'mong Autumn's sheaves;
Too soon will Winter sweep away
Love's blossoms with the withered leaves.

Romance

WHEN YOU BID me view the rose
In the scented garden shaded,
Why do my sad eyes upclose
When you bid me view the rose?
    (O loved face forever faded!)

When you bid me view a star,
Why do tear-drops weave a mist
And the heavenly vision bar
When you bid me view a star?
    (O dead eyes of amethyst!)

When you bid me view the swallow
Ere his summer songs be banished,
Why will not my sad eyes follow
When you bid me view the swallow?
    (O my love, forever vanished!)

JOSÉ-MARIA DE HÉRÉDIA
1842–1905

Oblivion

A RUINED temple crowns the promontory
Where marble goddesses and heroes stand,
Moss-girt and sunken in the ruddy sand
And barren weeds that mock their pristine glory.
In this lone spot only the herdsman strays,
To let his oxen drink, or, stretched at ease,
Waken the heavens and the resurgent seas,
Piping to hill and vale his antique lays.
Benignant nature, reverent of the gods,
Lifts every year, at spring's first falling showers,
Up the white stone her pale acanthus flowers.
But man, indifferent as the senseless clods,
Heeds not the dirge, borne on the south wind's
  breath,
Of moaning seas that mourn the Sirens' death.

Jason and Medea

WHERE THE RICH foliage sheds its odorous balm
And mystic whispers breathe from fainting flowers,
The happy lovers passed enchanted hours
In shadowy groves of laurel and of palm.
Bedded in bloom charged with narcotic scent,
Lulled by soft speech that flowed with witching
  charms,
The hero lay despoiled of his bright arms
And golden-glancing fleece magnificent.

Great birds flew through the blossom-laden trees,
And silver dewdrops glassed the azure skies,
Lighting, like far-flung jewels, the dim woods.
Love smiled on them; but in Medea's eyes
Strange portents shone, for she bore overseas
Her Asian philtres and barbaric gods.

The Chase

THE SUN-GOD's car, by four white stallions drawn,
Rides the meridian. His trampling steeds
With breath of flame sear all the golden meads
And the brown herbage of the parching lawn.
Vain is the oak-tree's green appareling.
Slant sunbeams through the quivering leafage
    stray,
And in the shade where silver fountains sing
They glide and dart and gleam in magic play.
It is the noontide hour: through bush and briar,
Girt by the band of her fleet-footed maids
And a shrill pack of fierce Molossian hounds,
With twanging bows and blood and bellowing
    sounds,
Her tresses streaming back in golden fire,
The huntress Dian scours the forest glades.

Nymphaea

APOLLO's GOLDEN chariot nears the deep;
Dim headlands fade beneath his circling wheels;
His foaming steeds rush down the western steep
And spurn the crimson clouds with brazen heels.

Seaward they plunge, and ocean's hollow sigh
Echoes along the purple sunset's trail,
While slowly through the blue night's glistening
    veil
A crescent moon climbs up the darkened sky.
The buskined nymph beside a silver fountain
Throws her loose bow and empty quiver down
Nor heeds the stag's hoarse baying on the moun-
    tain:
She dreams of revels and the floral crown,
Of dancing dryades and laughing Pan
Roaming by reedy banks Arcadian.

Pan

THROUGH DIM ravines and forest paths untrod
Save by shy nymphs and white-limbed dryades
Glides eager-eyed beneath the towering trees
The goat-foot Pan, half satyr and half god.
He stops to hear the softly murmured sound
Rising at noonday from deep-hidden rills
When Phoebus, wheeling in diurnal round,
Dispels the shadows from the misty hills.
A nymph with silent footfall speeds across
The flowery dell, scattering silver drops
Of morning dew still sparkling on the moss;
But, with one bound, Pan from the echoing copse,
With mocking laugh and clattering uproar,
Grasps her and flees—then silence reigns once
    more.

Bath of the Nymphs

WHERE BILLOWY Euxine washed the Argo's prow
The fountained crags 'neath somber laurels gleam.
A sportive nymph sits on a swaying bough,
Touching with timid foot the icy stream:
Lured by her call, her sisters golden-tressed
Cleave the blue water with their snow-white limbs,
And here a torso, there a rose-tipped breast,
Half unseen in the cooling current swims
While all the wood with silver laughter rings.
But suddenly two eyes with baleful light
Blaze in the copse—the Satyr! In mad flight
The nymphs disperse, like swans with beating wings
When from the quivering reeds with strident scream
A raven hovers on Caÿster's stream.

The Vase

WHAT CUNNING HAND wrought this fair master-
    piece?
Here carved in ivory gleams the Colchian grove;
Here Jason to Medea tells his love,
While lustrous-eyed she views the Golden Fleece;
Here ancient Nilus lies, immortal head
Of thousand streams. Here, mad with nectared
    wine,
Wailing Bacchantes, ivy-garlanded,
A snow-white bull with trailing wreaths entwine.
Here show the clash of steeds and armored cars,
Brave warriors slain, borne homeward on their
    shields,

And mourning men and maids in ravaged fields.
Here, sinuous-curved, divinely shaped, are seen
Smooth breasts that light the ivory like pale stars
Where on its rim two white Chimaeras lean.

Andromeda and the Monster

PALE-FACED Andromeda, scarce half alive,
Maddened with terror by the leaping sea,
Bound to a jutting rock, moans piteously,
Each ivory limb locked in a brazen gyve.
The winds tempestuous that shoreward strive
Wash her cold feet in white foam ceaselessly,
While her dim eyes through tears obliquely see
Fierce jaws agape her tender flesh to rive.
Then, like unwonted thunder in clear skies,
Loud neighing rends the air, and her glad eyes
Behold descending toward her from above,
Through the bright heavens with steady flight
    and true,
The wingèd horse, steered by the son of Jove,
Casting his shadow on the liquid blue.

Perseus and Andromeda

STOPPING HIS flight above the foam-flecked tide
He stains the rock with the foul dragon's blood;
Then, swift as one might cull a lily-bud,
The hero lifts her up, sitting astride
Of his immortal steed, that fiery-eyed
Paws the salt spray and hangs upon the flood
Which the blue heavens with thousand stars be-
    stud,

While the pale girl clings sobbing to his side.
He clasps her tight. The mad waves roar and hiss.
Smiling through tears, she lifts her icy feet
From the white waves and their unkindly kiss;
And the glad horse no mortal hand could tame,
Feeling the spur, with movement lightning fleet,
Leaps through the dazzled air with wings of flame.

The Flight of Andromeda

UP THROUGH the starlit air, without a sound,
The wingèd horse steers on its steady flight
Through azure spaces of ethereal light
Where wheel the planets in eternal round.
Below them Afric deserts, mountain-bound,
And fertile Asia loom, and, lost in night,
Dim cloud-girt Lebanon; then, shining white,
The mystic sea where luckless Helle drowned.
They float from star to star across the void,
By those vast wings as by a sail convoyed,
In whose warm interspace they lie embraced
While world on world rolls slowly into view,
And from the deep, majestic and far-spaced,
Their constellations rise into the blue.

The Goatherd

RASH HERDSMAN, do not climb these steep ravines,
Following the wild bounds of your wandering goat;
The twilight deepens, and the dusk clouds float
Where frowning Maenalus the valley screens.
Bide here with me; I have ripe figs and wine;
Await the daybreak in my moss-thatched cot;

But whisper low: shy wood-gods haunt this spot,
Great Hecate speaks here with voice divine,
And yonder where the tinkling fount upwells
Yawns the dark cavern where the Satyr dwells.
If we creep slyly toward it we may chance
To hear his piping while the pale moonlight
Gilds his crook'd horns and his wild notes incite
My leaping kids to foot the pastoral dance.

The Shepherds

COME WHERE the steep Cyllenian valleys spread;
Here high in air the pillared pine-trees loom;
Here bedded deep in thyme and clover-bloom
The lazy wood-god props his slumberous head.
From silver springs the ewe has drunk her fill,
And ere a month of summer days glides by
She'll yield rich milk and cheese and e'en supply
With woolly store the nymphs who haunt this hill.
Be gracious to us, O goat-footed Pan,
That lead'st thy flocks by streams Arcadian,
And heed our prayers beneath these rustling trees!
Now let us hence—the sun flames in the west,
And though no marble shrine, with blossoms drest,
Rise in this grove, our gifts nathless may please.

The Cicada

PAUSE, TRAVELLER, where the green cicada sleeps
Which little Helle through two seasons fed:
Its wings are folded, its blithe music dead,
And by its grave the sad-eyed maiden weeps.
No more she hears from cistus-bloom or pine

This tiny muse among the furrows singing
Or through the sunlit meadows gaily winging.
Lay lightly down your spray of eglantine
And do not waken from its peaceful dreams
That airy sprite whose tombstone whitely gleams
Above the thyme-clad sepulchre! Though oft
We die unmourned, for thee the tender tear
Of childhood flowed—its small hands shaped this
    bier,
On which the morning dew falls warm and soft.

The Shipwreck

FROM OUT THE NILE, too trustful of fair skies,
Seeing through nodding masts the Pharos pass,
He seaward sailed, watching Arcturus rise,
Proud of his bark all lined with shining brass.
Alas! no more the Alexandrian quay
Shall he behold! Where the bleak dunes arise
'Mong wind-swept reeds, beside the moaning sea,
In his lone grave the shipwrecked sailor lies.
Engulfed by a brown ridge of heaving sand,
In dawnless sleep unlit by star or moon,
He rests at last on the Hellenic strand.
There may his anxious spirit be at ease!
O earth, on which his hapless bones are strewn,
Lie light on him, and softly sing, O seas!

The Dead Bride

STRANGER, CRUSH NOT these pallid flowers, but pass
The verdant mound where sleeps my dolorous
    shade,
Which from its low bed hears the murmur made

By creeping ivy and fresh-springing grass.
And yet you pause? I hear a moaning dove,
Poor victim you would offer on my tomb:
Nay, heed me! Loose it in the clover bloom—
Life is so sweet! Ah, let it live and love!
While myrtle wreaths still garlanded my door
I died untimely on my wedding day
And closed my eyes to the sun's gracious light,
So near, yet far from him whom I adore,
Doomed, hapless virgin bride, henceforth for aye
To dwell in Erebus and dawnless night.

The Runner

As DELPHI SAW HIM, foremost in the race,
Fly through the stadium, leaving all behind,
So Ladas runs still on this brazen base.
With wingèd foot, fleet as the Boreal wind,
With arms flung out and body forward bent
And dripping brow, he rushes uncontrolled,
As if the sculptor's art were impotent
To lock that leaping life within the mold.
He palpitates with flux of hope and fear,
Drinking with gasping lips the too thin air;
The muscles on his shining limbs lie bare,
While, borne resistless in his swift career,
He from his pedestal seems rushing down
To clear the goal and snatch the victor's crown.

Othrys

THE AIR GROWS COOL; the sky is one red rose;
The cattle fear no more the gadfly's sting.
On Othrys' slopes day still is lingering.

Zeus guides you here, my guest; here find repose.
Drain this warm milk, and at my hearthstone
    doze,
Lulled by the lazy tinkling of the spring,
Or view through the pale glow of evening
Towering Olympus and Thymphrestes' snows,
Or farther yet Eubaea's circling seas
And somber Callidrome and Oeta's crest,
The pyre at once and shrine of Heracles,
Or, outlined by the incandescent West,
Parnassus, where 'neath shining laurel trees,
From dusk to dawn, proud Pegasus finds rest.

The Flute

T IS TWILIGHT and the white doves streak the sky.
Come, amorous goatherd, quit the darkling meads.
Here the cool fountains plash among the reeds,
And here my tender flute-notes swell and sigh.
Under this shady plane-tree let us lie
In the soft herbage, while your wild goat speeds
Through clover dells and thyme-clad hills, nor
    heeds
Its timid kid that calls with quavering cry.
Come, hear my flute, of seven hemlock stems,
Wax-joined. Now gay, now grave, it sings or moans
In joyous carols or sad requiems.
Come, learn Silenus' art, his melting tones;
And those deep sighs that hint love's secret wounds
Shall be transmuted to melodious sounds.

Trebbia

PALE DAWNS the direful day upon the hills;
The camp awaits. Far down, the river rolls
Where the Numidian horse drink at the rills
And trumpets blare among the leafy knolls.
Though Scipio warns, and gloomy augurs frown,
Though streams are flooded and the skies hang
    wan,
Sempronius, scornful of his foe's renown,
Lifts high the fasces, and the host moves on.
With shafts of flame that toward the black clouds
    stream,
Far to the north Insubrian hamlets gleam;
Loud swells the Afric elephant's hoarse cry.
Hid in the rondure of a shadowy arch,
Hannibal, jubilant, hears drawing nigh
The heavy tramp of legions on the march.

The Cydnus

THRONED IN triumphal azure glows the sun,
Through somber waves the silvery trireme flies,
On the still air the flute-notes fall and rise,
And rustling silks perfume the galleon.
Keen as the hawk that like a gonfalon
Rides at the prow, with her devouring eyes
Proud Cleopatra 'gainst the evening skies
Gleams like a bird of prey no flight may shun.
Now Tarsus looms, where Antony disarmed
Awaits the swart Egyptian, whose warm breast
Shines roseate in the rosy-glowing West
Mid kissing Zephyrs by her beauty charmed—
Nor feels, lifting the flower-strewn seas, the breath
Of those twin deities Desire and Death.

Imperator

AFTER FIERCE battle-shock and bloody rout,
Rallied by tribune and centurion,
The cohorts stood. The loud triumphal shout
And smell of carnage told of victory won.
They, numbering their dead, with clouded eye
Beheld, like leaves swept by an autumn gust,
Far off the archers of Phraortes fly
In whirling eddies through the desert dust.
Then sudden loomed above the ensanguined
     ground,
Crimson with gore from many a gaping wound,
While earth and sky rang with the trumpets' blare,
Mid purple flags, in shining panoply,
Checking his rearing horse that pawed the air,
In sunset flame the blood-stained Antony.

Antony and Cleopatra

ON THEIR HIGH terrace throned triumphantly,
They watched the sun-god over Egypt ride
And lordly Nilus through the delta glide
Past Sais and Bubastis to the sea.
The Roman in his brazen panoply,
Like one who lulls a child at eventide,
Held the voluptuous body by his side
Fast and more fast in trembling ecstasy.
Her pallid face, ringed round with odorous hair
That shed its perfume on his quickened sense,
Proffered red lips and azure eyelids fair;
But in her eyes imperial Antony
Saw, leaning toward her kiss, on an immense
High-tossing tide a hundred galleys flee.

The Fountain

THE ALTAR LIES half hid by grass and thorn.
The nameless fountain trickles drop by drop
With murmuring sighs. O weeping naiad, stop
Thy plaints, nor thy lost lover longer mourn!
The glassy pool that was your trysting-place
Is scarcely rippled by the flitting dove
When the wan moon, sole witness of your love,
Looks down at eve to mirror her white face.
More rarely the swart goatherd stoops to drink
And on the mossy marble of thy brink
Sprinkles libations from his hollow hand,
No longer seeing on this Roman shrine
The silver vase girt with a golden band.

Stained Glass

THIS SHRINE HAS SEEN fair dames and barons high,
Splendent in azure, gold, and glistering pearl,
Bow 'neath prelatic hands that sanctify
The armorial pride of marquis and of earl.
They rode to chase with horn or clarion strain,
With sword held high and falcon at the wrist,
Or fared toward distant lands, as to a tryst,
Where paynim cities front the Orient main.
Today these lords and their proud chatelaines,
With couchant greyhounds leashed in carven
    chains,
On lofty tombs of marble, black and white,
Lie moveless, voiceless, lapped in leaden dreams,
Turning their stony eyeballs, void of sight,
Toward the rose-window where the sunlight
    streams.

The Lady with the Viol

IN THE HIGH balcony whose arches give
Dream visions of Italian hills and plains,
Pale, olive-crowned, she sings melodious strains,
Frail flower that has so little time to live.
The viol, which her slender fingers play,
Beguiles the fever of her pulsing blood.
Alas! her heedless lover, far away,
Leaves this fair rose to wither in the bud.
Upon the vibrant strings, the soul divine
Of her he called his lovely Angevine
Breathes to the wandering winds her amorous woe,
As if her poet's too oblivious ear
In dusty Roman streets might haply hear
The Winnower's Song he rhymed so long ago.

The Dogaressa

ALONG THE vaulted marble portico
Stroll the magnificos, superbly stoled
In red dalmatics, splendent with the glow
Of massive collars of relucent gold.
Idly they gaze into the calm lagoon,
Their cold eyes glittering with patrician pride,
While 'neath blue skies the Adriatic tide
Lies stagnant in the hot Venetian noon.
The brilliant swarm of noble cavaliers
Trail their rich gold and purple down the stair,
Where, severed from their group as in disdain,
A beauteous dame in flowing garb appears
Of red brocade, and with ironic air
Smiles at the negro dwarf who bears her train.

The Conquistadors

LIKE FALCONS flying from their rocky nest
Whom lure of quarry on a sudden stirs,
From Palos de Moguer the mariners,
Captains and troopers, sailed into the West.
Gaily they steered, with white sails all unfurled,
To seek the gold Cipango's hills conceal,
And the bland breezes drove their steady keel
Toward the dim shoreline of the island world.
The silver moon illumed with magic gleams
The phosphorescent blue of tropic seas
That lapped their transient sleep in golden dreams,
Or drew them to the caravel's high prow
To watch the rise of unknown galaxies
From trackless tides no ship had cleft till now.

To a Dead City
Cartagena de Indias

O MOURNFUL CITY, once the ocean's queen!
In thy untraveled bay the sharks disport
While clouds hang over thy deserted port
And silent shores and oozy inlets green.
Thy ruined towers are pierced by cannonade
Of bigot foes; the moaning water swirls
Against their base and weaves a crown of pearls
Round crumbling battlement and balustrade.
Between these flaming skies and languorous seas,
Lulled by their noontide spell of slumberous ease
Or by the tropic night's lethargic calm,
Thou dreamst of the Conquistadors of old
And the dead glory of the realms of gold
In the dim shadow of the waving palm.

The Coral Reef

THE SUN illumines like a misty dawn
The watery floor of the Arabian deep,
Where shelving sands and coral caverns spawn
Strange shapes that in the weedy flora creep,
While, stained with bitter salt and iodine,
Moss, shaggy algae, sea-anemones,
Curl purple-hued and wrought in strange designs
Round crimson reefs washed by exotic seas.
A glistening fish, with ruddy scales besprent,
Midst branching madripore roams out and in,
Through the translucent azure, indolent;
Then sudden, sweeping wide his flaming fin,
Shoots down the gleaming tide, an aureoled
And quivering shaft of emerald, pearl, and gold.

Sicilian Medal

AETNA STILL yields the gold and purple wine
That warmed the verses of Theocritus,
But what Lethean cavern hides from us
That antique charm, that loveliness divine,
That face of Arethuse, or Proserpine,
Who thrilled with love the lord of Erebus,
That purple blood of old so generous,
Crossed now with Saracen and Angevine?
All things decay; the marble turns to dust;
Girgenti is a tomb, and Syracuse
Sleeps shrouded in its haze of changeful blues.
Only the antique medal or the bust
Can bring back from the pallid realm of shades
The deathless beauty of Sicilia's maids.

Funeral Lament

ON PHOCIS' STRAND, where soaring temples rise
And Pytho's dome defies the lightning's wrath,
When the spent hero trod death's somber path
Still Hellas' beauty cheered his closing eyes;
Still he beheld, set in the moonlit night,
The Ionian isles which silver billows kiss,
And round tall promontories bathed in light
Surged the low-singing seas of Salamis.
But I, the child of latest time, must lie
Mewed in a lidded coffin's close confine,
While slow chants sound and ghostly tapers shine.
Yet I too as a hero dreamed to die
On sunlit fields, and join the ancestral shades
Still young and mourned by warriors and fair maids.

The Siesta

No BUZZING insect stirs, no pilfering bee;
In the dun woods no whispering branches toss;
The dimly outlined ferns droop languidly,
Soft-pillowed on wet banks of emerald moss.
High-domed in azure deeps the noonday sun
Weaves on my lids, half closed in slumberous ease,
A roseate net, of fretted sunbeams spun,
That cross and recross in the sultry breeze.
All rainbow-hued the vagrant butterflies,
Drunk with the booty of the nectared flowers,
Whirl in a gauzy maze of flaming dyes,
While, in the golden network of the hours,
Melodious huntsman, lured by magic gleams,
I try to snare my swarm of wingèd dreams.

Sunset

DEW-DRIPPING FURZE lights up the granite dome
And paints its towering peak with sunset glow
Where, faintly streaked by shining bars of foam,
Round the last cape the soundless waters flow.
Still night descends. The cottage-haunting bird
Lies nestled in the smoke-wreathed thatch asleep;
Through gathering mists the Angelus is heard
Above the tumult of the heaving deep;
As from abysmal gulfs, the hollow dells
And black ravines resound with tinkling bells
Of weary lambs that creep into the fold.
The wind-swept clouds steer their dusk caravan
High overhead, and the sun shuts the gold
Flamboyant branches of its crimson fan.

Sea Breeze

WINTER HAS MADE the hills and meadows bare.
Nature lies dead. On these gray Breton rocks
That brave the wild Atlantic's ceaseless shocks
The burnished weeds hang shivering in the air.
Yet from far off a faint aroma comes,
Borne on the wind across the trackless seas;
Its perfume breeds delicious ecstasies,
And its strange spell my wondering senses numbs.
Whence does it rise? It drifts three thousand miles
From shores remote where shining Indian isles
Swoon in the radiance of the westering sun;
And gazing seaward from my beacon tower
On Cymric reefs where streaming ebb-tides run,
I breathe the fragrance of a tropic flower.

On a Broken Statue

THE CLEMENT MOSS has veiled those mournful
    eyes,
Since in this pathless wild no hand benign
Pours offerings of white milk and ruddy wine
To the carved Pan that marked its boundaries,
And all around the half-hid marble rise
Green myrtle-sprays and multicolored vine
Whose trailing blossoms cling and intertwine
In tangled splendor of autumnal dyes.
The slanting shafts of light that pierce the trees
Burnish his eyes like gold; his face, o'errun
By ivy red and clustered goldenrod,
Shines with new life; and the caressing breeze,
The fitful shadows, and the moving sun
Make of the ruined stone a living god.

GABRIEL VICAIRE
1848–1900

Comes My Love

TRIPPING through the meadowland
Where it joins the Bettaut grove,
Bearing wildflowers in her hand,
Comes my love, my love, my love.

Iris seems she or Aurora,
Or the garden goddess Flora,
Bringing me the daybreak's gold
In her mantle's dewy fold.

When I see her emerald eyes
And her bosom's veilèd snows,
I am like the bee that flies
Round and round a budding rose.

Queenly blossom! I'm her lover,
Gladly lifting up my head
Like the humble sprig of clover
Springing where her footsteps tread.

Cherries red that ripest be
On the branches' bending tips
Seem less ruddy ripe to me
Than the redness of her lips.

Sing, my heart, till now unstirred,
Sing as gay as yonder bird.
How the waters brighter gleam
As she leans above the stream!

O green bushes, hedges high,
Coverts apt for lovers' hiding
When in grassy beds they lie
With the pale moon o'er them gliding!

Do not let your somber shadows
Darkly round her fall and float
When she trips across the meadows
In her scarlet petticoat.

Here she comes, my sweet, my darling,
Dazzling me with sparkling glance,
Blackbird, wagtail, linnet, starling,
Piping music to her dance.

All the charms of thousand springs
With their magic grace enfold her,
All the joys the season brings
Thrill my heart when I behold her.

JEAN RICHEPIN
1849–1926

Speak Not to Me of Spring

SPEAK NOT TO ME of Spring when the warm sap,
  Teeming in nature's veins, swells, buds, and
    blooms;
Nay, speak of Winter, whose snow-covered lap
  Hints of unending sleep in marble tombs.
Hail, Winter! In the spirit's dismal deeps
  Thy melancholy wakes an answering rhyme,
Season of death that in the darkness weeps,
  Wearing funereal weeds for Summer's prime.
Too gay is April aureoled with flowers,
  Flame-helmeted July, or August swart;
My somber spirit loves a sky that lowers
  And fields as barren as my own tired heart,
Horizons dark with snow whose steadfast flakes
  Form a white lint that sifts in still repose
Down o'er my melancholy dreams and makes
  Them sleep like a hurt child whose eyelids close.
We dream, O snow! to see thy avalanche
  Bury life's empty hopes and vain remorse,
To see thy spreading shroud the champaign blanch
  Till all the world appear a white-robed corse.
Nature, outworn by myriad transformation,
  Shuts her tired fingers, that at last rebel
Against the sterile task-work of creation,
  And sounds unto the world its funeral knell.
Then, making the vast universe her tomb,
  Outstretched with closed eyes and impassive mien,
Draped in a shroud of snow, she waits her doom,
  And quenches stars and moon that she may die
    unseen.

STÉPHANE MALLARMÉ
1842–1898

Apparition

SAD SHONE the moon, and tearful seraphim,
Adream mid dew-drenched flowers, calmly drew
From sobbing viols notes that seemed to swim
White in the pale corolla's swaying blue.
It was the blessèd day of your first kiss.
My thought-sick fantasy, so fain to feast
On perfume of old woes in hours of bliss,
Played with sad dreams that come when joy has
     ceased
And its sweet blossom has been culled and scented.
But wandering lone and vaguely discontented,
Sudden I saw your sun-illumined hair,
And in the evening light you stood before me
So wreathed in happy smiles you seemed to be
That old-time fairy floating on the air,
With golden chaplet crowned, who sportively,
Breaking my infant sleep, from shining jars
Showered me with white bouquets of perfumed
     stars.

PAUL VERLAINE
1844–1896

The Nightingale

LIKE TWITTERING birds in scattered flight
Old memories in my soul alight,
And the lone fountain of regret
Tosses in air its lessening jet
With silvery notes that faint and die
Into a melancholy sigh.
Then silence falls on wood and wold;
No linnets pipe, no sparrows scold.
Yet one bird sings, the lonely one
Whose voice I loved in days bygone,
That voice, the sweetest ever heard,
Whose music mourns an absent bird,
Singing as on that far-off day,
But languid now its plaintive lay.
In silver mists the solemn moon,
Set in the sultry air of June,
Hangs heavy on the silent night,
Locked in a pale of azure light,
Outlining in its windless deeps
The branch that sighs, the bird that weeps.

Love's Melting Mood

TEACH ME, love, thy melting mood
In this forest solitude
Where the wind-tossed blossoms dance—
Languid love with drooping wings,

Like the birdling choir that sings
In gray twilight's lulling trance.

O the murmur fresh and faint,
Twittering note of soft complaint,
Like the gently plashing sound
Of the grasses and the stones
Where the winding brooklet moans
On the golden-sanded ground!

Whose this voice that seems to weep
Where lone meadows lie asleep?
Tell me, sweetest, is it thine?
How the love-notes wind and wend
Through the balmy night and blend
Mine with thine, and thine with mine!

Moonlight

YOUR SPIRIT is a landscape exquisite
Where masks and mummers flutter merrily,
Strumming the lute and dancing, yet a bit
Sad in their quaint fantasticality.
In minor key the fluting notes express
Victorious love more joyous than our dreams;
Yet, half mistrustful of this happiness,
The lute-strains faint among the pale moonbeams—
Calm, pallid beams that sorrowfully mount
Where leaf-hid songbirds twitter drowsily,
And tossed in silver spray the slender fount
Among white marbles sobs in ecstasy.

After Three Years

Pushing the loose-hinged gate, again I view
The old familiar paths across the lawn,
The shrubbery all rosy in the dawn,
And glistening flowers top-heavy with the dew.
Nothing is changed or gone: the humble bower
Buried in climbing vines, the melody
The gurgling fountains made, and hour on hour
The plaintive sighing of the aspen-tree;
The rose still trembles as of old; I see
The stately lily bending in the breeze,
And every lark seems the same lark to me,
While yonder from the avenue of trees
Peeps out Velleda's battered statuette,
Slender, in the faint-scented mignonette.

Cat and Lady

A lady playing with her cat—
What sight more pretty, pray, than that?
The hand so light, the paw so white,
Thrust and parry in the night.
The lady hides in silken glove,
So fine her pet can scarcely graze her,
Pink agate nails that darting move,
More sharp and shining than a razor.
The sly cat, too, in velvet paws
Hides momently her deadly claws—
But ah! the devil claims his share.
His loud laugh rends the veil of night,
While twinkle in the sulphurous air
Four spots of phosphorescent light.

Sentimental Duo

IN THE OLD solitary park
Two vague forms wandered in the dark.
Their eyes seemed dead, their lips ice-cold,
Their speech was like a tale twice-told.
In the old solitary park
Their past walked with them in the dark.

"Do you recall that night, moonlit?"
"Nay, why should I remember it?"

"Does not your heart thrill at my name
With dreamy joy?" "Time cooled our flame."

"Here in that blessèd long-ago
Your lips touched mine!" "Ah, did they so?"

"How sweet was love, how dear our past!"
"But love is fled; it did not last."

Thus walked they through the dewy grass;
Only the lone night heard them pass.

Lady Mouse

LADY mouse trots
Black in the evening gray,
Lady mouse trots
Gray in the darkling day.

Chimes the loud bell:
Ye good prisoners, sleep!
Chimes the loud bell:
May your slumbers be deep.

Let come no bad dreams;
Dream only of love;
Let come no bad dreams
While the stars shine above.

How brilliant the moonlight!
Now all are asleep.
How brilliant the moonlight!
The shadows how deep!

A cloud hangs o'erhead,
How black lies the lawn!
A cloud hangs o'erhead,
Lo! now comes the dawn.

Lady mouse trots
Pink in the moonlight blue,
Lady mouse trots,
Lazy slumber, adieu!

Snowflakes

In the unending
Monotonous plain,
Stray snowflakes descending
Shine white through the rain.

The sky it is ashen
With never a glimmer
Of Pleiad's pale passion
Or Dian's faint shimmer.

Like nebulous clouds
The gray oaks are swaying,
With mist-woven shrouds
Their dead boughs overlaying.

The sky it is ashen
With never a glimmer
Of Pleiad's pale passion
Or Dian's faint shimmer.

How wild the winds blow,
O ravens hoarse-throated!
How deep lies the snow,
O wolves so thin-coated!

In the unending
Monotonous plain,
Stray snowflakes descending
Shine white through the rain.

Moonbeams

THE MOONBEAMS blanch
The woods that glitter;
On every branch
The birdlings twitter,
Perched just above
My love, my love.

The pool begets,
When dies the breeze,
The silhouettes
Of willow-trees,
Through which wind streams
And wakes strange dreams.

A tender peace, infinite, soft,
Folds like white fleece
Round us from aloft,
Where Mary's star
And the angels are.

Autumn Music

MY heart-strings throb
When violins sob
  In autumn woods;
Again relive
Days fugitive
  And languorous moods.

Vainly distraught
By haunting thought,
  I cannot sleep;
But all alone,
All woebegone,
  I dream and weep.

And then I go
Where wild winds blow,
  Drifting in grief
Now here, now there,
I ask not where,
  Like a dead leaf.

In Darkness I Grope

IN darkness I grope,
  Night's candles expire;
Sleep, every hope!
  Sleep, every desire!
So somber my mood,
  Without thought, without aim,
Things evil, things good,
  To me are the same.
Like a nest set adrift on the wave,

Like a cradle that's rocked in a cave,
   Where the night mists hang deep,
Where the shadows lie chill,
   Softly, softly, I sleep.
Be still, oh, be still!

Rain

O SOFTLY dropping rain,
Falling on earth and roof;
For a heart filled with pain,
O the soft-singing rain!

Tears well within my heart
Like rain that softly falls;
'Tis the rain's counterpart,
This weeping in my heart.

O tears without a cause!
O my disheartened heart!
Heart that obeys no laws—
O tears without a cause!

O heart so full of pain,
Unmoved by love or hate,
Why weep as weeps the rain?
O heart so full of pain!

Wisdom

I SEE THE quiet heavens outspread,
      So blue, so calm;
A tall tree overhead
      Sways like a palm.

The bell high-hung in cloudless sky
    Melodious rings,
And in the tree-tops nigh
    A birdling sings.

O God, O God, were this life mine,
    Simple and still,
Then might this peace divine
    My spirit fill.

Tell me, thou doleful one,
    So full of tears,
Tell me, what hast thou done
    With thy lost years?

CHARLES VAN LERBERGHE
1861–1907

The Rosary

REFLECT, O soul serene,
Blue-eyed as heaven above,
That here there lives no pain,
But only love!
We dwell in solitude,
No care shall here intrude,
Let peace descend on all
When nightly shadows fall.
Forget the world, forget
Its toil and fret,
And to the happy gardens come;
Come to the still retreat
Where in their flowery home
The light-winged choir of hours beget
The smiling hopes and dreams that yet
Shall make life wholly sweet.

Circling the basin in their round,
As 'twere a brow with blossoms crowned,
A rosary of maidens blond
Turns and eddies round the blue
Waveless waters of the pond.
Then they halt,
And with slow return renew
The chain of blossoms that they strew
In the basin's sunlit blue
Imaging the azure vault.
Each one gives her tiny hand

To her neighbor in the band,
And they march in circling rank
Round and round the flowery bank,
Singing ever as they go
Where the crystal waters flow,
Singing soft a liquid hymn,
Whilst their faces, fair and blond,
In the fountain, white and wanned,
Dance and swim
Mid the glimmers yellowish
Of the darting golden fish.

MAURICE MAETERLINCK
1862–

The Quest

THIRTY YEARS I've sought him, sisters,
    When will he appear?
Thirty years I've wandered, sisters,
    Yet he draws not near.

Thirty years I've journeyed, sisters,
    Tired, through stony ground;
Everywhere he calls me, sisters,
    Yet is never found.

Now my heart grows fainter, sisters,
    Loose your sandal-shoon;
Now the day is dying, sisters,
    Soul and body swoon.

You are new-fledged virgins, sisters,
    My vain quest renew;
Take my pilgrim-staff, sweet sisters,
    Go and seek him, too.

PAUL FORT
1872–1931?

Mystic Eyes

How CLEAR the streamlet's bed I see!
Or is it I myself am seen?
The forest seems a single tree
Reflected in the watery sheen.

The cloudless sky above my head
Is hidden by a swaying bough,
Whence mystic eyes austerely shed
A radiance never known till now.

Are they arboreal eyes that ope
Through wind-swept leaves of shimmering gold,
Outlining 'neath the starry cope
Diana's statue, marble cold?

Where Is Happiness?

It is in this meadow nigh;
Run there quickly, run there quickly!
It is in this meadow nigh;
Run there quickly, ere it fly.

If you'd catch this passer-by,
Run there quickly, run there quickly!
If you'd catch this passer-by,
Run there quickly, ere it fly.

In the barley or the rye,
Run there quickly, run there quickly!

In the barley or the rye,
Run there quickly, ere it fly.

Where the hornèd rams you spy,
Run there quickly, run there quickly!
Where the hornèd rams you spy,
Run there quickly, ere it fly.

Where the streamlet hurries by,
Run there quickly, run there quickly!
Where the streamlet hurries by,
Run there quickly, ere it fly.

Where red cherries hang on high,
Run there quickly, run there quickly!
Where red cherries hang on high,
Run there quickly, ere it fly.

Leap that hedgerow just ahead,
Run there quickly, run there quickly!
Leap that hedgerow just ahead,
Run there quickly—it has fled!

CHARLES GUÉRIN
1873–1907

Elegy

O TRAGIC NIGHT! O night of black despair!
I stifle in my cold cell's chambered air,
Where hour on hour unrestingly I pace
And find in grief no lucid interspace.
My casement, flung wide to the invasive moon,
Reveals the soaring mountain-top aswoon,
With its pale retinue of clustering clouds
In the dim azure, joining star to star.
Light zephyrs fan my brow, and faint and far
A cascade tinkles down some hidden hill,
And dreamily I hear the watchdogs bark.
Leaning upon the granite hard and chill,
Absorbed in solitary grief, I stand
Cursing these blue skies and this verdant land
Where earth and heaven seem blent in whispered
    love,
For life's rich tides through barren shallows move,
Becalmed in havens of lethargic ease,
Or roll in riot down to unplumbed seas.
I have not known the calm thoughts that appease,
Nor those high moods the smiling gods approve!
My valiant pride is gone, my sighing breath
Invokes the dream of love, the hope of death.
    Do I behold you, virgin, shadowy bride,
Loved apparition standing at my side,
Like a spent lamp whose faintly glimmering ray
Dies on the air? Ah, do not fade away!
So sweet your silence and your eyes so bright

That my too blissful sobs die on the night!
Is't you, indeed? You, whom my somber mood
So vainly yearned for in my solitude?
My love, my angel bride? Do these rich charms,
These snowy limbs, lie pillowed in my arms?
You shall be mine forever, you shall sleep
Beside me wrapped in heavenly bliss so deep
That joy shall live immortal in your soul
And love shall find in love its perfect goal.
   O God! I thank thee. By thy mercy blest,
I hold my living dream clasped to my breast.
Speak to me, love! Nay, rather, do not speak,
But hover silently, till your warm cheek
Pale in the radiance of yon lingering star
That hangs upon the morning's orient bar.
The dew already gilds the laden grasses,
And Dawn, that in her magic mirror glasses
With doubled charm the beauty day discloses,
Pours on the earth her apronful of roses.
Far off the anvil rings its Angelus,
And thousand cattle slowly file past us,
Bell after bell, while, on the breezes borne,
Clamor the shrill notes of the shepherd's horn.
The valley now lies bathed in emerald light,
The hamlet in green meadows flashes bright,
Window to window throws responsive flames,
And morn's fresh life pours through their vine-clad
    frames.
Trembling with joy, I kiss the morning dew
From your wet lids, and bid the fleeting hours
Bind your white brow with wreaths of odorous
    flowers
That bloom immortal in the land of love.
Youth's ruddy wine throbs in our pulsing veins,
Bliss springs anew, our ancient sorrow wanes,

And Destiny, in morning's splendent cope,
Borrows the flaming monstrance of the sun
To bless two wedded souls that, blent in one,
Thrill with the selfsame dream, the selfsame hope,
And, while the paling stars grow faint above,
Weep in the speechless ecstasy of love.
   Love! Love! Alas! Behold the slow day rise
From the vale's lunar blue. See these cold skies,
This river, murmuring in the sighing breeze,
While I, forlornly reft of sweet heartsease,
Have only in vain dreams clasped my pale bride.
Her throbbing bosom was this barren stone;
The tremulous poplars by the fountainside
Fooled my sick fancy with their tender tone;
And all these deep delights that seemed so sweet
Bloomed in a heart too skilled in self-deceit.
Nay, close the casement! Stifle all desire!
Lean o'er this gloomy hearth where burns no fire;
Its twin chimeras are the counterpart
Of the sad dreams that brightened my sad heart.
And since all things are vain, since fortune dashes
The cup from parched lips, since the poet's art
Can still no pain, since love's flame burns to ashes,
And darkness swallows all that man has wrought,
Seek man's sole refuge from insensate thought:
Make your lone bed a sepulchre, and sleep
Where vanquished souls their voiceless concourse
   keep.

ROSEMONDE GÉRARD
(Mme Rostand)
1870–

The Sleeping Beauty

Ringed by her golden hair the princess sleeps
On her white pillow with a face of snow,
And vaguely smiles at the sweet dream that peeps
From lids that closed a hundred years ago.
Her head droops sidewise in the pale moonbeams
Which through the colored panes impearl her brow,
While magic stillness seals the founts and streams
And songless birds sit tranced on every bough.
Near-by her little page has drowsed yearlong,
Clasping numb fingers round his mouldering flute,
That once had lulled with many an old-time song
The maid that sleeps now, like its music, mute,
Still waiting for Prince Charming to appear
And kiss her back to life this hundredth year.

JEAN MORÉAS
1856–1910

Proserpine among the Violets

IN THIS BLITHE vale where thy light footsteps
   stray
Among the beds of tender violets,
O Proserpine! beware the fatal nets
Of that dark fowler come to snatch away
A bride to people Hades. Pluto's heart
Is pierced by Eros with the selfsame dart
That thrills in spring with love's delicious fear
The migrant bird and the fleet-footed deer.
List! At his wild shouts the infernal steeds
Toss high their quivering heads that shun the light
And crush with iron hoof the nodding reeds
And asphodels that girdle all in white
The marshy meads where Camarina lies.
In Enna's vale low droop the fainting flowers,
And where Cyane's crystal waters rise
Her fountained tears congeal in sudden showers.
Soon of a sunless realm shalt thou be queen,
Blond Ceres' child, far from the meadows green,
Doomed evermore, among the voiceless dead,
The radiance of those peerless eyes to shed
On amorous ghosts who pace that pale demesne
And, seeing thee, renew those ancient woes
That by black Lethe's water sought repose.

O Airy Heavens

O AIRY HEAVENS that pour your golden light
Upon the shining girdle of blue seas!
O curling smoke whose wreaths hang silver-bright
On my loved cot, set in black cypress trees!

O olive-clad Cephissian stream antique,
Still vocal of the Sophoclean age,
Temples, and shattered marbles that yet speak
Of Attic glories marred by Time's fell rage!

Parnes and proud Hymettus, that still soar
Out of the shadows toward the flaming sun,
I love your mossy ruins, your curved shore,
Your loveliness that braves oblivion.

After Long Years

AFTER LONG years again I see my home,
Its nest-filled poplars, its bird-haunted lawn,
And this same arbor through whose rose-clad dome
Shone Venus' star, and Sirius, and the dawn.

But the green turf where sanded pathways meet,
The old familiar outline of the shore,
And the bright flowers, more golden than the
    wheat,
Gaze in my face, but know me now no more.

Acolyte

HERE STRETCHED the pathways where my foot-
  steps roamed
When leaves embrowned on wind-tossed stems
Flung to the ceiling azure-domed
Their golden-tinted diadems.

Here languid autumn moves with measured tread
By somber wood and reedy mere,
And wounded memories yet uncomforted
Here find their past, their dead dreams here.

O fading leaves, O blossoms crimson-hued!
Your pale smile yields me no delight,
No semblance of your still beatitude
To me, mute sorrow's acolyte.

Compensation

I COMMUNE with the dead and dwell in tombs,
Foe to myself; I neither get nor keep;
My glory is men's mock; the crow exhumes
The grain I plant but never come to reap.

Yet I lament not, though the north wind's ire
Conjoin with the world's scorn to fret and sting,
Since, when I touch Apollo's golden lyre,
Ever its learnèd notes more purely ring.

This Shadow of a Dream

SAY NOT: Life is a flowery bed of ease;
Heart, speak not so, by noble impulse fired.
Nor do not say: Life is a long disease;
That speaks an unstrung heart, too quickly tired.

But smile when spring leads in her flowery train,
Weep with the north wind and the moaning stream;
Taste every pleasure, suffer every pain,
And say: How sweet—this shadow of a dream.

The Rose

O LOVELY ROSE, quick blown and quickly faded,
To Cypris dear and to the poet's lyre,
The garden's pride, whose transient charms per-
  vaded
The odorous air your damask leaves suspire;

O queen and darling of the tender spring,
When autumn's rust embrowns your vermeil hues,
Your warm heart, opening to the winter's sting,
Will hail sweet death as if she were your muse.

Ah, Could I Too!

THE GARDEN ROSE that I had plucked, half-
  scorning
Its paling hue, vaunt-courier of decay,
Divorced from the blue sky and dewy morning,
In this small vase has lived its little day.

But when chill evening came to cancel all
Its fragile bloom and blanch its damask dye,
It bowed its head and let its petals fall,
Indifferent if Death pause or pass it by.

Ah, could I too so calmly play my part,
Nor let old memories cloud the passing hour!
Too much of ancient grief bides in this heart
That views with pain the specter of a flower.

Discord

THE ROSE I loved doth hourly fade away;
Not every season is the time of flowers;
Too long the Zephyrs have prevailed; today
Belongs to chilling winds and icy showers.

Ah, Joy! why will you cross my melody
With lilting strains? Know you not it is folly
To steal into my music and to tease
Strings consecrate to tristful Melancholy?

The Ivy

I LOVE TO SEE the rustic ivy wreathe
Some ruined monument,
And in its tendrils gracefully ensheathe
A plane-tree earthward bent.

Yet most I love cool fountains overhung
With somber foliage
Where plaintive waters softly plash among
Rocks grey with age.

Dead Leaves

WHEN THE DEAD leaves, by russet autumn burned,
Strew the dark pond behind the ruined mill,
When whirling winds the gaping doorways fill
And the blank space in which the mill-wheel turns,

Then will I come and seat me on this bank
Beside the wall where reddening ivies gleam,
To view hour-long beneath the leafage dank
My image and the sun's die on the stream.

O Sister Spirit

O SISTER SPIRIT, toward your cloudless brow,
While dreary Autumn haunts the withering bough,
And toward the shimmering haven of your eyes,
My wingèd thoughts in melancholy guise
Mount like a whitening fountain in the blue—
The tender azure, pale October's hue,
That paints its soundless languor on the tide
O'er whose clear depths the sere leaves deathward
   glide,
Breeze-borne down channeled basins crystal-bright
Where a gilt sunbeam trails its lengthening light.

The Lament of Hyagnis

GREEN REALM of Cybele, whose waving trees
Gave airy perch to the shy nightingales,
How thin your shadows now where the cool breeze
Scarce moves sere boughs whose once-fresh verdure
   pales!

Like thee, autumnal wood, I sadly wait
The melancholy turn of the spent year,
And bid farewell to my dear spring, which late
Mirrored its graces in thy silver mere.
No more upon my pipe with pleasing pains,
    Bedded in thyme and lush trefoil,
I cheer the wood-nymph with my rustic strains
    Or goatherd at his toil.
Belovèd pipe, blest source of my sweet song,
Thy merry notes are mute, and thy soft sigh
No more the echoing hills and glades prolong,
Poor useless reed, grown sapless now and dry.

The Fairies

WEE GOLDILOCKS in shining frocks,
That lapped my soul in slumber deep,
Wee Goldilocks in shining frocks,
That brought me blessèd balm of sleep
In magic woods where sweet content
By magic rites is brewed and blent,
And gentle gnomes that in my sleep,
Above my flowery pillow bent,
So courteously did present
A golden scepter in my sleep—
I know it was but cheat and lure,
These songs and scepters in the wood,
Yet still in dreams I hold it sure
And would not waken if I could,
For all it be but cheat and lure.

ALBERT SAMAIN
1858–1900

My Soul Is an Infanta

MY SOUL is an Infanta, purple-robed,
Lone as a phantom ship on phantom seas,
Glassing strange semblances of royal ease
In sculptured mirrors shining golden-globed.

Couched by her chair, and waiting her command,
Two carven hounds with melancholy eyes
Dream of the chase they nobly symbolize
In some untrodden vale of fairyland.

Her darling page, called Once-Upon-A-Time,
Chants amorous songs o'er which she fondly
    lingers,
Seeking the mystic meaning of his rhyme
In the red tulip clasped by her white fingers.

The long lawns vanish in the fronded green;
White statues, fountains, soaring balustrades,
And thousand mystic charms all unforeseen
Draw her grave eyes along the wooded glades.

Her even mood is gentle and resigned,
Unruffled by the iron laws of fate,
Yet full of wistful pity, intertwined
With pride that holds aloof inviolate.

Quiet her voice, yet thrilled with sobbing notes
Of sad lament at some impending doom,
When through her dream the proud Armada floats,
Bearing its freight of heroes to the tomb.

By the long twilight's purple tranced, she sees
Visions of pomp imperial, castle walls
On which the light in mellow splendor falls,
And pictured knights in shining panoplies.

These ravishments, snatched from oblivion,
Soothe her sick heart, so long to joy denied,
While the glad vision and the golden sun
Irradiate her soul with regal pride.

Thus wanly smiling on her fevered dreams,
She finds new calm in still soliloquies,
Bidding the world, like far-off murmuring seas,
Lure her sad soul with transitory gleams.

No passion stirs the pale deep of her eyes,
Haunted by visioned ghosts of cities dead,
As, gliding through the silent halls, she spies
The spectral trace of times forever fled.

Holding her budding tulip, purple-lobed,
While the spent fountains sing low monodies,
She stands between tall mirrors, golden-globed,
In the bright oriel 'neath the marble frieze,
Lone as a phantom ship on phantom seas.

My soul is an Infanta, purple-robed.

Watteau

MISTY woods shine amethyst,
Venus' star mounts overhead,
Violins call to the tryst
Maids by singing lovers led.
Hands in fond hands lingering lie,
Trancèd eyes reflect the sky,

Rosy-hued the fountains flow,
And diaphanous through the trees
Floats upon the odorous breeze,
Between Estelle and Cydalise,
The shining spirit of Watteau.

Kindling with magic spells love's tender fire,
He touched with glowing tints its pretty folly,
And lent a soul to languorous Desire,
Seating it at the feet of Melancholy.

Down forest glades, their gold-tipped canes a-
     swinging,
Slim shepherds pace with mincing shepherdesses,
Where echoing groves and silver fountains singing
Add finer grace to trailing courtly dresses.

The dying roses scent the bluish air,
And the hushed garden woos to amorous thought
That soothes with quick-snatched kisses love's
     despair,
And pensive hopes with nature's beauty fraught.

Love's pilgrims seek a lovers' fairyland;
Their gold-rimmed galley steers in seaward flight;
The dreaming lover hears from the far strand
A dying flute-note thrill the crystal night.

Ah, could I, too, to those bright mansions go,
And live one hour in that enchanted world,
Where by the silver shore the sails are furled
And dim Cythera lies in moonlit glow.

Fans coquettishly eclipse
Love-notes shaped on ruby lips,

While white fingers snatch and prop
Curls that down white foreheads drop.
Soft the twilight shadows fall;
Silence hovers over all;
Agnes smiles; Lothario
Lays his viol on his cloak;
And above these gentle folk
Floats past branching elm and oak
The shining spirit of Watteau.

Pannyra

DEEP SILENCE holds all in a sudden trance
As golden-heeled Pannyra treads the dance.
The flute invites her with its silver sound,
Fold upon fold her white veils gird her round,
Forward she darts; her light steps cross and twine;
Her circling arms in movement serpentine
Shake the thin gauze into fantastic curves;
It billows out, and leaps, and spreads, and swerves
In rhythmic splendor over breast and thigh;
She seems a flower, a flame, a butterfly;
Breathless they stare; she sways, she floats, she
    swims,
The madness of the dance invades her limbs,
Wilder she whirls in ever swifter flight,
Aureoled in fire by the bright torches' light,
Then sudden stops—and in the silent hall
They watch the waving draperies slowly fall
In narrowing spirals, and, subsiding, flow
Round her high-pointed breast and limbs of snow,
Till in a light divine the golden-heeled
Pannyra's naked beauty stands revealed.

Xanthis

THE TENDER GRASS and the fresh morning breeze
Are wet with mist that floats upon the hills,
And in the woods, beneath wide-branching trees,
Thin shining webs o'erhang the tinkling rills.
Through darkling thickets stealing unespied
The placid waters cast a furtive gleam,
Where Xanthis, robe and sandals thrown aside,
Clasping a birch that hangs above the tide,
Half-leaning, views her beauty in the stream.
All white she stands, all white her image dances,
And the clear brook paints to her circling glances
Her rounded bosom and her milk-white arms,
Her shining loins, her hair, her violet eyes,
While her quick hand, in innocent surprise,
From all onlookers save the woods and skies
Tries modestly to veil her glowing charms.
But suddenly a bellowing cry resounds,
And Xanthis, trembling like a hunted deer,
Sees in the glassy pool, with headlong bounds,
From the blue depths a hornèd faun uprear.

The Soap Bubble

BATHYLLUS in the clucking poultry-yard
Sits by his foamy bowl, and long and hard
Blows through a straw. The soapy waters bubble
And rise and overflow. Vain the child's trouble,
And only acrid savors burn his tongue.
But no—at last a dancing bubble, hung
From his wet straw, is lengthened, thinned, dis-
    tended;

It floats in air, a filmy globe suspended;
And still he blows and still the globule grows
And shines prismatic. In its orb are seen
The rainbow tints of dawn. The meadow's green
Shifts on its crystal wall in whirling course
With trees, and house, and road, and flying horse.
More marvelous it shines, more roseate:
Behold it loosen, veer, and oscillate,
Then, pink and paling green, soar toward the sky
Farther and farther, high and yet more high
And higher still—until with dazzled eyes
Bathyllus seeks in vain his glittering prize.

HENRI DE RÉGNIER
1864–1936

The Vase

My heavy hammer rang in the clear air.
Here was the brook, the orchard there,
The meadow and the wood,
Under a sky more blue from hour to hour,
Then rosy-hued, then brown at dusk.
I rose in happy mood
At the completed rosary of hours,
Though numb with laboring from dawn to dark
Upon the marble block from which I hewed
With heavy hammer-strokes the vase yet crude—
Strokes ringing loud and glad in the bright air,
Rhythmic with the clear morn and day so fair.
The vase was issuing from the obscuring stone,
Still formless in its unshaped slenderness.
I waited now
With idle hands and furrowed brow
Day after day, still turning round
To left, to right, intent on every sound.
The marble lay untouched, the hammer dumb.
The streams
Leapt from the fountainhead all out of breath;
And still as death,
Like one who dreams,
I watched the breeze across the meadow come,
Shaking ripe fruit that fell from branch to branch.
I breathed the wind-blown scents that bore the
    tale
Of far-off flowers in some deserted vale;

Low voices floated into my daydreams,
And from the meadows and the lulling streams
Soft wailing notes of flutes.
At last I saw,
Between the gold and ochre of the leaves,
Sweep russet-legged into the golden dawn
A russet faun.
Again,
While in the greenery I watchful stood,
I saw him, newly issued from the wood,
Perch on a rock and indolently try
On his crook'd horn to catch a butterfly.
Another time
A swimming Centaur steered across the stream,
And, while the water dripped from breast and
     mane,
Pawed at the leaves that quivered all agleam,
Then snuffed the wind, and stopped, and fled
     again.
But on the morrow in the trampled grass
I saw his hoof-prints plain.
One day, again,
I saw three women pass,
Three naked nymphs with baskets full of sheaves,
Far off where the lone mountain
Impends with jutting eaves.
And there one morning by a crystal fountain
These three nymphs sported in the reeds. And one
Spoke to me, saying: "Fashion me in stone.
Even as you see my body in your thought
Let me be wrought,
And let my blithe face in the marble shine.
See how my sisters mime the dancing hours
With circling steps that twine
And recombine

And with wild strains of music intertwine."
Then two warm lips imprinted upon mine
A touch divine.
And lo! the orchard vast, the wood, the plain
Shook with strange noise, and gushing forth again,
The fountain leaped and all its waters laughed,
While the three nymphs that its clear liquid quaffed
Clasped hand in hand and danced among the
    rushes.
The ruddy fauns came thronging from the bushes,
And voices sang behind the orchard trees
With sound of flutes upon the light-winged breeze.
Sleek centaurs shook the earth with thunderous
    tread,
And the broad heavens resounded as they sped,
Bearing astraddle on their arching spine,
With thyrsis green and bellying skins of wine,
Lame satyrs bursting through a cloud of bees.
Then hirsute mouths and vermeil lips appease
Love's sting with kisses, and the maddened rout,
The heavy hoofs, the nimble feet, the snout
Protuberant, the arching back, the mane,
The flowing tunics, in swift dance insane
Rolled past me while I gravely watched their flight
And in the carven marble's glowing white
Fashioned in stone this tidal whirl of life.
The exhalations of the teeming earth
Unto a passioned ecstasy gave birth,
And, smelling odorous fruits and vintage grapes
And fetors rank that oozed from bestial shapes
Of goats and stallions, quick I followed after
Each hurrying scene to carve it in the stone,
To fix each mingled motion, tint, and tone,
Charmed by the eddying dance and pelting
    laughter,

The warm effluvium of wild flesh,
The snorting mouths and red lips dewy-fresh.
Then night descended and I turned away,
My madness dying with the dying day.
The vase was finished, body, base, and rim.
It stood there, shining in the twilight dim,
Carrying in spirals on the living stone
The circling figures, while the wind's low tone
Still brought the echoes of the dancing rout
That on the polished marble in and out
Wound silently around the massive base
'Neath white acanthus leaves that crowned the
      vase.
So in the night, where thickest shadows slept,
I cursed the dawn and in the darkness wept.

Versailles

No more, Versailles, in thousand fountains
      sings
Your wealth of waters set in myriad flowers;
No more, entwined in crowns of ancient kings,
Shine the white lilies of your odorous bowers.

No more, half-hid, the nymph glides through your
      shade;
The years have tarnished now the silver tide
That glassed in floating sheen the masquerade
Of kingly glory in its hour of pride.

Your greening basins 'neath the giant trees
Slumber in silence and oblivion,
And by their marble ledge the wandering breeze
Seeks vainly for the grace of days bygone.

But it is not your pageant and your glory
I miss, nor jewelled crown nor sceptered rod,
Nor do I scan the page of ancient story
To greet a monarch in each marble god.

What though no cascades fall with echoes strident
Round Neptune towering in his arid fount,
Lifting with regal hand his shattered trident
From wind-swept leaves that to his ankles mount.

Let but your lessened streams sing monodies
Where glooming boughs impend, and in sad pity,
With dying notes among the moss-clad trees,
Mourn your decay, O many-fountained city!

Love's Hour

I WILL NOT SPEAK the passion lodged in me
Till your dear image, in the fountain glassed,
Has palely writ in watery charactery
How brief a time your beauty's date shall last.

I will speak only when those gentle hands
Are redolent of all the season's bloom,
And when your smiling spirit understands
The tearful joy that mocks at mortal doom.

I will speak only when the flitting bees
That in the warm air tilt the drooping flowers
Have thrilled your ear with murmurous melodies
And rustic scents that blessed the sunlit hours.

I will speak only when the last red rose
Sets your white arm a-tremble on my own,
And when the shadow of the dim day's close
Subdues your spirit to a twilight tone.

The intermingled balm of night and day
So tenderly your tremulous heart shall move
That it will blend in the soft words I say
My voice, your voice, and the sweet voice of love.

The Fountain

IF YOUR STEPS lead you to this happy vale
Where through the reeds the silver fountains sing,
Remember that its tenuous charm and frail
Comes from the coolness of the bubbling spring.
And if perchance you spy the water-sprite
Sleeping, bare-limbed, lulled by its melodies,
Where, lifted on the tide, the lilies white
Flash their pure radiance through the circling trees,
Avert your eyes, and, silent, steal away,
Pleased with the music that the fountain gave,
The grateful shelter in the hot noonday,
And the cool draught drawn from the silver wave.

Troy

NOW, BY THE WHIP and heavy oar made old,
A white-haired slave, I dream of that far town
That from its hills beheld the seas unfold.
Barren are now those shores from which flow down
Slow tides that creep across the ash-strewn sand.
Cool Simois' waters and Scamander's wave
No longer slake my thirst, and if, sad slave!
Drunk with stol'n wine, I see in dreams that land
And touch with gladsome foot my native strand,
Its climbing pathways and its pastoral vales,
I know too well how soon the vision pales

And how, poor wretch, with transitory joy
I see behind long rows of Grecian sails
Shine in the evening sky a phantom Troy.

Cupid and Psyche

WHILE SOMNUS lulled you with Lethean rod
Cupid leaned toward your face in the dim night,
Holding his lamp and smiling through its light . . .
Not vainly did you dream you loved a god!
Cock-crow and dawn! But your chaste maiden-
     hood,
Pale child, could nevermore have guessed aright,
Had not the god dropped, as he turned in flight,
Three golden arrows tinct in virgin blood.
'Twas he then! 'Twas the tender god of love,
Whom Venus' cunning plots could not enmesh,
Who left resplendent in your ivory flesh
His lamp's translucent glow, as if to prove
In its soft rondure and its sinuous line
The amorous imprint of his bow divine.

Chrysilla

WHEN ON MY latest day the sun is setting,
O let not tardy Time with his sharp knife
Steal toward my couch, dry-eyed and unregretting,
To cut the thread of my too lingering life.
But may Love come? Nay, Love too was my foe,
And unappeased the cruel god were fain
To see this wounded heart in its death-throe
To life's last flower impart a crimson stain.
No, at that hour let me behold in dream,

Silent and bare and beautiful, my Youth,
Holding a rose and tossing on the stream
Its last pale petals, severed without ruth,
While sobbing fountains moan farewell, and I,
Unscathed by scythe or arrow, calmly die.

The Reed

I PLUCKED a reed, a tiny thing,
And, blowing, set the grass aquiver,
The meadowland,
The willow tree,
And, far away, the rippling river—
A little reed, a tiny thing,
Sufficed to make the forest sing.

The passers heard the song at eve,
It echoed in their thoughts;
The silence bore it and the breeze.
Subdued or clear,
Far off or near,
The passers still this music hear,
And in their heart as in the trees
Still ring its melodies.

I had no need
Save of my tiny reed,
Plucked by the fountain Love frequented,
There to retrace
With tear-stained face
The sorrows he lamented,
To make the passers weep
And the grass quiver by the stream.

A little reed, a tiny thing,
Sufficed to make the forest sing.

COMTESSE DE NOAILLES
1876–1933

The Dancer

THE SUNLIT FIELDS with summer's beauty teem,
Drenched with the scent of lemon, mint, and pine,
While June, entranced by her own sensuous charm,
Glasses her face where sleeping waters shine.

Bright butterflies weigh down the languid flowers,
Clover and balm and many an odorous plant,
Round whose sleek stems, green from the summer
      showers,
The golden shafts of sunlight glide aslant.

How gay the season! How the meadow smiles!
The lilac-bloom and the empurpled fig
Hum with wild bees, and down the woodland aisles
Swift whirring wings stir every dancing twig.

Brightening the morning with her eyes,
Bitto, the dancing-girl, with measured beat
Whirling her crotals, past the hedgerow hies,
The pebbles burning 'neath her sandaled feet.

With linen veil, green as the budding grape,
And tunic flashing round her dainty limbs,
She dances on, a frail and lovely shape,
Thrilled by the meadow-lark's exultant hymns.

She hears her mirror and her perfume-box
Rattle metallic in her osier basket,
And counts the bees that in the nodding phlox
Gleam on each flower like jewels in a casket.

What strange desires allure your dancing feet
To dare the perils of the morning hour?
Eros lies hidden in this green retreat,
And his sweet poison lurks in every flower.

Return to ply the tasks that you forsook;
Soon the hot noonday sun will ride o'erhead;
Go, sprinkle your parched oyster-plants and look
If night has chilled your seeded garden bed.

But, clasping her two hands behind her neck,
The dancer smiles; the sage advice is lost;
Tumultuous breezes lift the folds that deck
Her swaying form; her veils fly zephyr-tossed.

Heady aromas through the blue air flit
And swathe her light soul in an amorous dream;
She steals between the waving wheat to sit
By the calm pool and watch its silvery gleam.

To the warm sun, as to a wanton lover,
The peony lays bare her flaunting charms,
And blushful windflowers languorously uncover
Their odorous breasts and faint in summer's arms.

What lubric ardor in the herbage stirring
Clings round your feet and steals into your breast?
What febrile breezes on your flushed cheeks erring
Make your soul quiver like a pendulous nest?

Down the rough slope, where the blue cassia
     weaves
Its silken net, young Crito leads his goats
To the cool fount where, girt by lily leaves,
Sweet Bitto's image on the water floats.

"Sweeting," he cries, "here your glad goatherd
     comes,

Bearing rich gifts: white cheese like the round
  moon,
An osier crate all full of purple plums,
And this smooth pipe which graven flowers festoon."

He does not woo with timid words alone;
His arm steals round her, and his amorous play
Charms her soft sense. In melting undertone
She whispers Yes, who should have answered Nay.

Love's fiery ordeal leaves her grave and pale,
Her tender body racked, her sweet dream lost.
Ah, Bitto! many a day will you bewail
Your fond delusion and its heavy cost.

These burning kisses that the poets sing
Lure the tired soul through love's dark labyrinth—
Your pangs came from the fecund season's sting,
From smell of mulberry and terebinth.

Seeking to cure with passion's untried charms
A love born of the fields and the sun's fire,
You clasped the goatherd in your naked arms,
Who left you cloyed and wan with sick desire.

In love with the fresh morn, the glancing light,
You sought on the rude herdsman's wheedling lips
The season's spell, the thrill, the dear delight
Of tossing blossoms where the wild bee sips.

You dreamed your heavy heart was like the nest
That bends the tender branch where it reposes;
You hoped that, falling on the goatherd's breast,
'Twould shed its petals like the ripened roses.

The cunning spell by which your soul was moved
Could bring to your lorn heart no anodyne:
It was the tender summer that you loved,
The aromatic bloom, the odorous vine.

Invocation

PRIAPUS, god benign of orchard bloom,
I bring these wreathèd orange flowers and these
Green sprigs of parsley, fresh from earth's dark
    womb,
And firstling pods where swell the tender peas.

Thou garden-god, whose smile all lovers court,
Bring Daphnis to me, that too timid swain,
That foe to Eros and to amorous sport,
O cruel Eros, cause of all my pain!

Belovèd, in the sultry noontide hour
Come to me, come, the while your wild goats
    browse,
Kiss upon kiss on my red lips to shower
And in my cup of ash to pledge our vows.

My bare feet like two snowy pigeons rest
Perched on the sandals' edge, my shining arms
Are smooth as polished reeds, and my white breast
Is redolent of thousand perfumed charms.

Behold my woolly lambs: their downy fleece
Lines the soft bed where love shall find repose,
Noting the gradual season's slow increase
In smell of ripening pear and budding rose.

O syrinx-player! when the violet light
Of evening stills the lone cicada's song,
Steal through the silent woods and moonlit night
And hour on hour love's happy rites prolong.

When the new dawn whitens the shining meads,
We'll pluck red roses from the trailing vine
And golden crocus gemmed with dewy beads
To hang in garlands on Priapus' shrine.

To Faunus

Shattered, dying garden-god—
Faun, reflect me in your eyes;
Let my image dance and nod
'Mong Elysian deities.

Go and tell the pensive dead,
Whom my childish sports delight,
How the yew trees shade my head
As I wander robed in white.

Tell them how my sunny brow
Under woolly fillets shines,
How my lips and fingers now
Smell of herbs and ripening vines.

Tell them how each nimble gesture
Shifts with every shifting shade
On the meadow's verdant vesture
By the swaying branches laid.

Tell them then how all too soon
Slumber comes to seal my eyes
While I dance beneath the moon,
Tranced by mystic melodies.

Tell them how, all white and nude,
On my snowy coverlet
My lissom limbs gleam golden-hued,
Ringed by veins all violet.

Tell them how my loosened hair
Shines like plums all wet with dew.
Tell them I am wondrous fair,
And have eyes of lunar blue.

Tell them how, when idly lying
By the fountain's brink at rest,
For a love immortal sighing
I have clasped them to my breast.

Biographical Notes and Index

BIOGRAPHICAL NOTES

ANONYMOUS: Provençal, twelfth century, and Old French, twelfth century (pp. 3–6). The early love poems of southern France, which in Provençal found expression in the songs of the *troubadours*, were divided by theme or form into many different genres. The *alba*, or "dawn song," depicts the sorrows of the lovers who must part at break of day. This theme was popular also among the *trouvères* and *jongleurs* of northern France, where it was called an *aubade*. By the twelfth century the influence from southern France found its way north and mingled with the currents that were in fashion there. The old French pastorals and romances, or ballads, usually deal with the beauties of nature and the song of birds, which are closely associated with the loves of the shepherds and shepherdesses, or with the knight who meets and woos a peasant lass. The *reverdie*, as its name implies, reflects the coming of spring. At the hands of courtly and aristocratic poets, the simple themes were treated with an artistry of form which later became fixed in technical complexities and subtle conceits. From them developed the *rondeaux* and *ballades* of the fourteenth and fifteenth centuries.

GUILLAUME DE MACHAULT (pp. 7–8) was courtier, soldier, traveller, talented musician, and the most popular poet of his day. His most important composition, *Le Voir-Dit* ("The True Story"), written when he was past sixty, relates in prose and verse his belated romance with a young aristocratic lady of Armentières. He is remembered chiefly for his skilful handling of the fixed literary forms of the *ballade*, *rondeau*, *virelay*, and *complainte*.

JEAN FROISSART (p. 9) was famous chiefly as the chronicler of feudal life, but he owed some of the favor he found with the noble great, whose deeds he described in his *Chroniques*, to his poetic talent. Besides a long romance, *Meliador*, he wrote a number of *rondeaux*, *ballades*, *virelays*, and *pastourelles*, which show the influence of Machault.

EUSTACHE DESCHAMPS (pp. 10–11) was a soldier and diplomat who held some important posts under Charles V and Charles VI, and a widely travelled person. In old age, however, he experienced some severe hardships, which may account for the disillusion his poetry expresses. Abounding in references to the events of the day, his works are of historical rather than literary interest, save for the *ballades*, *rondeaux*, and *virelays*, of which he wrote a great number.

ANONYMOUS, fifteenth century (pp. 12–13). This period has left many popular poems of unknown authorship, frequently in ballad form, which were collected and preserved in *chansonniers*.

ALAIN CHARTIER (pp. 14–16) enjoyed an immense reputation as a prose writer and poet during his long career as secretary and historian to Charles VI and Charles VII. In his *Quadrilogue-invectif* he laid bare the abuses of the feudal army and the sad plight of the peasantry. In a diatribe entitled *Le Curial* he attacked the courtiers of Charles VII. His poetical compositions include *Le Débat du réveille-matin*, *La Belle dame sans merci*, and *Le Livre des quatre dames*, from which the translated selection is taken.

CHARLES D'ORLÉANS (pp. 17–19) was the son of Louis, duc d'Orléans, and of Valentine Visconti, a Milanese princess, both of whom were great patrons of the arts. At the battle of Agincourt (1415) he was taken prisoner, and spent long years of captivity in England, during which he found consolation in poetical composition. On his return to France he settled down in his château at Blois and surrounded himself with a group of poets and men of letters. In his *rondeaux* and *ballades* he managed to endow with sincerity and grace the conventional themes of court poetry.

FRANÇOIS VILLON (pp. 20–25), whose real name was perhaps de Montcorbier or des Loges, derived that of Villon from his benefactor, Guillaume Villon, a priest who recognized his genius and provided for his education. He studied at the University of Paris and earned the degree of Master of Arts in 1452. Three years later he was accused of having killed a priest, was banished from the capital, and for a time led the life of a vagabond with a group of scoundrels called the *"coquillards,"* in whose special idiom several of his ballads were written. After being pardoned he returned to Paris, where he was arrested for theft and imprisoned at Meung-sur-Loire (1461). On the accession of Louis XI he was set free, but before long was again sentenced, this time to death. Once more he was pardoned (1463). The place and circumstances of his death are unknown. *Le Petit Testament* (1456) and *Le Grand Testament* (1461), which contain some of the greatest ballads in the French language, were composed partly in prison. The latter collection, especially, is autobiographical in character. It expresses his laments over his youth and wasted opportunities, and contains vivid evocations of sickness and misery, of death, and intimations of the beyond.

CLÉMENT MAROT (pp. 26–28) was the son of the poet Jean Marot and a protégé of Marguerite de Navarre and her brother, Francis I. Because of his leanings toward the Huguenot doctrine he was twice jailed and eventually was forced to seek safety in Italy, where he died. His translations of the first fifty Psalms, in a great variety of metrical forms, were for a long time sung in Protestant churches. He was drawn to Calvinism, however, by his independence of mind, for by temperament he was rather a gentle epicure. As a court poet his reputation in his time was immense, and in his *épîtres*, *élégies*, *ballades*, and *rondeaux* he remained faithful to the style and spirit of the fifteenth century.

HUGUES SALEL (p. 29) was a protégé of Francis I, who made him abbot of Saint-Chéron. Besides various lyrics he wrote a translation of the first ten books of the *Iliad* in French verse.

JACQUES PELETIER (pp. 30–31) translated Horace and wrote an *Art poétique*, in which he advocated the use of a more simplified spelling. He was also the author of a sonnet sequence, *Les Amours des amours*, of *La Savoie*, and of various lyrics collected in his *Œuvres poétiques*.

PIERRE DE RONSARD (pp. 32–53) came of a noble family from the region of Vendôme. At the age of twelve he served as page to the royal princes, and later as a kind of secretary to the great humanist and ambassador Lazare de Baïf. A severe illness which left him deaf in early youth forced him to give up hope of a military and diplomatic career, and he embarked upon a program of classical studies under the famed Hellenist Dorat, which lasted seven years. Along with a group of young scholars and poets he conceived the desire of enriching the French language by borrowings from the Greek and Latin, and French literature by imitation of the genres of classical antiquity and of Italy. This was the professed aim of the *Pléiade*, whose members, besides Ronsard and Dorat, were Antoine de Baïf, Du Bellay, Belleau, Jodelle, and Pontus de Tyard. Ronsard's fame, however, does not rest today on his imitations of Pindar, or on his unfinished epic *La Franciade*, but on the shorter odes and the sonnets, where his love of nature and beauty and his sense of the transitoriness of earthly things are rendered with considerable charm and feeling.

JOACHIM DU BELLAY (pp. 54–61) came of an ancient family of Anjou. His meeting with Ronsard and a period of study with Dorat awakened him to the world of poetry and scholarship. His *Défense et illustration de la langue française* (1549) was the official manifesto of the *Pléiade* and served to introduce his sonnet sequence *L'Olive*, whose inspiration owed more to modern Italy, however, than to ancient Greece or Rome. His residence of four years in Rome as secretary to his cousin, the Cardinal du Bellay, resulted in the composition of *Les Antiquités de Rome*, which contain his meditations on the ruins of the Eternal City. He is best remembered, however, for *Les Regrets*, a sequence of sonnets in which he immortalized his friendship for Ronsard and his nostalgia for home and country.

ANTOINE DE BAÏF (p. 62) was, with Ronsard and Du Bellay, a pupil of Dorat at the Collège de Coqueret. He founded an academy with the aim of establishing a closer union between music and poetry, and elaborated a system for regulating French versification by quantity, as in Greek and Latin prosody. Of his *Œuvres en rime* only a few short pieces have survived.

RÉMI BELLEAU (pp. 63–65) was a member of the *Pléiade*. He published the first French translation of Anacreon, a learned commentary on Ronsard's *Amours*, and various collections of poems, of which *Les Bergeries*, a pastoral in prose and verse, is the most notable.

PONTUS DE TYARD (p. 66) was bishop of Châlon-sur-Saône and the last survivor of the *Pléiade*. His *Erreurs amoureuses* (1549) are characterized by a strong neo-platonic inspiration.

JEAN PASSERAT (pp. 67–68) is best known for his collaboration in the anonymous political pamphlet *La Satire Ménippée*. In his poems, printed posthumously in 1608, several pastoral poems, or *villanelles*, were found. These were meant to accompany a rustic dance, and the one for which Passerat is now chiefly remembered has become the type of its class; it is written in tercets, on two rhymes, the first and third line being repeated alternately in each tercet.

OLIVIER DE MAGNY (p. 69) was a protégé of Hugues Salel. During a stay in Rome he met and befriended Du Bellay. On his return to France he published *Les Soupirs*, which is as autobiographical in character as his friend's *Les Regrets*. His collection of *Odes* and his sequence of sonnets, *Les Amours*, contain some of his best work.

LOUISE LABÉ (pp. 70–73), was the most distinguished poetess of the French Renaissance. In her native Lyons she presided over a circle of gifted scholars and poets including

Maurice Scève and Pernette du Guillet. Her twenty-four sonnets, which are among the most impassioned and sensitive in
the whole range of French literature, are supposed to have
been inspired by her love for Olivier de Magny, and her
elegies probably express her grief at his absence. She also
wrote a prose dialogue, *Débat de folie et d'amour*, whose argu-
ment was summarized by La Fontaine in his fable *L'Amour et
la folie*.

JEAN VAUQUELIN DE LA FRESNAYE (pp. 74–75) was
the author of an *Art poétique français* (1605) which advocated
the return to the Christian and national tradition while pre-
serving the main theories of Ronsard. He wrote a number of
charming *Idillies* and also the first satiric French poem actu-
ally to bear that title.

DU BARTAS (p. 76), whose full name is Guillaume Salluste,
Seigneur du Bartas, was a convinced Huguenot from Gascony.
He planned a great epic in which biblical characters and
Christian sentiment should replace the pagan setting then in
fashion. *La Semaine* (1579), the first part of this uncompleted
work, relates the story of the Creation. Its grandiose style has
been more admired in England (by Spenser and Milton) and in
Germany (by Goethe) than in France.

PHILIPPE DESPORTES (pp. 77–78) was a disciple of Ronsard and an imitator of Petrarch, Ariosto, Sannazaro, and the
minor Italian poets. The serious side of his talent he reserved
for the poems inspired by his Catholic faith. His translation of
the Psalms is remembered chiefly for Malherbe's acid com-
ment: "*Votre potage vaut mieux que vos psaumes.*"

GILLES DURANT (p. 79) collaborated on *La Satire Ménippée* and wrote many odes, sonnets, *chansons*, and imitations of
the Psalms.

JEAN BERTAUT (p. 80) was a close friend and follower of
Desportes. He entered the Church at an early age and had a
share in the conversion of Henri IV, who made him Bishop of
Sées in 1606. He excelled in the writing of light verse celebrat-
ing the incidents of court life.

FRANÇOIS DE MALHERBE (p. 81) exerted a great influence as a critic of the *Pléiade*. By insisting on greater sim-
plicity and purity in choice of language and on stricter adher-
ence to the rules of versification, he paved the way for the
technical perfection of French classical poetry. Like Pope, he
subordinated everything to "correctness," and his poetical
work, if lacking in warmth, lyricism, and color, is always dis-

tinguished by an impeccable purity of style. The sonnet to Louis XIII was written to celebrate the defeat of the Protestant party at Montauban.

JEAN OGIER DE GOMBAUD (p. 82), one of the founders of the French Academy, enjoyed some popularity as a versifier during the course of his long life. He wrote a pastoral novel, *Amarante*, a tragedy, *Les Danaïdes*, and a collection of *Épigrammes*.

MATHURIN RÉGNIER (p. 83) is France's first and probably greatest satiric poet. In his philosophy of life he was a follower of Epicurus (as proclaimed in his epitaph), and he satirized, long before Rousseau, the restrictions imposed on human nature by social conventions. In the realm of poetry he was an independent disciple of Horace and defended the claims of untramelled inspiration, the *nonchalances* of the Muse, as he put it, against Malherbe's strict orthodoxy.

JEAN DE LINGENDES (p. 84) was among the first French poets to use the form called *stances*, and achieved a fair measure of popularity with his madrigals, odes, and sonnets. His most important work is *Les Changements de la bergère Iris*.

FRANÇOIS DE MAYNARD (pp. 85–86) was, like Racan, one of the favorite disciples of Malherbe, and in some of his sonnets and lyrics he showed a verve and sincerity that were denied to his master. The ode *La Belle vieille* was written when he was nearly fifty-five, and a widower.

THÉOPHILE DE VIAU (pp. 87–89) had a career almost as picturesque and tragic as that of Villon, to whom he has sometimes been compared. With Régnier, he opposed the rigidity of the reforms of Malherbe. His tragedy *Pyrame et Thisbé* was important in its day.

CLAUDE DE MALLEVILLE (p. 90) was one of the first poets to be elected to the French Academy. His sonnet *La Belle matineuse* made him famous, and he wrote also many elegies, songs, and *rondeaux*.

VINCENT VOITURE (p. 91), though of plebeian origin, became by his wit and cleverness the shining light of the Salon of Madame de Rambouillet. He enjoyed great popularity as the author of lively letters and light society verse.

TRISTAN L'HERMITE (pp. 92–93) was the author of some admirable lyrics, but was better known as a dramatist. His first tragedy, *Marianne*, had in its day a success almost as great as that of the *Cid* of Corneille.

ANONYMOUS, from *Le Misanthrope* of Molière (p. 94). This song is sung by Alceste as an example of true feeling.

JEAN DE LA FONTAINE (pp. 95–103) is universally known as the author of the *Fables*, which he wrote when he was past middle life. Silvestre de Sacy has said of them that they supply different delights to three different ages: the child rejoices in the freshness and vividness of the story, the eager student of literature in the consummate art with which it is told, and the experienced man of the world in the subtle reflections on character and life which it conveys. As an artist La Fontaine stands, with Racine, as the epitome of French classicism, and his *Fables*, with their complete mastery of all the resources of meter and rhythms, illustrate to perfection his own precept, *rien de trop*.

NICOLAS BOILEAU-DESPRÉAUX (p. 104), critic and satirist, formulated in his *Art poétique* the main principles of the classical doctrine, based on reason, truth, and a close study of antiquity. As a poet "who speaks always of verse and rhyme and never of poetry" (Théophile Gautier), Boileau's claims to a place among the French lyric poets rest upon a few fugitive pieces. The lines to Sylvia were inspired by his youthful love for Marie Poncher. They were set to music by Lambert in 1671.

GUILLAUME AMFRYE DE CHAULIEU (p. 105) was a poet and wit who continued the trifling school of Voiture and the Bacchic sect of Saint-Amant. His poetical compositions consist mostly of quatrains (such as the stances to the solitude of Fontenay) and of Pindaric odes.

CHARLES RIVIÈRE DU FRESNY (p. 106) was equally gifted in architecture, painting, and music. He made his literary reputation by writing comedies, which are forgotten today, and a great number of odes and fugitive lyrics. His novel of manners, *Les Entretiens ou amusements sérieux et comiques*, gave Montesquieu the idea for his *Lettres Persanes*.

ALEXIS PIRON (pp. 107–109) was famous for his talent in turning out epigrams, of which the best known is the burlesque epitaph on himself, ridiculing the Academy. He also wrote several tragedies, a number of light plays, and a comedy, *La Métromanie*, which enjoyed a great success.

FRANÇOIS AROUET DE VOLTAIRE (pp. 110–114) became famous in all the literary genres, but during the first sixty years of his life was celebrated primarily as a poet. His contemporaries put his tragedies on a level with those of Racine, and his epic *La Henriade* was considered the equal of the *Iliad* and the *Aeneid*. Some of his epistles and satires, his epigrams, and his short miscellaneous poems can still be read with pleasure for their wit and charm.

FRANÇOIS JOACHIM PIERRE DE BERNIS (p. 115) was known as one of the most talented epigrammatists in the gay court of Louis XV, and through his verses won the friendship of Madame de Pompadour.

PIERRE-AUGUSTIN CARON DE BEAUMARCHAIS (p. 116) won fame and immortality with his comedies *Le Barbier de Séville* and *Le Mariage de Figaro*. The song of Chérubin occurs in this latter play.

NICHOLAS-GERMAIN LÉONARD (p. 117), a native of the island of Guadalupe, is remembered chiefly for his *Idylles et poésies champêtres*, which betray the imitation of Tibullus and Propertius.

ÉVARISTE DE PARNY (p. 118) was born in the Isle of Bourbon and educated in France. Some of his best poems (collected in 1778 under the title of *Poésies érotiques*) were inspired by his love for a young compatriot whom he addresses as Eléonore. His fame rests chiefly on his early love poems and elegies, whose tenderness and grace had a strong appeal for Lamartine.

JEAN-PIERRE CLARIS DE FLORIAN (p. 119) wrote several tales, comedies, and romances, but is especially remembered for his collection of *Fables* (1792). Some of his lyrics, such as *Plaisir d'amour* and *C'est mon ami*, have been set to music and become widely popular.

ANDRÉ CHÉNIER (pp. 120–138) was born in Constantinople of a French father and Levantine mother, but was raised in Paris. His friends, the poet Lebrun-Pindare, the painter David, and the scholar Brunck, stimulated his interest in the classical revival that took place in France between 1748 and 1790. Most of his poems, from his early idyls and bucolics, such as *La Jeune Tarentine*, to the Iambes and *La Jeune Captive*, written during his imprisonment at Saint-Lazare, have the coloring of Greek mythology but an accent that is entirely modern. In a fragment called *L'Invention* Chénier summed up his artistic ideal: *Sur des pensers nouveaux faisons des vers antiques*. He was interested in the scientific knowledge of his day and tried to condense it into a didactic poem, *Hermès*, somewhat after the manner of Lucretius.

ANTOINE-VINCENT ARNAULT (p. 139) was a dramatist who also won a considerable reputation in his day as a writer of fables. He was a protégé of Bonaparte, who entrusted him, in 1797, with the task of reorganizing the Ionian Islands and made him secretary-general of the University. After the Hundred Days he was sent into exile by Louis XVIII. In the elegy which made him immortal he compares his fate to that of the wandering leaf.

CHARLES-HUBERT MILLEVOYE (pp. 140–141) gained great notoriety with his collection of *Elégies* (1812), which contained his two most famous lyrics, *La Chute des feuilles* and *Le Poète mourant*. He was a great admirer of Chénier, and gave poetic expression to the mood of sentimental melancholy that was prevalent in his day.

PIERRE-JEAN DE BÉRANGER (pp. 142–145) achieved an immense popularity with his songs, many of which passed from hand to hand and were sung all over France before they were printed. He used the *chanson* as a medium to voice his republican and, later, his socialistic sympathies, and to interpret the thoughts and the sentiments of the common people from whom he sprang. Béranger was not a mere improvisator, but a conscientious student of style and composition; his lyrical gift and occasional touches of pathos combine to lift some of his songs into the realm of poetry.

MARCELINE DESBORDES-VALMORE (pp. 146–147) was an actress by profession and the wife of a comedian, Prosper Valmore. Her elegiac poems, said to have been inspired by her unrequited love for Henri de Latouche (a poet and playwright, and editor of Chénier's works), were greatly admired by Hugo, Baudelaire, and Verlaine for their note of genuine passion and great purity of expression.

ALPHONSE DE LAMARTINE (pp. 148–164), whose career was divided equally between literature and politics, was for a time the most popular poet of his day, and after the Revolution of 1848 the nominal head of the provisional government of France. His chief claim to immortality still rests on his first collection of elegiac poems, *Les Méditations poétiques* (1820), which embodied a wealth of melody and a purity of utterance such as had not been heard in French literature since the days of the Renaissance. The beauty of nature, the brevity of human life and earthly pleasures, and the promptings of faith are the mainsprings of his inspiration. *Le Lac* and *Le Crucifix* were inspired by his youthful attachment to Madame Charles, whom he immortalized under the name of Elvire.

ALFRED DE VIGNY (pp. 165–183) came from a family of soldiers and he himself joined the army at the age of sixteen. In the enforced leisure of army life he wrote his first collection of poems, which was published in 1822. Six years later, disillusioned with his military career, he resigned, married an Englishwoman, and decided, after an unsuccessful attempt to enter politics, to devote himself entirely to literature. During his lifetime he attained some fame with his plays *La Maréchale d'Ancre* and *Chatterton*, his historical romance *Cinq-Mars*, and his semi-autobiographical accounts of army life, *Servitude et grandeur militaires*. His chief ambition, however, was to write poetry "in which philosophic thought is clothed in epic or dramatic form." This he has achieved in a number of poems in which his disillusioned outlook on life is given added significance by a genuine elevation and an occasional sublimity of utterance seldom achieved by other Romantic poets. Chamfort's saying that "there is a kind of melancholy which amounts to spiritual greatness" is nobly reflected in some of the poems included in *Les Destinées*.

VICTOR HUGO (pp. 184–212) was the most versatile of all the poets of the nineteenth century, and no doubt the greatest for sheer power of imagination, for matchless mastery of words, and for virtuosity in handling every form of rhyme and rhythm. His works fill innumerable volumes, in which almost every literary genre is represented: lyric and epic poetry, drama, fiction, criticism, travel, memoirs, and political pamphlets. In his youth he was primarily the apostle and spokesman of Romanticism, but in the endless variety of his compositions it would be possible to trace the germs of nearly every poetic movement that flourished from the end of the nineteenth century to our own day. He himself attached more importance, however, to his role as a social and philosophic poet, rejected the doctrine of art for art's sake, and asserted about himself, not without justification, "No one has created more art for society and for humanity."

ALFRED DE MUSSET (pp. 213–238) was exceptionally gifted not only as a poet but as a playwright and a graceful storyteller. In his poems he was led by a sensitive and intensely introspective nature to voice the romantic theme of love as the source of all joy and all sorrow ("Nothing is better than love, nothing is more true than suffering"). He also believed, like Shelley, that "the most beautiful songs are those that tell of saddest thought" and that the poet must draw from his own experience the subject matter of his art. Most of his poems are therefore autobiographical. The lyrics of *Les Nuits* were inspired by his unhappy love affair with George Sand.

GEORGE SAND (pp. 239–240) is not known as a poet, but is famous for her long succession of romantic and pastoral novels. The lines translated in this volume are a paraphrase of a song that occurs in one of her best novels, *Les Mattres Sonneurs*.

FÉLIX ARVERS (p. 241) is the author of *Mes Heures perdues* (1833), which contains the sonnet for which he is now remembered. The lines were intended as a veiled confession of love for the daughter of Charles Nodier.

GÉRARD DE NERVAL (pp. 242–244) travelled widely in Europe and the Near East, and his *Voyage en Orient*, with its artful mingling of truth and poetry, is a classic among travel books. He also wrote exquisite stories and sketches, which revealed his gift for making tangible the magic world of dreams his fancy inhabited. The few incidental lyrics included in *La Bohême galante* show his intellectual kinship with Baudelaire and Verlaine.

THÉOPHILE GAUTIER (pp. 245–263) was a journalist, traveller, novelist, and poet who never quite forgot that his original vocation was that of painter. ("I am a man," he said, "for whom the visible world exists.") He began as an ardent apostle of Romanticism, but his aversion for the expression of feeling in poetry, his indifference to problems of politics, religion, and science, and his conviction that art should be divorced from morality, led him to devote his energy to the creation of an impersonal form of poetry whose ideal should conform closely to that of plastic art. Baudelaire called him an "impeccable poet" and dedicated his *Fleurs du Mal* to him. *Emaux et Camées*, his masterpiece, contains some of the most vivid, most polished gems in modern literature.

CHARLES BAUDELAIRE (pp. 264–273) began his literary career as an art critic and devoted many years of his life to the translation of Poe's writings. But it is chiefly as a poet that he has gained his steadily increasing reputation as one of the most important and influential literary figures of the nineteenth century. Few poets had a more exalted notion of the importance of their calling than Baudelaire. Beauty in all its forms, whether it spring from Satan or from God, was his chief aim. For him "poetry is related to music by a prosody whose roots plunge deeper into the human soul than any classic theory indicated." In *Les Fleurs du Mal* he gave expression to a world of complex feelings and sensations in a style of utmost purity and suggestiveness.

LECONTE DE LISLE (pp. 274–285) spent part of his youth in his native Isle of Bourbon and part in Paris, where he settled definitely at the age of twenty-seven. Like Vigny, he first took an interest in politics, but the Revolution of 1848 provoked in him a revulsion of feeling and a disillusionment with life and society which is reflected in his poetry. As an artist he believed that "the poet must express the Beautiful through a complex, scholarly, and harmonious combination of lines, colors, and sound, no less than through all the resources of passion, science, and imagination." This explains in part the classical perfection of his style and his command of a recondite erudition based on the lore of India and Greece—also his use of Christian, Celtic, and Scandinavian myths. He excelled in poetic evocations of the strange and remote past, and his descriptions of exotic scenery and of animal life show an exceptional accuracy of observation and a remarkable power of imagination. As a master of versification he ranks with the greatest poets of his country.

THÉODORE DE BANVILLE (pp. 286–290) began his literary career at the early age of nineteen with the publication of *Cariatides*, but it was his *Odes funambulesques*, which revealed his peculiar skill for handling rhymed verse of various forms, by which he attained celebrity. He described himself as "a lyric poet who is an expert only in metrics," and his belief that "rhyme is the whole of verse" led him to revive with gusto such forgotten sixteenth-century genres as the *odelette* and the *ballade*.

SULLY PRUDHOMME (pp. 291–293) became, in 1901, the first recipient of the Nobel prize for literature. From 1865 to 1888 he had published various collections of poems, on which his fame rests securely, but thereafter he developed an absorbing interest in philosophy and devoted his time to writing abstract treatises on the problem of final causes, the true religion of Pascal, and other subjects. He had a love for great precision of style and minute notation of detail. In his shorter poems he describes sensitive shades of feeling at times so imponderable that they seem almost to defy expression.

HENRI CAZALIS (pp. 294–295) wrote first under the name of Jean Caselli, then became more generally known as Jean Lahor. He achieved fame with *L'Illusion*, a collection of poems whose underlying pessimism can be explained by the author's absorption in Buddhistic philosophy.

FRANÇOIS COPPÉE (pp. 296–297) achieved celebrity overnight with his one-act play *Le Passant* (1869), which also made the reputation of Sarah Bernhardt. As a poet he was first a disciple of Musset and Baudelaire, but found his true vocation as the interpreter of the simpler aspects of daily life and of the humble people that inhabited the crowded districts and suburbs of Paris.

JOSÉ-MARIA DE HÉRÉDIA (pp. 298–316) was born in Cuba of a Spanish father and a French mother. He received most of his education in Paris, and at the École des Chartes he acquired a taste for the severe discipline of exact scholarship. On a journey to Italy in 1864, Italian art made a deep impression on him, and throughout his life he moved in a circle of scientists, philologists, poets, and painters. He was a great admirer of Leconte de Lisle and an extremely fastidious craftsman. His single published volume, *Les Trophées* (1893), is a collection of sonnets which had appeared in periodicals over a period of thirty years and which he had polished and repolished with great care. He believed that "the supreme faculty of the artist, poet, historian, novelist, painter, sculptor, or musician is the gift of evocation"; and in order "to evoke the soul of others, the soul of the past, the soul of things and of epochs," he limited himself to the sonnet form, within whose restricted frame he could manage to compress, as Lemaître has said, "all the beauty of a myth, all the spirit of an age, all the picturesqueness of an epoch."

GABRIEL VICAIRE (pp. 317–318) was, like Lamartine, a native of Bourgogne. In his several collections of lyrics, *Émaux bressans, Au Bois joli,* and *Le Clos des fées,* he showed a liveliness and malicious tenderness that are somewhat reminiscent of Villon, La Fontaine, and Verlaine.

JEAN RICHEPIN (p. 319), who prided himself on his gipsy blood, led a colorful life as soldier, newspaperman, sailor, novelist, playwright, and poet. In *La Chanson des gueux* and *Les Blasphèmes* he sang his romantic love of freedom and hatred of convention with a vigor and exuberance that sometimes recall Walt Whitman.

STÉPHANE MALLARMÉ (p. 320) taught English for thirty years in various *lycées* so that he might devote his leisure to poetry and meditation. His poetical genius was revealed to a generation of worshipping disciples by a descriptive passage in Huysmans' *A Rebours.* For him the poetical ideal consists not in definite statement but in pure suggestion, so that three-fourths of the enjoyment of a poem reside in the pleasure of slow divination. "There exists a secret affinity," he said, "between the old processes of magic and the sorcery that poetry must ultimately remain." The limited number of poems on which he lavished infinite care and thought are therefore a challenge, and a choice reward, for the intelligent reader's intuition and esthetic sense and sensibility.

PAUL VERLAINE (pp. 321–329) led a troubled, adventurous, and, toward the end, very miserable existence which illustrates the fundamental inability of the poet and dreamer that he was to come to grips with reality. He began as a disciple of the Parnassians and of Baudelaire with his *Poèmes saturni-*

ens and *Les Fêtes galantes*. In his *Art poétique* he asserted that the essence of poetry must be sought in musical suggestion and in the search for subtle shadings and imprecise notation—an ideal he tried to achieve in his *Romances sans paroles*. While serving a prison term at Mons, in 1873, he underwent a religious conversion, and his newly found faith is the subject of *Sagesse*, perhaps the most admired and influential of all his poetical compositions.

CHARLES VAN LERBERGHE (pp. 330–331) was a native of Ghent and a friend of Maeterlinck. His *La Chanson d'Ève* revealed a remarkable gift for misty evocations of ethereal and intangible beauty, which makes him almost worthy of a place with Shelley and Keats.

MAURICE MAETERLINCK (p. 332) is more celebrated for his dramas (*Pélléas et Mélisande, L'Oiseau bleu*) and for his scientific and philosophical essays than for his poems. He began his literary career, however, with a collection of symbolistic poems, *Serres chaudes* (1889), to which he added, a year later, a series of lyrics entitled *Douze chansons*. The latter testify to his fondness for the naïve charm of the popular ballad.

PAUL FORT (pp. 333–334) began to publish, in 1897, a long series of "French Ballads" which in the course of twenty-five years filled nearly thirty volumes. He believed in "the superiority of rhythm over the artifice of prosody," and in his ballads cultivated a style of "rhythmic prose" which allowed him, according to the dictates of inspiration, to pass from prose to verse and from verse to prose.

CHARLES GUÉRIN (pp. 335–337) attracted critical attention with *Le Cœur solitaire*, which revealed his unusual gift for delicate self-analysis. After his return to Catholicism he wrote *Le Semeur de cendres* and *L'Homme intérieur*, which are pervaded by a brooding melancholy and reflect the conflict of a spirit torn by mental anguish and an uncontrollable fear of life.

ROSEMONDE GÉRARD (p. 338) is the widow of Edmond Rostand. Her first collection of poems, *Les Pipeaux*, was published in 1890. She has since written some occasional lyrics and has collaborated with her son, Maurice Rostand, on several idealistic and romantic plays.

JEAN MORÉAS (pp. 339–345) was a native of Athens and his real name was Papadiamantopoulos. His education, however, was wholly French from the beginning, and when only ten years old he conceived the ambition of becoming a French poet. He settled in Paris in his early youth and made his literary début with *Les Syrtes* (1882), in which the influence of the Parnassians and of Verlaine is evident. This was followed two years later by *Les Cantilènes*, in which he tried to recapture the naïveté and the rhythm of the Old French *complainte*. In 1891 he founded the *École Romane*, whose program consisted in a revival of Greek, Roman, and French poetry of the Renaissance and seventeenth century. *Les Stances*, a collection of short lyrics of two or three stanzas (nearly all quatrains), are supposed to embody this archaic ideal, whose underlying note, however, is the Romantic theme of the isolation of the artist, the brevity of earthly life, and the inevitability of death.

ALBERT SAMAIN (pp. 346–351) for a long time led an obscure and difficult existence in Lille and in Paris, devoting his spare time to poetical composition. He was of a shy and sensitive nature, extremely modest, and only the repeated exhortations of his friends could bring him to publish *Au Jardin de l'Infante*, whose tenderness and gentle melancholy made it widely popular. His two subsequent collections, *Au Flanc du vase* and *Le Chariot d'or*, also contain some of his best verse.

HENRI DE RÉGNIER (pp. 352–359) came from an old aristocratic family. He knew Leconte de Lisle, Verlaine, and Mallarmé, and he was a close friend of Hérédia, whose daughter, the poetess Gérard d'Houville, he later married. He began as a disciple of the Parnassians and the Symbolists, but achieved his best individual style after he had outgrown their influence. In *Les Jeux rustiques et divins*, *Les Médailles d'argile*, *La Cité des eaux*, and other works, he transposed ancient themes and legends, and voiced his modern and sophisticated impressions in a chastened and classic style that sometimes recalls that of Chénier.

LA COMTESSE DE NOAILLES (pp. 360–365) was the daughter of the Prince de Brancovan, a Rumanian nobleman who had married the descendant of a distinguished Greek family. She was born and raised in Paris, and her first collection of verse, *Le Cœur innombrable* (1901), revealed her poetical genius, which deepened and matured with *Les Éblouissements*, *Les Vivants et les morts*, and *Les Forces éternelles*. She has been called "The Muse of Gardens" because of her sensitive gift for expressing the emotions and impressions aroused in her by the contemplation of the variegated aspects of external nature, and her fondness for pantheistic reverie.

INDEX OF FRENCH TITLES
OR FIRST LINES

The names of the authors are arranged alphabetically. The titles, or first lines, are listed in the order in which the translations appear in the preceding pages. First lines are distinguished from titles by the use of italics.